T0311521

An Economic Philosophy of Production, Work and Consumption

An Economic Philosophy of Production, Work and Consumption presents a new transhistorical framework for defining production, work and consumption. It shows that they all share the common feature of intentional physical transformation of something external to the agent, at some point in time.

The book opens with a discussion of various theoretical traditions within economics, spanning mainstream and heterodox perspectives, and problems with production definitions in use today. Next, the author outlines various definitions in a more formal manner and provides a discussion on measurement and the production boundary. Unproductive work is redefined as socially reproductive, i.e. such that would not be performed on a Robinson Crusoe Island. Finally, the volume applies the new conceptual framework to various historical cases and discusses the future of production, work and consumption.

This essential volume will be of interest to scholars of economic philosophy and methodology, the history of economic thought, economic history and national accounting.

Rodney Edvinsson is a Professor of Economic History at Stockholm University, Sweden.

Routledge Studies in the History of Economics

For more information about this series, please visit: www.routledge.com/series/SE0341

An Economic Philosophy of Production, Work and Consumption

A Transhistorical Framework

Rodney Edvinsson

LONDON AND NEW YORK

First published 2023
by Routledge
4 Park Square, Milton Park, Abingdon, Oxon OX14 4RN

and by Routledge
605 Third Avenue, New York, NY 10158

Routledge is an imprint of the Taylor & Francis Group, an informa business

British Library Cataloguing-in-Publication Data
A catalogue record for this book is available from the British Library

Library of Congress Cataloguing-in-Publication Data
Names: Edvinsson, Rodney, author.
Title: An economic philosophy of production, work and consumption: a transhistorical framework / Rodney Edvinsson.
Description: Abingdon, Oxon; New York, NY: Routledge, 2023. | Series: Routledge studies in the history of economics | Includes bibliographical references and index.
Identifiers: LCCN 2022014105 (print) | LCCN 2022014106 (ebook) | ISBN 9780367522254 (hardback) | ISBN 9780367522247 (paperback) | ISBN 9781003057017 (ebook)
Subjects: LCSH: Production (Economic theory) | Consumption (Economics) | Labor. | Work. | Economics--Philosophy.
Classification: LCC HB241.E38 2023 (print) | LCC HB241 (ebook) | DDC 338.5--dc23/eng/20220323
LC record available at https://lccn.loc.gov/2022014105
LC ebook record available at https://lccn.loc.gov/2022014106

ISBN: 978-0-367-52225-4 (hbk)
ISBN: 978-0-367-52224-7 (pbk)
ISBN: 978-1-003-05701-7 (ebk)

DOI: 10.4324/9781003057017

Typeset in Bembo
by MPS Limited, Dehradun

Contents

1   Introduction[1]

The dilemma of "leprechaun economics"

There is a joke about two junior economists finding dog shit during their walk. The first economist says to the second: "I pay you one million dollars if you eat up the dog shit". The second economist does it. They keep walking until they find another dog shit. The second economist now says to the first: "I pay you one million dollars if you eat up that dog shit". The first economist does it. They do not feel so well. None of them own one million dollars. So, they visit a senior economist to explain to them how to evaluate the situation. The senior economist exclaims: "These are wonderful news. You have just increased the GDP by two million dollars".

Although a joke, the senior economist has a point. According to the international guidelines of national accounting, eating dog shit for payment may constitute a type of service, included in the production boundary given that it is performed for the market. Its gross output and value added would similarly be valued by the amount paid (there is no intermediate consumption in the joke).

Weird things also appear in the real world of official national accounting. For instance, in 2015, the Irish GDP suddenly increased by 26 per cent. Given that there are no indications of a sensational rise in Irish productivity, the Irish Statistical Office instead has used the adjusted gross national income as a substitute. The phenomenon was jokingly described as "Leprechaun economics" by Paul Krugman (2017):

> GDP might go up because lower corporate taxes will draw in foreign capital; but this capital will demand and receive returns, which mean that part of the gain in domestic production is offset by investment income received by foreigners. As a result, GNI – income of domestic residents – will rise less than GDP. And surely, as in Ireland with its leprechaun economy based on low corporate taxes, GNI is the measure you want to focus on.

Still, the solution of the Irish Statistical Office is ad hoc. The GNI is not an alternative production measure. It is an income measure. Measures of

DOI: 10.4324/9781003057017-1

productivity quantify the technological capacity and presuppose the concept of production. The GNI equals GDP plus net primary incomes from non-residents (United Nations et al., 2009, p. 34). A country that pays substantial amounts of interest to foreign lenders has a much lower GNI than GDP, and GNI then substantially underestimates the level of production.

Analysis of the Irish economy in 2015 shows that the growth mainly came from manufacturing, which almost doubled in nominal terms, while the labour force in this sector in 2015 only increased by 5 per cent. Although the sector "detail within the Industry Sector of Origin is suppressed for 2015 for confidentiality reasons" (Central Statistics Office [Ireland], 2016), it is evident that the growth came from three industrial activities: chemicals and pharmaceuticals, computers and instrument engineering, and medical and dental instruments and supplies. Analysis has shown that the sudden growth occurred because multinationals moved intellectual property to be registered in Ireland, in the Irish case probably mainly two companies, Apple and Allergan. Even if the actual manufacturing occurred in other countries, the "contribution" of the companies was registered in Ireland, so-called factory-less goods production. As argued by Tedeschi (2018):

> Value added comes from labour, capital and their productivity. Nothing else. All value added goes to labour and to capital in the form of income, in short gross wages and gross "profits", the latter with a number of complexities. Nothing is left, in the real part of the economy (excluding government, for simplicity). The physical capital can be moved between countries incurring in transport and disassembly/assembly costs. Intangible capital, or intellectual property capital, is wholly different from plants and equipment, but is just as "real". As a result of the growing share of IP [Intellectual Property] capital, the international mobility of "real capital" becomes smoother and frictions vanish. IP capital, once created, can be combined with physical inputs and labour in different countries with no trade/transport cost, as when producing a new life saving drug on the basis of a chemical formula. The location of the "capital" changes when the owner changes, by a simple book entry or registration. So, the residence of the owner of the intellectual property brings with it the value added it produces, it is difficult to argument for the contrary.

Still, Tedeschi's view is mixing up transfer and production. Intellectual property is more accurately the holding of monopolist power since it hinders other people from accessing particular technology. Knowledge is non-rival, and no real costs occur for more people accessing it. Copyrights only exist in people's minds. In contrast, a machine is real as it has an existence of its own independent from the observer, although owning a machine is also a social construction.

The central quandary raised by the Irish case is theoretical, i.e., concerning where to draw the production boundary, the distinction between productive and unproductive activities, which for national accounts are decided by the international guidelines of *System of National Accounts (SNA)* (United Nations et al., 2009). For example, if foreign companies in Ireland had recorded the income flows from intellectual property as interest rate payments, the national accounts would have recorded such flows as transfers and not as production. In national accounts, paying a risk-free interest rate or tax is considered a transfer, and therefore not classified as payment for actual productive output. However, payments above the risk-free interest, as well as remuneration for the use of intellectual property, are considered expenses of actual productive additions.

Many activities included in the production boundary according to SNA are harmful to people today and to future generations. In the documentary, *The Social Dilemma*, Justin Rosenstein, former engineer at Facebook, expressed that (IMDb, 2020).

> We live in a world in which a tree is worth more, financially, dead than alive, in a world in which a whale is worth more dead than alive. For so long as our economy works in that way and corporations go unregulated, they're going to continue to destroy trees, to kill whales, to mine the earth, and to continue to pull oil out of the ground, even though we know it is destroying the planet and we know that it's going to leave a worse world for future generations. This is short-term thinking based on this religion of profit at all costs, as if somehow, magically, each corporation acting in its selfish interest is going to produce the best result. This has been affecting the environment for a long time. What's frightening, and what hopefully is the last straw that will make us wake up as a civilization to how flawed this theory has been in the first place, is to see that now we're the tree, we're the whale. Our attention can be mined. We are more profitable to a corporation if we're spending time staring at a screen, staring at an ad, than if we're spending that time living our life in a rich way. And so, we're seeing the results of that. We're seeing corporations using powerful artificial intelligence to outsmart us and figure out how to pull our attention toward the things they want us to look at, rather than the things that are most consistent with our goals and our values and our lives.

A particular weakness with national accounts is that activities directed towards coercing or even violence are regarded as productive as long as they are allowed by the state. As Nordhaus and Tobin (1973, pp. 7–8) point out:

> No reasonable country (or household) buys "national defense" for its own sake. If there were no war or risk of war, there would be no need for defense expenditures and no one would be the worse without them. [...]

> From the point of view of economic welfare, an arms control or disarmament agreement which would free resources and raise consumption by

10 per cent would be just as significant as new industrial processes yielding the same gains.

During wars, GDP can substantially increase when spending on military increases, which was the case during the 1940s in the USA. Such periods are permeated by destruction. In contrast, professional murders, terrorism and robberies are categorised as unproductive activities. Is there an essential difference between state and non-state-sanctioned violence? As argued by Edward Said (2003):

> Every empire, however, tells itself and the world that it is unlike all other empires, that its mission is not to plunder and control but to educate and liberate. These ideas are by no means shared by the people who inhabit that empire...

Many dictatorships perform far more cruel acts than violent groups working outside of the legal system. The Holocaust would be regarded as a productive activity by SNA 2008 since a state performed it. What would be the measure of "productivity" of such genocidal acts? The atrocities performed by Russian soldiers in Ukraine in 2022 would likewise be considered productive. Early in state-making, many parties shared in the use of violence, for example, feudal lords with private armies, and sometimes these entities came into conflict with each other.

The paradox of national accounting is that when violent groups become the most successful, i.e., win state power, their violent acts are suddenly placed within the production boundary. Violence and coercion are by definition practised by one part of the population against another part, irrespectively of whether one thinks that such acts are morally justifiable (for example, as self-defence) or not, or as expressed by Adam Smith (1999, p. 302):

> The rich, in particular, are necessarily interested to support that order of things which can alone secure them in the possession of their advantages. Men of inferior wealth combine to defend those of superior wealth in the possession of their property, in order that men of superior wealth may combine to defend them in the possession of theirs... Civil government, so far as it is instituted for the security of property, is in reality instituted for the defence of the rich against the poor, or of those who have some property against those who have none at all.

The Covid-19-crisis posed new challenges to national accounting. Suddenly, protection of human life came to the forefront, which cannot simply be reduced to market value, or as argued by Simon Mair (2020):

> Capitalism is challenged if, in responding to the crisis, things other than market value are prioritised. In the case of COVID-19, the response is

about protecting life. The value of life can be conceptualised in many ways; however it is done, the value of life is messy and resistant to being reduced to a single monetary metric. Consequently, when the protection of life becomes a societal priority, the dominance of markets is challenged. By prioritising life over exchange value, COVID-19 is challenging key assumptions of neoliberal capitalism…

It is not just health that suffers from the attempt to compress all value into exchange value: similar dynamics exist within the labour market. Many of the best-paid jobs in neoliberal capitalist societies exist only to facilitate exchanges; to make money. These jobs serve no wider purpose to society: they are what the anthropologist, David Graeber, called "bullshit jobs". Jobs in crucial services do not tend to be the highest valued in market terms, which can be shown by examples in health care.

While many activities within the official production boundary do not seem to contribute anything to society or are destructive, an opposite drawback is that GDP excludes many activities that could be considered productive, most importantly unpaid domestic services and human capital formation. Although GDP mainly includes activities for the market, there are inconsistencies. Goods and services are treated differently so that all non-market goods production is included in GDP, while most unpaid services are not, except, for example, services provided by owner-occupied dwellings (United Nations et al., 2009, p. 98). As reasoned by Wood (1997):

> The SNA's explanation of the exclusion of services is also problematic because the basis for distinguishing goods and services remains unclear and arbitrary. Why is hauling water the production of a good, but cooking a meal is a service? There are many meals prepared in third world contexts which are meant partly for the market and partly for home consumption. Is the distinction to be made based on whether the meal is primarily intended for the market so that "leftovers" are consumed at home, or it is primarily meant for home consumption, and leftovers are for sale? If a meal is cooked with some idea of how much will be marketed and how much will be consumed, is only part of the labor involved in producing that meal excluded? How much? There is surely a large percentage of water hauled which is meant exclusively for home consumption, with the "possibility" of selling the water no more important to the person doing the work than its use in washing clothes or caring for children. Why is this process considered a good rather than the transportation of a good, which is explicitly excluded?

Notions of production, work and consumption

The notions of production, work and consumption have been discussed for several centuries and even millennia. The gross domestic product (GDP), labour productivity and private consumption are used as measures of economic development and welfare across countries and periods. Yet, defining these concepts, and finding suitable measures, are deeply problematic. As discussed in Chapter 2, past beliefs, including non-Western philosophy, are not necessarily inferior to modern Western thinking. Pre-industrial economic ideas around the world were formulated in the context of other social and economic relations than modern ones, for example, other value systems than the market price. Even if the contemporary world has the advantage of knowing more, it has not yet proven compatible with long-term sustainability. This book seeks to apprehend the unity of various intellectual traditions, past and present.

Principles of national accounts and different classifications have changed over time and are contingent on the theoretical perspective (Coyle, 2014; Perrotta, 2018; Shaikh & Tonak, 1994; Studenski, 1958). The trouble is that the SNA is "designed for purposes of economic analysis, decision-taking and policymaking" (United Nations et al., 2009, p. 1). Despite that GDP is not specifically intended for scientific purposes, social science researchers use it for analyses of economic development and social relations. Corresponding with a growing recognition of the difficulty to measure GDP, there have been efforts to present alternatives. These alternatives, some of which are designed for political purposes as well, have been shown to spawn new problems.

This book argues that there is no point in replacing the current *System of National Accounts*. SNA has developed over the decades. Each revision results in all numbers having to be recalculated backwards. One of the revisions in SNA 2008, the inclusion of intellectual property in the notion of capital formation (United Nations et al., 2009, p. 206; Inter-Secretariat Working Group on National Accounts, 1993, p. 180), has generated new snags, such as the "Leprechaun economics" of the Irish case. For the near future, it would probably be advisable to revise as little as possible, to have time series that are not permeated with various breaks. Instead, statistical offices should publish as much disaggregated data as possible, so as to allow alternative constructions of national accounts.

One category of alternatives to GDP is welfare measures (Stiglitz et al., 2009; Jones & Klenow, 2016). Welfare, for example, life expectancy can be increased from the same production level by distributing output more equally. We need measures of both production and welfare, not to confuse the two as often occurs in the public debate (Hoekstra, 2019, p. 15).

Many attempts exist to reconstruct so-called satellite accounts for SNA by expanding the production boundary. The definition of production proposed by feminist economics, first formulated by Reid (1934), is labelled as the third-party (or person) criterion. According to the criterion, an activity is defined as productive if it can be delegated; if not, it is considered unproductive. Sleeping cannot be delegated, so it is unproductive. Cooking a meal can be delegated and is therefore productive. The criterion has been widely used among economists critical of the mainstream approach (Goldschmidt-Clermont, 1993; Gershuny, 2011; Hanly & Sheerin, 2017). Becker (1980) likewise includes unpaid domestic services in the production concept, although he does not explicitly discuss its definition. Including human capital in growth models (Becker, 1994) indirectly implies that the production boundary is expanded to include learning. Notwithstanding, human capital formation is incompatible with the third-person criterion.

A common feature of some satellite accounts is the underlying neoclassical schema that non-market activities can be reduced to or likened to a perfect market system with no transaction costs, no social power and perfect information. It has contributed to some of the failures of these attempts. Some feminist economists have raised criticism against the third-party criterion because it follows a market logic (Wood, 1997). Estimates of the value of unpaid domestic services vary substantially, depending on which shadow price is used, i.e., which market activity those non-market services are compared to. As Bourdieu (1986) brings up, mainstream economic theories of human capital formation ignore the crucial determinant of education investment, namely the domestic transmission of "cultural capital".

Mainstream environmental economics follows the Coase theorem that the most efficient solution (under the assumption of no transaction costs) to externalities is not government action but to let the various parties negotiate a solution. A price tag is put on these externalities. However, attempts to put a price tag on environmental degradation are very difficult, given that various agents value externalities differently. The contribution to the human welfare of nature is free, without a price tag, and cannot be likened to human activity.

Ultimately, these difficulties in formulating alternatives to GDP often rest on social prejudice, a difficulty imagining human phenomena different from the present predominate capitalist relations. Studying the economic thought of non-capitalist societies can be an essential intellectual exercise to overcome such social prejudice.

In the neoclassical and feminist traditions, production and work have sometimes been equated, but it is crucial to separate the two analytically. Marxists have long argued that only labour contributes to value added, not capital, which goes back to Classical economists' distinction between productive and unproductive labour and the labour value theory. National accounts are inconsistent in this respect. Taxes are regarded as transfers, which are treated differently from capital income. However, there is no central difference between taxes and profits. Treating tax as income from a physical asset is not far-fetched, given that states control territory. Taking the assumptions of neoclassical economics literally, it is not the rich that exploit the poor, nor women and ethnic minorities that are discriminated at the market, given that everybody is paid according to their marginal productivity. As asserted by Becker (1980, pp. 22–25):

> Men have been less biologically committed to the care of children, and have spent their time and energy on food, clothing protection, and other market activities... Since the biological natures of men and women differ,

the assumption that the time of men and women are perfect substitutes even at a rate different from unity is not realistic... Complementarity implies that households with men and women are more efficient than households with only one sex, but because both sexes are required to produce certain commodities complementarity reduces the sexual division of labor in the allocation of time and investments... Wage rates are lower for women at least partly because they invest less than men in market human capital, while the productivity of household time is presumably greater for women partly because they invest more than men in household capital.

The labour value theory tells a different story, in that the unprivileged transfer embodied labour to the privileged. For example, women work more than men but earn less income and own less capital. Historically, contrary to the claims of Becker, women have been active in food and cloth production for the market. Women were drivers of the first industrial revolution. Early factory owners in England strongly preferred women and youth workers, while more restrictions on female workforce outside the home in China prevented widespread adoption of machinery (Goldstone, 1996). Although both machines and territories are physically necessary for production to occur, their control rendering income streams is a social construction, not a physical necessity. Furthermore, according to Marx, as discussed in Chapter 2, there is not only a transfer from the workers to capitalists but correspondingly between capitalists. The growth of housing markets, financial services and intellectual property further demonstrate that perspective's relevance.

In need of greater precision and formalisation

The purpose of this book is to show that trans-historical definitions of production, work and consumption are possible to formalise. This study proposes a conceptual framework that shows that various definitions of the production boundary can be perceived as variations of a common understanding across different theoretical traditions of how humans consciously change external nature in order to satisfy human needs.

Finding greater precision to terms such as production, work and consumption, should be related to the analytical purpose of such conduct. Since the current national accounts use a quite eclectic definition of the production boundary, greater precision may enable us to understand the limits of the concept of GDP as applied today and of alternative formulations. As discussed in chapter 2, Marxist economists only consider labour that produces a surplus value for the capitalist as productive. They have never presented an unambiguous articulation of productive and unproductive labour or even of work itself. The weakness of satellite accounts where unpaid domestic services are included is that they still rely on putting a shadow market price on those activities. The growth of the service economy, various intangible products and rapid qualitative development of individual goods and services have increasingly generated difficulties for the concept of GDP that largely rests on a physical notion of measuring the quantity of goods of constant quality. Reconstructions of historical national accounts and accounts of poorer countries have revealed that the present production boundary is inadequate and needs a more trans-historical reformulation, where non-market production is accounted for at equal footing with market production (Edvinsson & Nordlund Edvinsson, 2017).

In contrast to Classical and Marxist writers, but along the neoclassical and feminist traditions, this book focuses on what is production in general. It would be desirable that the concepts of production, work and consumption can be linked to the primary conditions of economic and social evolution. However, such a conceptual framework may not serve the narrower purpose of formulating adequate economic policy for present-day nations dominated by capitalist relations.

Whether a trans-historical definition of production is possible or appropriate is related to the perception of value. A completely value-free articulation is not promising given that a productive activity presupposes that an addition to value is made. Value is a social construction, and what is considered valuable has changed through history. Nevertheless, trans-historicity only means that the same notion is applied over the course of history. Some values are shared across human societies, even if they are not universal for all possible conscious beings. Value reflects a material reality, although not in an absolute deterministic manner. Production, work and consumption are purposeful actions, and, as Austrian economists have argued, explaining human action cannot rest on history alone as some of those features are universal (Selgin, 1988). These features cannot entirely be studied empirically but must be analysed through reason as well. The utilitarian tradition of defining production, i.e., that production ultimately contributes to human needs, can provide a trans-historical concept of production. How a conscious being is defined, and whether the notions of production, work and consumption could be expanded to include animals or even all life, is further explored in Chapter 5. In contrast to the mainstream tradition, it is argued that it is necessary to move beyond price as a general measure of value of production. It must also be considered that some human needs can be satisfied at the expense of others.

For production, the main challenge consists in ascertaining where to place the production boundary. The third-person criterion is consistent, but needs further development; furthermore, it is a definition of work and not of production. While soldiering is destructive, it is still work (Lucassen, 2021, p. 2). Other critical issues concern how to deal with violence, double counting of transaction costs, human capital formation, non-market activities and causation of final consumption.

This book is about the qualitative aspects of economics. A theory of human evolution is not necessarily mathematical. As stated by Amartya Sen (1999, p. 3):

Mathematical exactness of formulation has proceeded hand in hand with remarkable inexactness of content.

This book applies formal logic to reconceptualise various definitions of production, work and consumption, although the presentation is made in natural language. The research method has followed a kind of hermeneutic circle between the parts and the whole (George, 2021), oscillating between (1) formulating tentative formal definitions based on various theoretical traditions and practices in national accounting (the whole), (2) critically evaluating their concrete, but hypothetical, applications on ambiguous cases that may reveal flaws and inconsistencies in the original formulation (the part), and (3) reformulating the definitions to better fit these ambiguous cases (back to the whole). In the research process, the circle continues until a kind stable stage has been reached between definitions and applications on borderline cases. The objective is not to go higher and higher, but deeper and deeper. This process is not portrayed in this book, but the results are presented in Chapter 4.

Marxists argue that production is the driving force of history. Neoclassical economists emphasise the centrality of utility. Institutionalists point out that institutions set the stage for history. These claims are very difficult to test empirically because they are so generalising. The starting complication is that there is no common agreement on production, utility and institutions. Only with conceptual clarity can we move on to measure various variables and investigate different causal mechanisms, for example, between social forms – or institutions – and growth of productive capacity, or why capitalism has been more successful than socialism.

This book shows that production, work and consumption all share the common feature of intentional physical transformation of the intrinsic properties of a subject matter. The object transformed during the productive activity and work must, at some point in time, be exterior to the agent. For work, the purpose of changing an exterior object must not lie in the transformation of the agent. A productive activity must potentially be able to cause the satisfaction of human needs, usually final consumption, which is not a condition for work or required by the third-person criterion. Consumption typically implicates destruction of the desirable properties matters have, which is opposite to production. The concept of utility is associated with final consumption, which is primarily directed towards satisfying human needs, i.e., reproducing human life in its varied forms. It involves the transformation of the matter that is a final purpose for the consumer or serves as a purpose for transforming the consumer. Work can be seen as a negative utility or negative reproduction. It is through work humans typically produce, but not necessarily so. The possibility of production without any involvement of work, or leisure production, should be considered, entailing that production occurs without negative utility for the agent of production.

The concept of institution is related to sociality. The Classical distinction between productive and unproductive work mirrors the dissimilarity of what is technologically and socially necessary. Using a criterion applied by the institutional economist Cheung (2005) to identify transaction costs, as costs that would not occur in a Robinson Crusoe economy, this study defines social reproduction as an activity either transforming a person against that person's wishes or transforming a person's intentional actions. It relates to a distinction made by Aristotle (*Ethics*, 5, 1130b32–1131a22) between voluntary and unvoluntary transactions. Productive activity contributes to the physical process of transforming matters beyond making others to work, the latter instead being a type of social reproduction. If you pay an artist to paint, it is not you who have created the drawing, even if the latter would not have been materialised without your money. Theoretically, in an example from Senior (1850, p. 8), somebody can claim to own the sun or wind and enforce everybody else to pay for the "service" provided by the sun or wind. However, "ownership" of the sun or wind is not the same as causing the positive effects of the sun or wind on the beings of Earth. Social reproduction as the reproduction of social relations should here be distinguished from how the term is used by Marxist feminists to discuss the reproduction of labour (Bhattacharya & Vogel, 2017).

Making formalised distinctions, such as specifying the production boundary in national accounting, is sometimes associated with Western individualism. It can be contrasted to Eastern philosophy that highlights the unity of opposites and the equality of all things (Ho, 1995), early Western thought, and the criticism of individualism by various heterodox economists. In the antique Greek Sorites paradox, it is asked when an individual heap of sand stop being a heap of sand if individual grains are removed one at a time (Hyde & Raffman, 2018). Distinctions, such as between heaps and non-heaps, can still fulfil central analytical purposes as long as they are not interpreted as absolute and the investigation opens for some lack of precision and multiple meanings. It will always be possible to construct examples for which formalisation is ambiguous, and where intuitive meaning can be superior. That is not by itself undesirable as we need a language that retains some flexibility for the user, even within the field of science.

The rest of the book has the following structure. Chapter 2 overviews the historical evolution of economic thoughts on production, work and consumption, from the pre-modern to modern mainstream and heterodox views. Chapter 3 examines the system of national accounts, alternative frameworks and problems encountered in these systems. Chapter 4 presents the overall trans-historical framework of this book and discusses how various definitions of production can be logically viewed as variations of a common theme. Chapter 5 explores possible applications of the framework focusing on measuring production, growth modelling and stages in the evolution of intelligent life. Finally, chapter 6 reflects on the purpose of this book and the limitations of formalised definitions. It is chapter 4 that is the main contribution of this book, while chapters 2 and 3 give a background and chapter 5 contextualises the framework.

Note

1 The publication of this book as open access has been generously funded by Konung Gustaf VI Adolfs fond för svensk kultur (project id A631–2020), Magnus Bergvalls stiftelse (project id 2020–03988) and Åke Wibergs stiftelse (project id H20–0201). The work on this book has also been financed by the Swedish Collegium for Advanced Study (SCAS) and Riksbankens Jubileumsfond during my time as Pro Futura Scientia VIII Fellow. I finally want to thank participants at the seminars at SCAS, Uppsala University, the Department of economic history and international relations, Stockholm University, and the Institute for Economic and Business History Research, Stockholm School of Economics, for many valuable comments.

2 Production, work and consumption in the history of economic thought

Evolving perspectives on the production boundary and value

This chapter presents past and present views on production, work and consumption. Many controversies in economics are related to discussions of where to draw the production boundary. A modern view takes the monetary valuation of production, work and consumption as almost self-evident. However, a study of the history of economic thought, especially before the 20th century, reveals how this idea is historically contingent. Many of today's discussions have antecedents. For example, some of the problems of evaluating the contribution of financial services discussed in the next chapter have been already recognised by antique philosophers.

Historically, there are three main traditions of how to set the production boundary: the surplus, the utilitarian and the market principle traditions. In the first tradition, productive activities are described as productive of surplus or accumulation of wealth, in the second of utility or satisfaction of human needs and in the third of incomes from the market. Studenski (1958, p. 11) similarly distinguishes between the restricted material production concept, which includes only "material goods" (and possibly some "material services"), the comprehensive production concept, which includes all commodities and services, and the restricted market production concept, which only includes goods and services produced for the market. The restricted material production concept was dominant among Classical economists, while neoclassical economists advocated the comprehensive production concept. Modern national accounts rest on the restricted market production concept, which goes back to the Keynesian revolution.

Measuring aggregate production presupposes a perception of value. Only activities that generate new value are considered productive – in the surplus tradition, it is surplus value, in the utilitarian tradition, new utility, and in the market tradition, gross output (while value added can be negative). There is a long debate amongst economists about value. A related issue concerns which production factors are productive. Classical economists distinguished between labour, capital and land. French economists of the 18th century developed a

DOI: 10.4324/9781003057017-2

land theory of value. A modern version is ecological economics, which emphasises the natural constraints on production. Marxist economists instead advocated a labour value theory, according to which only labour is productive, reproducible capital is past labour and nature is not productive of its own. Neoclassical economists emphasised that both labour and capital are productive. The value added is divided between the contributions of capital and labour. Later theories added new production factors such as knowledge, human, social and cultural capital.

Next follows a presentation of pre-capitalist economic thought, including ideas of economic relations in religious texts, early modern economic thinking and Classical economics. The rest of the chapter is a comparison of various mainstream and heterodox traditions: Marxism, Neoclassical economics, Keynesianism, Post-Keynesian economics, Austrian economics, Schumpeterian economics, Feminism, Institutionalism and Ecologism.

Pre-capitalist economic thought

Pre-capitalist thought on production, work and consumption is not coherent, but some themes are reoccurring across time and continents. Many ideas and debates in modern society on economic growth, consumption and the environment can, at least in a rudimentary form, be traced far backwards in time.

The term economics is derived from the Greek term *oikonomike*, household management, reflecting that the household was the main production unit at the time. It is, therefore, a historical perplexity that most household production today is not considered part of economic activity, as if only money can give value to a product.

Anthropologists have shown that the predominant exchange in pre-monetary societies was not bartered trade, and took more varied forms, for example, as a gift economy among non-strangers. Graeber (2011) writes that the barter myth "makes it possible to imagine a world that is nothing more than a series of cold-blooded calculations"; trade is turned into a physical necessity, rather than a specific social form. Some of the views of these societies have become known through contact with modern societies. For example, William Charles Mariner, who as a teenager lived on the island of Tonga 1806–1810, in his later account quoted a chief named Fīnau 'Ulukālala (Martin, 1827, pp. 213–214):

> … Finow … thought it a foolish thing that people should place a value
> on money, when they either could not or would not apply it to any useful
> (physical) purpose. "If," said he, "it were made of iron, and could be
> converted into knives, axes, and chisels, there would be some sense in
> placing a value on it; but as it is, I see none. If a man," he added, "has
> more yams than he wants, let him exchange some of them away for pork
> or gnatoo. Certainly money is much handier, and more convenient, but
> then, as it will not spoil by being kept, people will store it up, instead of

sharing it out, as a chief ought to do, and thus become selfish; whereas, if provisions were the principal property of a man, and it ought to be, as being both the most useful and the most necessary, he could not store it up, for it would spoil, and so he would be obliged either to exchange it away for something else useful, or share it out to his neighbours, and inferior chiefs and dependents, for nothing." He concluded by saying "I understand now very well what it is that makes the Papalangis [white men] so selfish – it is this money!"

Several ancient texts explicitly warn about technological progress (Cosimo, 2019, p. 2). According to the *Book of Genesis* (Douy-Rheims_version, 1609, pp. 13–14), when people attempted to build a tower that would reach heaven, God decided to confound the tongue of men. The myth of Icarus has sparked the idiom "don't fly too close to the sun". A negative view of wealth accumulation was common in the agricultural society, across various cultures and epochs, reflecting that these societies were not based on fast economic growth (Perrotta, 2003). Lao Tzu (1988, pp. 19, 33, 44, 80) counterposes economic and wealth growth to a happy society, fore-shadowing the modern degrowth debate:

> Throw away industry and profit, and there won't be any thieves … If you realize that you have enough, you are truly rich … If your happiness depends on money, you will never by happy with yourself.… If a country is governed wisely, its inhabitants will be content. They enjoy the labor of their hands and don't waste time inventing labor-saving machines. Since they dearly love their homes, they aren't interested in travel … There may be an arsenal of weapons, but nobody ever uses them. People enjoy their food, take pleasure in being with their families, spend weekends working in their gardens, delight in the doings of the neighborhood.

In the pre-capitalist era, it was considered that the main purpose of economic activities was to satisfy human needs. The myth of King Midas that rejoices when he turns everything to gold until he realises that he cannot eat, reflects such a standpoint. *Quran* (Itani, 2014, p. 150) recognises the centrality of reproduction:

> … Allah originates the creation, and then reproduces it …

Pre-capitalist thinking was not hedonistic, with some exceptions, such as *Charvaka*. Human needs were considered to be limited, with some similarities to today's criticism of consumerism.

The Bible, the Quran, Vedic texts, Sutra texts and Buddhist Jatakas express negative views on usury and advocate either complete prohibition or restricted use (Visser & McIntosh, 1998). For example, the *Quran* (Itani, 2014, p. 16) states:

> … Allah has permitted commerce, and has forbidden usury.

The ancient Indian materialist school of *Charvaka*, opposing both Buddhism and Hinduism, developed an early utilitarian viewpoint, preceding Bentham's ethics of maximising pleasure and minimising pain by more than 2000 years. In *Sarva-siddhanta Sangraha* (Shankaracharya, 1909, p. 6), written in 7th century AD, the school's views are described as followed:

> The experience of (the miseries of) hell consists (only) in the pain caused by enemies, by injurious weapons, by diseases and other causes of suffering … It is only a fool that becomes thin and worn out to dryness by performing penances, and by fasting, etc … By adopting only those means which are seen (to be practical) such as agriculture, the tending of cattle, trade, politics and administration, etc., a wise man should always (endeavour to) enjoy pleasures (here) in this world.

Preceding Maslow's hierarchy of needs, in the ancient Indian collection of animal fables *Panchatantra*, Vishnu Sharma states (Ryder, 1955, p. 467):

> Until a mortal's belly-pot Is full, he does not care a jot For love or music, wit or shame, For body's care or scholar's name, For virtue or for social charm, For lightness or release from harm, For godlike wisdom, youthful beauty, For purity or anxious duty.

The negative opinion of wealth accumulation was not universal. For example, ancient Mesopotamian laws regulated the very high interest rates charged for loans (Nagarajan, 2011). With the rise of agrarian society, accumulation of material wealth became prominent. Land was an imperative investment. Storage is a kind of capital accumulation. A passage in the *Epose of Gilgamesh* (Sîn-lēqi-unninni, 1998, p. tablet VI) provides a noteworthy statement concerning the storage of food supplies in an agrarian society:

> Anu addressed princess Ishtar, saying: "If you demand the Bull of Heaven from me, there will be seven years of empty husks for the land of Uruk. Have you collected grain for the people! Have you made grasses grow for the animals?" Ishtar addressed Anu, her father, saying: "I have heaped grain in the granaries for the people, I made grasses grow for the animals, in order that they might eat in the seven years of empty husks. I have collected grain for the people, I have made grasses grow for the animals."

Arthashastra, sometimes translated as the "science of wealth", credited to have been written by the Indian philosopher Chanakya around 300 BC, is a treatise on economics, policy and military strategy. It was partly influenced by *Charvaka*'s rejection of supernatural explanations. The work does not condemn interest rates but proposes regulation. It remarks that higher risk premiums justify higher rates. It emphasises the role of wealth accumulation for further accumulation, foreshadowing contemporary growth theory and input–output analysis of national accounts (Kautilya, 2000, p. 419):

> Men, without wealth, do not attain their objects even with hundreds of efforts; objects are secured through objects, as elephants are through elephants to catch them.

Arthashastra's (Kautilya, 1915, p. 12) discussion on *Varta*, which could be translated as livelihood or economics, resembles the later utilitarian tradition in setting the production boundary:

> Agriculture, cattle-breeding and trade constitute *Varta*. It is most useful in that it brings grains, cattle, gold, forest produce (*kupya*), and free labour (*vishti*).

In the ancient Chinese work *Yue jue shu*, the usefulness of both agriculture and trade is similarly recognised (Milburn, 2007, p. 36):

> If farmers are harmed then grass and trees are not cleared, if tradesmen are injured then goods are not put on the market.

With the rise of writing and public administration, an education system developed for the elite outside of the family. *Arthashastra* (Kautilya, 1915, p. 12) has an appreciative and utilitarian view of human capital formation. It advises students to study systematically and the king to be well educated and disciplined in sciences. Confucius (2015) similarly emphasises the usefulness of systematic and reflective studying. However, other thinkers consider the negative impact of knowledge, reflecting a negative opinion of technological improvements and economic growth. In the book of *Genesis* (Douy-Rheims_version, 1609, p. 5) God forbids Adam and Eve to eat from the tree of knowledge of good and evil. Lao Tzu (1988, pp. 48, 59, 71), a contemporary of Confucius, states:

> The mark of a moderate man is freedom from his own ideas ... Not-knowing is true knowledge. Presuming to know is a disease.

Greek philosophers lived in a society that knew money, but it took the form of commodity money. The coins made of previous metal had intrinsic value and alternative uses. Nevertheless, the primary purpose of commodity money is its use in exchange due to its rarity. Plato formulates the so-called value paradox (*Euthydemus*, 304b, translated by W.R.M. Lamb):

For it is the rare ... that is precious, while water is cheapest, though best ...

Although Aristotle did not have a clear perception of the production boundary, his naturalistic ideas of what is natural and what is not is a precursor to the distinction later made between productive and unproductive labour in Physiocratic and Classical economics. He distinguishes between production and destruction as opposites (*Topics*, 1.9), and between activities that create wealth on their own and those that transfer wealth between people by consent and through force (*Oeconomica*, 1.1343a–1343b, translated by G.C. Armstrong):

> Of occupations attendant on our goods and chattels, those come first which are natural. Among these precedence is given to the one which cultivates the land; those like mining, which extract wealth from it, take the second place. Agriculture is the most honest of all such occupations; seeing that the wealth it brings is not derived from other men. Herein it is distinguished from trade and the wage-earning employments, which acquire wealth from others by their consent; and from war, which wrings it from them perforce. It is also a natural occupation; since by Nature's appointment all creatures receive sustenance from their mother, and mankind like the rest from their common mother the earth.

In contrast, the methodological individualism of neoclassical economics tends to conflate the two. In *Politics* Aristotle made his famous distinction between the use of a good for its material properties and as an item of exchange, which later was developed into the distinction between use value and exchange value. From this categorisation he (*Politics*, 1.9, 1257a–1257b, translated by William Ellis) next brings up that while exchange for the sake of satisfying one's needs is natural, accumulation of monetary wealth is unnatural and not part of the economy (household management):

> The uses of every possession are two, both dependent upon the thing itself, but not in the same manner, the one supposing an inseparable connection with it, the other not; as a shoe, for instance, which may be either worn, or exchanged for something else, both these are the uses of the shoe; for he who exchanges a shoe with some man who wants one, for money or provisions, uses the shoe as a shoe, but not according to the original intention, for shoes were not at first made to be exchanged.
>
> ... acquisition of those possessions which are necessary for a happy life is not infinite ... There is also another species of acquisition which they particularly call pecuniary, and with great propriety; and by this indeed it seems that there are no bounds to riches and wealth ...

Money then being established as the necessary medium of exchange, another species of money-getting soon took place, namely, by buying and selling, at probably first in a simple manner, afterwards with more skill and experience, where and how the greatest profits might be made …

Thus in the art of acquiring riches there are no limits, for the object of that is money and possessions; but economy has a boundary, though this has not: for acquiring riches is not the business of that, for which reason it should seem that some boundary should be set to riches, though we see the contrary to this is what is practised.

Scholastic thinker Thomas of Aquinas argued that trade is unnatural, but it is necessary in a non-perfect world, as long as a just price prevails. Fabio Monsalve (2014) contends that early scholastic thinkers tried to combine two conflicting theories of value, a cost-of-production theory, which links the value of goods to their cost of production (primarily labour input) and the subjective utility theory, which associated the value of goods to their satisfaction of human needs.

Preceding some of the problems in modern national accounts on double counting, Aquinas (1981, pp. II–II, Q78, A1) purports:

… To take usury for money lent is unjust in itself, because this is to sell what does not exist, and this evidently leads to inequality which is contrary to justice. In order to make this evident, we must observe that there are certain things the use of which consists in their consumption: thus we consume wine when we use it for drink and we consume wheat when we use it for food. Wherefore in such like things the use of the thing must not be reckoned apart from the thing itself, and whoever is granted the use of the thing, is granted the thing itself and for this reason, to lend things of this kin is to transfer the ownership. Accordingly if a man wanted to sell wine separately from the use of the wine, he would be selling the same thing twice, or he would be selling what does not exist, wherefore he would evidently commit a sin of injustice. In like manner he commits an injustice who lends wine or wheat, and asks for double payment, viz. one, the return of the thing in equal measure, the other, the price of the use, which is called usury.

What Aquinas recognises is that there is a difference between the usefulness of wine and the usefulness of acquiring wine. The latter is ultimately a social relation. Aquina's classification is related to the Classical economists' later distinction between productive and unproductive labour. The pitfall of double counting is recognised in current national accounts. For example, the concept of value added, defined as output less intermediate consumption, has been developed to avoid double counting. If the output equals intermediate consumption, the value added is zero. National accounts similarly distinguish between a transfer and productive activity to avoid double counting.

Schumpeter (1954, p. 61) purports that Aristotle came close to formulating a labour-cost theory, but it was not explicit. While classical Greek philosophers regarded labour as a waste of time, reflecting the point of view of free slave-owners that could devote their full attention to philosophy, art and politics. In the *Bible*, labour was not considered degrading (Sedlcek & Havel, 2011, p. 86). Work as a specific human activity is noted in the *Book of Job* (Douy-Rheims_version, 1609, p. 642):

> Man is born to labour, and the bird to fly.

Work as the consumption or even destruction of the worker is noted by several ancient thinkers. In the *Epic of Gilgamesh*, Gilgamesh, the ruler of Uruk, attempts to increase his subject's productivity to raise his protective wall, preventing them from even having contact with their children and wives (Sedlcek & Havel, 2011, p. 21), exemplifying the disutility of work. Zhuang Zhou (2013, p. 252) similarly writes:

> If the body is made to labor and take no rest, it will wear out …

Much later, Marx described how the absolute surplus value could be enlarged by increasing the hours worked per day, but there is a physical limit to such exploitation. The Jewish Sabbath is a recognition of that limitation. Even God had to rest after six days of work creating the world. In *Muqaddimah*, chapter 5, section 1, Ibn Khaldun (1967) alludes that labour generates profit, coming close to Marx' theory of exploitation:

> (Man) obtains (some profit) through no efforts of his own, as, for instance, through rain that makes the fields thrive, and similar things. However, these things are only contributory. His own efforts must be combined with them … human labor is necessary for every profit and capital accumulation. When (the source of profit) is work as such, as, for instance, (the exercise of) a craft, this is obvious. When the source of gain is animals, plants, or minerals, (this is not quite as obvious, but) human labor is still necessary, as one can see. Without (human labor), no gain will be obtained, and there will be no useful (result) … If the profit results from something other than a craft, the value of the resulting profit and acquired (capital) must (also) include the value of the labor by which it was obtained. Without labor, it would not have been acquired.

Early modern economic thinking

When capitalist relations developed during the early modern period, a more positive assessment of money wealth appeared, which mercantilist thought exemplifies. As Marx (1965) puts it:

> Buying in order to sell, or, more accurately, buying in order to sell dearer, M-C-M', appears certainly to be a form peculiar to one kind of capital alone, namely, merchants' capital.

With the rise of merchant capitalism, especially in foreign trade after the discovery of America by Europeans and the inflow of silver into Europe, the old scholastic thought became untenable. Late scholastic thought, such as the Spanish Salamanca School, and mercantilism dropped ideas about the just price and ban on the interest rate. The Salamanca school developed various arguments in support of interest rates (Rothbard, 1976). The exchangers must be allowed to make profit and cover their losses. It is a risk premium and involves opportunity cost. Money is a merchandise and has a price. Similar ideas were formulated much earlier, for example, in *Arthashastra*.

The surplus tradition advanced during the merchant capitalist epoch. Production came to be regarded as activities that are productive of surplus. During this period, the distinction between productive and unproductive activities disseminated, recognising the conflict between public and individualist interests. Already in 1516, in *Utopia* Thomas More (More, 1516, p. 98) notes:

> Then consider how few of those that work are employed in labors that are of real service, for we, who measure all things by money, give rise to many trades that are both vain and superfluous, and serve only to support riot and luxury: for if those who work were employed only in such things as the conveniences of life require, there would be such an abundance of them that the prices of them would so sink that tradesmen could not be maintained by their gains ...

While many mercantilists emphasised the importance of trade, for example, that only agrarian production destined for export was productive, physiocrats considered only agriculture to be productive of surplus and Classical economists considered both agriculture and manufacturing to be productive. This reflected an evolution of capitalist relations, from mainly being located within foreign trade, to agriculture and finally to manufacturing.

According to Studenski (1958, pp. 13–15), William Petty and Gregory King advocated a comprehensive concept of production as early as the late 18th century. Petty developed an input-based theory of value, where value can be reduced to labour and land. To keep track of the population, statistical methods and political arithmetics were founded in the 17th century by Petty. It laid the groundwork for modern national accounts and equilibrium analysis. Petty presents the first calculation of national income and national wealth. National wealth consists of non-human resources (capital and land) and humans. He shows that national income is the same by income and by expenditures. National income equals the payments for all production factors (land, capital, labour). Wealth is valued in relation to income. Petty considers landowners, theologians, doctors, pharmacists, lawyers, administrators, philosophers, gamblers, cheats, prostitutes, entertainers, menial servants, and beggars as unproductive, as well as soldiers, traders and retailers, although the latter were the pillars of the nation (Cosimo, 2019, p. 7). Gregory King presents more developed national accounts (Holmes, 1977).

Mercantilist thinkers developed value theory. They introduced the concept of an "intrinsic value" as distinct from the price and proposed a causal connection (Meek, 1973, p. 15). William Petty (1662) remarks that:

> all things ought to be valued by two natural Denominations, which is Land and Labour ... we should be glad to finde out a natural Par between Land and Labour, so as we might express the value by either of them alone as well or better then by both.

This framework laid the foundation for the evolution of two distinct theories of value.

Richard Cantillon (1680–1734) mentions that while value is determined by labour and land, labour can ultimately be reduced to land, stating "that the real value of everything used by men is proportional to the quantity of land used for its production, and for the upkeep of those who produced it" (Cantillon, 2010, p. 115). According to Brewer (1988), Cantillon proposes a land theory of value, analogous to the labour theory of value of Ricardo and Marx. Land was the vital production factor in an agricultural society. In emphasising the restraint posed by land, Cantillon could be seen as a precursor to ecological economics. Emphasising the restraint of nature on the size of production is related to a more pessimistic view of population growth. Foreshadowing Malthus, criticising Petty's standpoint that new land could always be found, Cantillon (2010, pp. 92–93) states that:

> The increase of population can be carried furthest in the countries where the people are content to live the most poorly and to consume the least production of the soil. In countries where all the peasants and laborers are accustomed to eat meat and drink wine, beer, etc., not many inhabitants can be supported ... Men multiply like mice in a barn if they have unlimited means of subsistence.

Cantillon contends that the population becomes stationary. The labour is therefore endogenous, while land is exogenous.

In his emphasis on land, Cantillon was a forerunner to the Physiocrats, which were part of the French Enlightenment. In contrast to mercantilism, they argued that only agriculture is exclusively productive. Land is the only source of wealth. Physiocrats did not consider manufacturing productive because it does not create something new but only reshapes objects. The farmer is the only worker that produces more than he consumes, while the artisan produces what he consumes. Quesnay points out the following about the activity of the shoemaker (translated in Cosimo (2019, p. 19)):

> is there not, one will ask, the production of a pair of shoes? No, because if you distinguish the raw material of this pair of shoes from the form of the product, you find only the processing carried out by the shoemaker, the value of this is pure expenditure made for his subsistence.

The mercantilists, Physiocrats, and Classical economists tended to consider only activities that produce a surplus to be productive, which was the mainstream perception of production up to around 1870. Marx (1969, pp. 153–154) explains the common standpoint of the surplus tradition:

> … Adam Smith … is following a course that was taken by the Physiocrats and even by the Mercantilists; he only frees it from misconceptions, and in this way brings out its inner kernel. Though wrong in thinking that only agricultural labour is productive, the Physiocrats put forward the correct view that from the capitalist standpoint only that labour is productive which creates a surplus-value; and in fact a surplus-value not for itself, but for the owner of the conditions of production; labour which produces a net product not for itself, but for the landowner, For the surplus-value or surplus labour-time is materialised in a surplus-produce or net product … Surplus-value itself is wrongly conceived, because they have a wrong idea of value and reduce it to the use-value of labour, not to labour-time, social, homogeneous labour. Nevertheless, there remains the correct definition that only the wage-labour which creates more value than it costs is productive. Adam Smith frees this definition from the wrong conception with which the Physiocrats linked it.

> If we go back from the Physiocrats to the Mercantilists, there too we find one aspect of their theory which contains the same view of productive labour, even though they were not conscious of it, The basis of their theory was the idea that labour is only productive in those branches of production whose products, when sent abroad, bring back more money than they have cost (or than had to be exported in exchange for them); which therefore enabled a country to participate to a greater degree in the products of newly-opened gold and silver mines …

Classical economics

Classical economists had a very long-term perspective on production, work and consumption. They explain the evolution of history by the development of material conditions, which later Marx overtakes in his theory of historical materialism. In contrast to later growth theories of neoclassical economics, stage theory does not universalise capitalist relations to all historical epochs and does not reduce production to one commodity. Adam Smith considers there to be five ends for humans: self-preservation, procreation of the species, order, happiness, and the perfection of the species (Alvey, 2003). Society passes through four stages: the stage of hunters, shepherds, agriculture and commerce. The epochs consist of "modes of subsistence", related to the means of self-preservation.

Adam Smith (1979, p. 430) considers only those activities that generate a surplus of material products that could be consumed at a later stage as productive, which restricts the concept of productive work to goods production. Smith's arguments reveal the connection between surplus and the "materiality" of production in this tradition:

> A man grows rich by employing a multitude of manufacturers: he grows poor by maintaining a multitude of menial servants. The labour of the latter, however, has its value, and deserves its reward as well as that of the former. But the labour of the manufacturer fixes and realizes itself in some particular subject or vendible commodity, which lasts for some time at least after that labour is past. It is, as it were, a certain quantity of labour stocked and stored up to be employed, if necessary, upon some other occasion. That subject, or what is the same thing, the price of that subject, can afterwards, if necessary, put into motion a quantity of labour equal to that which had originally produced it. The labour of the menial servant, on the contrary, does not fix or realize itself in any particular subject or vendible commodity. His services generally perish in the very instant of their performance, and seldom leave any trace or value behind them for which an equal quantity of service could afterwards be procured.

An interpretation is that Adam Smith regards labour as productive only if it increases the physical capital stock, which could consist both of stored goods and fixed capital. Labour that contributes to surplus that the capitalist immediately finally consumes is therefore not productive either. The Classics wrote in the pre-Einsteinian world, where it was not yet known that energy is material.

John Stuart Mill similarly defines productive labour as "labor productive of wealth", and unproductive labour as such "which terminates in a permanent benefit, however important, provided that an increase of material products forms no part of that benefit" (Mill, 1885, p. 60). He remarks that both types of labour are useful, but both could be wasted. Mill distinguishes between production and distribution. Whereas production is independent of social structure, distribution is socially determined. Physical circumstances determine the laws of production. The laws of distribution of wealth are "a matter of human institution solely" (Mill, 1885, p. 155). Vardaman Smith (1985, p. 278) points out that Mill's classification is rooted in his philosophical distinction between two empirical laws, the laws of physics and the laws of the mind. While the laws of production and the consequences of a given distribution are linked to the laws of physics, the laws of distribution depend on the laws of the mind.

According to Marx (1965), the notion that only labour contributes to value and surplus developed together with the rise of free labour, which came into fruition in Classical economic thinking:

> The secret of the expression of value, namely, that all kinds of labour are equal and equivalent, because, and so far as they are human labour in general, cannot be deciphered, until the notion of human equality has already acquired the fixity of a popular prejudice.

Ricardo advocated a labour theory of value and analysed when relative prices did not correspond to relative labour inputs. In Niehans' (1994) reinterpretation, this analysis is made in three stages: (1) If commodities are produced by labour only, relative price corresponds to relative labour input. (2) If commodities are produced with means of production, but there is no interest rate, prices also depend on relative labour costs, but then indirect labour must be added. (3) In the third stage, Ricardo introduced time and interest. Say output accrues after the time delays θ_1 and θ_2 in two different sectors. Then, labour theory of value ceases to be exact. Only if $\theta_1 = \theta_2$ are we back in the world of the pure labour theory of value. This analysis foreshadows the Marxist distinction between labour values and production prices, and the discussion on the transformation problem.

The topic of long-term growth occupies a prominent place in classical economics. In contrast to the mainstream economics of today, classical economists focus on the possible limits to long-term growth (Eltis, 2000), of the attainment of the so-called "stationary state", recognising as Mills (1885, p. 514) puts it "that the increase of wealth is not boundless". It reconnects to Aristotle's discussion of the impossibility of infinite growth.

According to Maddison (1991, pp. 11–12), Malthus only considered two factors of production, natural resources and labour, without allowance for technical progress and capital formation. Since population grows geometrically, while natural resources can only grow arithmetically, the consequence is recurrent overpopulation and a subsequent check on population. Henceforth, living standard is kept down to the level of the means of subsistence (Malthus, 1989, pp. 9–15).

In contrast to Malthus, Ricardo (1969, pp. 263–264) clearly recognises the augmentation in productive power that machinery could bring. However, he stresses, influenced by Malthus, that productivity growth is slower in agriculture than in industry because the supply of land is fixed, which leads to, due to growing population, increased use of less fertile land. In contrast to Adam Smith's view of growing competition as a cause behind a falling profit rate, Ricardo instead seeks the cause of this fall in the sphere of production; it is a consequence of the decreasing labour productivity of agriculture labour, which in the long run causes increased rents and wages, both eating up the profit of the capitalist (Ricardo, 1969, pp. 192–200).

According to classical economists, when the profit rate falls below a certain level, incentives to expand capital would not exist. Then, a so-called stationary state would be attained. In contrast to Malthus and Ricardo, who regard the stationary state pessimistically as an economy at a subsistence level, John Stuart Mill (1885, pp. 514–517) has a more positive outlook. He considers it a stagnant economy, which is associated with a higher level of production and a fairer distribution of wealth than before. Such an economy would be stationary only when considering production and capital accumulation, not stationary in human improvement.

While Malthus' and Ricardo's more pessimistic scenarios have later been proven wrong, they illustrate how the growth of a system can be eroded in the long run as the endogenous result of the dynamics of the system itself.

Marxism

Historical materialism is the cornerstone of Marxist analysis. Marx (1977) distinguishes between the economic base and the superstructure and between the productive forces and the relations of production. Different stages in economic development correspond to different economic laws. The mechanisms are other under capitalism than under feudalism.

The Marxist tradition largely belongs to the surplus tradition. Like many classical economists, Marxists distinguish between labour that is productive and unproductive of surplus. Although Marx does not explicitly relate this distinction to historical materialism, the focus on productive labour is consistent with emphasising material conditions as a driving force of history.

In *Grundrisse*, Marx (1993, p. 85) points out that "all epochs of production have certain common traits" and that "[p]roduction in general is an abstraction, but a rational abstraction in so far as it really brings out and fixes the common element and thus saves us repetition". However, Marx next states that some determinations only belong to some epochs and "there is no production in general". One interpretation is that since production involves an addition to value, and value systems differ between social and economic systems, a definition of what is productive and unproductive is variable in the same way as value systems are variable.

In *Theories of Surplus Value*, Marx (1969, pp. 152–304) presents two concepts of productive labour, labour that is "productive because it is reproductive; that is to say, because it constantly replaced the values (equal to the value of its own labour-power) which it consumes", and labour that is productive in a capitalist sense, of surplus value, when "the worker not only replaces an old value, but creates a new one". The focus in the Marxist tradition has been on labour that is productive of surplus value. According to Marx, productive labour for capital includes not only goods production but also services that create a use value that can be sold for profit.

Marx (1969, pp. 152–153) remarks:

> The mere existence of a class of capitalists, and therefore of capital, depends on the productivity of labour: not however on its absolute, but on its relative productivity. For example: if a day's labour only sufficed to keep the worker alive, that is, to reproduce his labour-power, speaking in an absolute sense his labour would be productive because it would be reproductive; that is to say, because it constantly replaced the values (equal to the value of its own labour-power) which it consumed. But in the capitalist sense it would not be productive because it produced no surplus-value …

> Productivity in the capitalist sense is based on relative productivity—that the worker not only replaces an old value, but creates a new one; that he materialises more labour-time in his product than is materialised in the product that keeps him in existence as a worker. It is this kind of productive wage-labour that is the basis for the existence of capital.

This notion theoretically includes some non-capitalist production provided that the output is above the value of wages, intermediate consumption and capital depreciation.

What constitutes productive and unproductive labour has been widely debated among Marxist economists (Laibman, 1992, pp. 71–87; Shaikh & Tonak, 1994; Mohun, 1996; Cámara, 2006; Lambert & Kwon, 2015; Cronin, 2001; Olsen, 2017; Moraitis & Copley, 2017; Houston, 1997). Some Marxists argue that the processes of deindustrialisation and financialisation are accompanied by a growing share of unproductive labour (Lambert & Kwon, 2015).

According to Olsen (2017), productive labour in the Marxist sense satisfies two conditions: it is production labour and it is labour employed by capital. Among Marxists, it is recognised that it is difficult to distinguish between productive and unproductive activities empirically as unproductive work is likewise performed in productive activities (for example, commercial work in manufacturing enterprises) and vice versa. Savran and Tonak (1999, p. 142) make the following point in this respect:

> It is true that at the *empirical* level some difficulty may arise when calculating the ratio of production activities to circulation activities in commercial enterprises, but at a *conceptual* level the distinction is crystal clear.

Moraitis and Copley (2017, p. 93) write that the "attempt to classify labour into the spheres of productive and unproductive has managed to create more confusion than clarity". Laibman (1992; 1999) identifies seven different meanings of the distinction between productive and unproductive labour, of which four really matter: (1) the physicalist definition considers labour productive only if it results in a tangible good, (2) the socio-economic definition only if it is employed by capital, (3) the evaluative definition, if it does not reproduce exploitative or alienated conditions according to an exterior standard, for example, a rationally ordered society, and (4) the analytical definition, only if it produces surplus value. Laibman concludes that all these meanings are problematic and should be abandoned by Marxist economists.

A shortcoming of Marxist economics is that the distinction between productive and unproductive labour is made in terms of what activities generate a surplus. It narrows the notion of production to one social form and does not provide a trans-historical framework. Even if Marx opens for the possibility for a broader definition, neither he nor later Marxists develop that point.

In volume I of *Capital*, Marx (1965, p. 35) advances the labour theory of value. He overtakes the distinction between use and exchange value from earlier thinkers. The exchange value of a commodity is a function of the socially necessary labour time it takes to produce it, including raw materials and the tear and wear of the machines. But use values become a reality only by use or consumption. Thus, new technology, assuming labour time in society is constant, contributes to increasing the amount of use values, but not to the amount of exchange or labour value. Likewise, Marx (1965, p. 317) considers the productivity differences between labourers:

> Skilled labour counts only as simple labour intensified, or rather, as multiplied simple labour, a given quantity of skilled being considered equal to a greater quantity of simple labour.

The labour theory of value is the foundation for Marx theory of exploitation. The value of labour power is determined in the same way as the value of other commodities, by the labour time it takes to produce it, or in this specific case, by the labour time contained in the commodities that labourers and their families consume. The extraordinary attribute of labour power compared to other commodities is that the use value of labour power, when the capitalist consumes it (i.e., puts it in the production process), is generally higher than its exchange value. Marx illustrates this by showing that the worker works for himself one part of the day and the other part for the capitalist.

Marx distinguishes between constant capital (c), variable capital (v) and surplus value (s). The invested capital can be divided between constant capital – raw materials, the wear and tear of machines and buildings, etc. (though not-produced commodities, as land, are generally not included in this category) – and variable capital, the expenses on wages. The constant capital does not contribute to any new labour value but only transfers its old labour value to the new product. The variable capital transfers its old value and creates new value, i.e., surplus value.

The rate of exploitation (e) is a relation between variable capital and surplus value, algebraically: $e = s/v$. The rate of profit (p) is a relation between surplus value and total invested capital, algebraically: $p = s/(c+v)$. These two algebraic relations imply that the rate of profit is always lower than (or, in the exceptional case of no constant capital, equal to) the rate of exploitation.

Marx introduces the concept of the organic composition of capital (k), which is the relation between constant and variable capital, algebraically: $k = c/v$. The profit ratio can then be seen as a function of both the organic composition of capital and the rate of exploitation.

In volume II and III of *Capital*, Marx (1967; 1966) further elaborates his theory of labour value. There is no mechanical relationship between price and labour value; the determination is mediated. The analysis becomes even more complicated when the model is made to approach closer and closer to the reality in a series of approximations. Marx (1967, p. 167) clarifies that the turnover time of capital is a determinant of the profit ratio, and so is the ratio between fixed and circulating capital. Similarly, in modern growth theory, it is the accumulated capital stock that is analysed. Marx claims that the price of non-produced commodities, like land, often does not reflect any labour value content.

In volume III of *Capital*, Marx (1966, p. 142) introduces the concepts of cost and production price. The different organic compositions of distinct capitals imply that the competitive production prices of a commodity systematically deviate from their labour values, which was already shown by, for example, Ricardo. This is a consequence of the equalisation of the profit rate between different capitals, assuming competitive conditions. Through such an equalisation of the profit rate, Marx claims there is a transfer of value from the more labour-intensive capital to more capital-intensive capital. In other words, more capital-intensive capital appropriates not only the surplus value of its own workers but also part of the surplus value produced by the workers of more labour-intensive capital. To the individual capitalist, this would appear as if the amount of constant capital contributes as much as the amount of variable capital to his/her profit. Marxists do not judge capitalism in this individualistic manner; they see capitalism at an aggregate level. Shaikh and Tonak (1994, p. 35) distinguish between profit on alienation and profit on surplus value. Profit on alienation arises due to transfers in the exchange, so-called unequal exchange, and not from surplus value production, which does not involve unequal exchange given that labour is paid its value, i.e., paid what workers consume.

Neoclassical economics

Classical economics strived to lend economics an objective foundation, representing a kind of empiricism. Jevons, Walras and Menger propelled the neoclassical or marginalist revolution in the 1870s. They rejected the objectivist theory of value (whether based on land or labour) and the differentiation between intrinsic and market price. In the simplest neoclassical model, there is only one price, which, in turn, is determined by a perfectly competitive market. The term "neoclassical" is problematic (Colander, 2000), given that those labelled as such often are conscious of the limits of the simple neoclassical model. However, most of the labels of various economic schools are problematic, but these labels are needed as rough generalisations of various models.

Utility is a central notion in neoclassical economics. According to Stanley Jevons (1871), the economy can be analysed as a calculus of pleasure and pain, but only actual choices reveal preferences. He solved the value paradox. Water has little value because its marginal utility, i.e., the last consumed unit, is close to zero. Since marginal utility is diminishing, the total utility of water can still be very high. In this way, the distinction between use value and exchange value was no longer necessary (Cohen & Harcourt, 2003).

Although early neoclassical economists focused on the marginal analysis of the demand side, neoclassical economists later introduced the assumption of diminishing marginal productivity (Cohen & Harcourt, 2003; Persky, 2000). It was an extension of Ricardo's assumption of diminishing marginal productivity of land for the whole economy, based on the distinction between fixed and variable costs. Neoclassic economists developed the concept of a production function with continuous variable factors. Marginal product is the price in real terms. The amount of work put into a product is not what determines the price. Marginal productivity determines the distribution of output between capital and labour. Companies hire workers until the marginal labour product is equal to the salary. The marginal productivity of capital similarly determines capital income. According to the Cobb-Douglas function, the profit share is always the same, even if mainstream economists also present other types of functions where this is not the case. There is no exploitation of labour since labour is paid what it contributes (at the marginal). Clark (1891, p. 312) argued that "what a social class gets is, under natural law, what it contributes to the general output of industry". Böhm-Bawerek (1907) maintains, in opposition to Marx's theory of exploitation, that interest arises because people value contemporary goods more than the future ones, i.e., there are time preferences. In this sense, neoclassical economics abandoned the surplus tradition, given that no surplus is assumed to appear under perfect competition after all factors of production are paid (although under monopoly, there is a rent).

Late neoclassical economics is not interested in actual utility as in traditional utilitarian thought, but in how preferences reveal themselves at the market, an analytical tool pioneered by Paul Samuelsson (1938). Such models assume that consumers' preferences can only be revealed by their actual purchases at the market under a budget constraint. They are based on various axioms, such as that everybody has a constant preference order. Why agents have such preferences is considered outside the field of economics. The concept of utility was robbed of its psychological element. At the same time, as shown by psychological experiments, agents may not behave in accordance with these models (Grether & Plott, 1979). For example, an agent's subjective preferences may not follow a preference order. If A is chosen over B and B is chosen over C, A may not necessarily be chosen over C. The assumption of constancy in the preference order should be questioned given that such order often depends on the context, and agents could act irrationally.

By defining utility as revealed preferences, neoclassical economics, although having certain advantages to delimit the analysis, retreats from analysing the purpose of the economic activity itself – human reproduction. Why do people want to maximise pleasure less pain? There is an objective side to this. If somebody grieves because of the death of a loved one, is the problem the grief or that the loved one has died? Would we really consider a society that does not care about those who have died better than today's society? At the heart of the neoclassical approach to environmental economics is to turn resources into commodities that could be priced at present value. The ecosystem can be modelled as a constraint in the maximising process (Dore, 1996). Since there is a time preference, the neoclassical models conclude that future utility decreases by a certain per cent per time interval. For a sufficiently long period, the future utility decreases towards zero. If action is entirely guided by such a model, it is not worth doing anything to stop changes that are negative for humanity in the very distant future. The worry is that if humans would act like that, humanity may eventually cease to exist. Most people see that there is a positive utility in humanity's long-term survival. As argued by Stiglitz et al. (2009, p. 252):

> Discounting is unavoidable from a practical point of view (to avoid infinite sums), but is ethically problematic: in principle, all people should be treated equally, irrespective of their date of birth.

Neoclassical scholars criticise the Classical conviction that only goods production is productive, showing that goods production is not essentially dissimilar from providing services. They consider the concept of unproductive labour as meaningless, given that labour only exists if it generates revenue (Cosimo, 2019, p. 1), which is related to the assumptions (in the underlying model to which reality is perceived to conform reasonably well) of perfect information, perfect rationality, individual utility-maximisation and no externalities. Unlike Marx, they regard all services as productive, including trade and financial services. Carl Menger (2007, p. 190) mentions that:

> Because they [intermediaries in trade] do not contribute directly to the physical augmentation of goods, their activity has often been considered unproductive. But an economic exchange contributes … to the better satisfaction of human needs and to the increase of the wealth of the

participants just as effectively as a physical increase of economic goods. All persons who mediate exchange are therefore—provided always that the exchange operations are economic—just as productive as the farmer or manufacturer.

Marshall similarly points out that traders are involved in physical transformation (1890, p. 116):

> It is sometimes said that traders do not produce: that while the cabinet-maker produces furniture, the furniture-dealer merely sells what is already produced. But there is no scientific foundation for this distinction. They both produce utilities, and neither of them can do more: the furniture-dealer moves and rearranges matter so as to make it more serviceable than it was before, and the carpenter does nothing more.

Marshall (1890, p. 117) wants to go beyond the Classical differentiation between productive and unproductive labour, with a caveat:

> We may define labour as any exertion of mind or body undergone partly or wholly with a view to some good other than the pleasure derived directly from the work. And if we had to make a fresh start it would be best to regard all labour as productive except that which failed to promote the aim towards which it was directed, and so produced no utility.

Neoclassical economics applies a market perspective on the non-market sector as well. Marshall's definition implicates that production is regarded wider than the modern definition of GDP. Although, as Jane Whittle (2019) notes, Marshall did not want to include household work in the concept of national income, the concept of income should be distinguished from productive labour. Pigou (1920, p. 33) mention the paradox that "if a man marries his housekeeper or his cook, the national dividend is diminished", but similar to Marshall, states that since unpaid services cannot be measured, it should be excluded from national income.

Becker (1980) later applies the neoclassical model to household production, which de facto widens the production boundary. In contrast to the standpoint held by Pigou, Becker considers it possible to put a price tag on various unpaid activities. Including human capital in the analysis (Becker, 1994) widens the production boundary further. It is not a new insight. Already Adam Smith (1979) notes that "acquisition of such talents, by the maintenance of the acquirer during his education, study, or apprenticeship, always costs a real expense, which is a capital fixed and realized, as it were, in his person".

In neoclassical economics, an externality is a cost or benefit incurred by a third party that does not choose to incur this cost or benefit, which potentially widens the borders of national accounting and opens for welfare studies

(Coase, 1960; Pigou, 1920), but imposes a market logic on those effects. There are both positive and negative externalities.

The development of models of long-term economic growth from the late 1950s onwards has mainly been based on a neoclassical framework. The Solow growth model is the simplest, which therefore is the reference point for the other neoclassic growth models. Solow (1956) uses the label "neoclassical":

> Everything above is the neoclassical side of the coin. Most especially it is full employment economics – in the dual aspect of equilibrium condition and frictionless, competitive, causal system. All the difficulties and rigidities which go into modern Keynesian income analysis have been shunted aside. It is not my contention that these problems don't exist, nor that they are of no significance in the long run. My purpose was to examine what might be called the tightrope view of economic growth and to see where more flexible assumptions about production would lead a simple model.

The Harrod–Domar growth model (Harrod, 1939; Domar, 1946), first developed by Harrod in 1939, is the best-known Keynesian growth model. It assumes a fixed capital-output ratio, which is related to the accelerator, implying that an increase of a unit of output requires an increase in the capital stock by a fixed amount. The model assumes a fixed saving rate. Such assumption of rigidities, determined by institutional factors, allows, in contrast to the neoclassical growth models, formulated later, for endogenously generated unemployment and slump. For saving to equal investment, the capital stock must, according to the Harrod–Domar model, grow with a fixed percentage, the warranted growth rate. However, if efficient labour, a measure of the labour force in efficiency units to allow for technical progress, grows faster than the warranted growth rate, unemployment grows steadily. Only if the growth rate of efficient labour equals the warranted growth rate is it possible for a constant percentage of the labour force to be employed. This is what is labelled as the "knife-edge" of the Harrod–Domar model.

Solow (1956) criticises the Harrod–Domar model for studying "long-run problems with the usual short-run tools" and for not allowing for the possibility of substitution between labour and capital in production. If the latter assumption is abandoned, the knife-edge notion of instability disappears. In the long run, the Keynesian rigidities are not valid and one "usually thinks of the long run as the domain of the neoclassic analysis, the land of the margin".

The main variables of the Solow model are output, Y, population, N, capital, K, labour, L, technical level, A and (gross) saving rate, s, where all these are functions of the point of time, t. Population is assumed to grow at rate n, technological level at rate g and capital to depreciate at rate δ. Output, Y, includes depreciation of capital, δK. The growth rate of capital is a function of these variables. It takes population, technical level and the saving rate as exogenously determined (with n, g and δ being constant). Only capital and labour are determined endogenously. This is why the Solow model is labelled as an exogenous growth model, while in endogenous growth models saving rate and/or technical level are determined endogenously.

According to the Solow model, the economy follows a "balanced growth path" in the long run, with output and capital stock growing at a constant and equal rate. The economy returns to the balanced growth path in the long run, though on different capital-output levels (Solow, 1956; Romer, 1996, pp. 15–16). The capital-output ratio is endogenously defined within the Solow model (Solow, 1994). A two-sector growth model, developed by Uzawa (1961), showed that balanced growth equilibria are stable under the assumption of two produced commodities.

In the growth models, it is recognised that there is a golden rule saving rate that maximises consumption in the long run (Phelps, 1961) along the steady-state path. The golden rule saving rate entails that we act today for future generations in a way that we would have preferred past generations to act for us, which interestingly is contrary to the capitalist logic of profit maximisation.

The original Solow model has some problems in explaining the differences in productivity between countries (Breton, 2004), mainly because capital does not seem to have the diminishing return predicted by the neoclassical assumptions. In the late 20th century, the importance of knowledge and education has been underlined by various extensions to the Solow model to improve the explanation of the difference between countries, which reflect broad changes within the economy (Foray, 2004). The endogenous growth models open up for constant or increasing returns to scale and imperfect competition, and the broadening of the production boundary.

One type of model emphasises the importance of the accumulation of knowledge. In one model, the economy is divided into two sectors, a goods-producing sector, where output is produced, and a Research & Development sector, where additions to the stock of knowledge (ΔA) are made. Thus, the growth rate of A will vary with how large the latter sector is (Romer, 1990). A related model of knowledge accumulation is known as the learning-by-doing model, first formulated by Kenneth Arrow (1962). The central idea is here that as individuals produce goods, they develop new ways of improving the production process. The simplest case is when learning occurs as a side effect of the production of new capital.

In both of these models, temporary increases in the saving rate or the population size (or rather the increase in the size of the market) can increase the long-term growth rate. In contrast, in the Solow model, an increase in the saving rate only affects the growth rate over a certain period but limits the long-term growth rate, which is determined by the growth rate of the technological level, a quite unsatisfactory assumption. That population size affects the level of growth in the models emphasising accumulation of abstract knowledge can be seen as a consequence of more knowledge being produced if the population, or the market, is larger and knowledge being a non-rival good in contrast to physical capital. Paul Romer (1990, pp. S98-S99) qualifies this point by stating that "what is important for growth is integration not into an economy with a large number of people but rather into one with a large amount of human capital".

Abstract knowledge, which is a non-rival good, can be distinguished from so-called human capital, which consists of the abilities, skills and knowledge of particular workers and that, as conventional economic goods, are rival and excludable (though knowledge could be excludable, it is less likely to be so). In some models, the stock of human capital plays a similar role as K. As in the Solow model, the economy reaches, in the long run, a balanced growth path, on which physical capital stock, human capital stock and output grow at the same and constant growth rate (Mankiw et al., 1992; Lucas, 1988) and the neoclassical assumption of decreasing returns to scale of capital is retained. The main difference between human capital and Solow growth models is that the share of capital (physical and human capital) in total output becomes larger in the former than in the latter case. This fact allows for the great differences in output per labour between various countries to be explained by differences in the stock of capital per labour (in the case of the human capital model, the stock of human and physical capital).

There are several challenges to operationalise new growth theory. It is not easy to put a fictitious price tag on these types of capital. Expanding the concept of capital has repercussions on where to draw the production boundary and how national accounts are to be constructed, but this is not always considered. Although Marshall admitted there could be failed production, perfect information is not compatible with such a possibility. In practice, neoclassical models assume that there is no failed production. Modern growth theory incorporates knowledge into accumulation, thus acknowledging that there is no perfect information, but next, the assumption is made that we have perfect knowledge about the impact of the accumulation of knowledge on long-term growth.

Growth models are usually formulated for the industrial period but do not explain pre-industrial economic growth. The neoclassical assumption of perpetual economic growth can be contrasted to Classical economists' hypothesis of a future long-term stagnation. The unified growth theory has developed to address the failures of endogenous growth theory in explaining world income inequalities and the lack of per capita economic growth in the poorest countries by combining a Malthusian theory for the pre-industrial period with an expanded version of the Solow model for the industrial period (Galor & Weil, 2000; Galor, 2011). The early economy is assumed to follow a Malthusian mechanism, where technological progress due to population growth is offset by diminishing returns on land, which generates a tendency towards stagnation and an economy close to subsistence level. In the modern period, the transition triggers investment in human capital, which in turn causes a decline in fertility levels, further permitting technological advances and a continual improvement in living conditions in accordance with the Solow model.

Keynesian and post-Keynesian economics

The Great Depression and the Second World War played a decisive role in increasing the state's economic role, later theoretically underpinned by Keynesian economics. In the early stages of the American Great Depression, there was no desire to have statistical data, reflecting the predominant view that government intervention was unnecessary as the market would solve the crisis by itself (Hoekstra, 2019, p. 32). It was not until 1934 that Kuznets (1934) published the first estimates of the national income of the USA during the depression.

The restricted market concept reflects the growing importance of monetary and fiscal policy. With such a changed focus, only the part of the economy directed towards the market is relevant. With its focus on market activity to formulate economic policy, the modern SNA definition of GDP has its roots more in Keynesianism than in neoclassical economics (Stiglitz et al., 2009, p. 86). Keynes himself emphasised the importance of collecting aggregate statistics (Tily, 2009). However, as Studenski (1958, p. 25) points out, Keynes himself was not particularly skilful in formulating statistical concepts, but his followers were, and the application of national accounts gained moment after the turn towards Keynesianism.

Keynes (1973) deals with the relation between production, work and consumption, but only for the market economy. The ultimate purpose of production is consumption. If there is no sufficient demand, there is a risk the economy will fall into a depression. Paid work is related to market production. Unpaid domestic services are ignored, given that the focus of Keynesian economic policy is to accomplish full employment at the market. Labour is defined as market labour. Since the purpose of economic policy is to stimulate employment, national accounts regard transfer as different from production, or as Keynes (2010, p. 382) puts it, "these are merely out of one pocket into another". While Kuznets wanted to subtract what represents "dis-service" to society – for example, armaments, advertisements and financial and speculative activities – from the national income, this advice was not followed (Coyle, 2014, pp. 12–16). One reason may be the focus of combatting unemployment in Keynesian economics.

Keynes main target was Say's law, i.e., that supply creates its own demand. In the neoclassical model, what is produced will be automatically demanded; there is no failed production. There is no involuntary unemployment. Keynes opens for the possibility of a general glut and for fiscal policy to stimulate demand to increase production and employment. Insufficient demand reflects the notion that the ultimate purpose of production must be consumption. Production is discontinued if it cannot find consumers.

Keynesian economics has some similarities to mercantilism. Both argue that money is not neutral for the economy. Keynes himself writes positively about mercantilism. Both Keynesianism and mercantilism tend to disregard the parts of the economy which are less relevant to state policy. While mercantilists favoured trade before agriculture, Keynesians tend to disregard unpaid domestic services. While both for Marxist and neoclassical economics, the price is just a veil reflecting underlying conditions such as labour value or marginal utility, for Keynesian and mercantilist economists, price takes a real existence of its own.

Post-Keynesian economics originated from criticism of mainstream interpretation of Keynes, focusing on the hypothesis that there is no natural or automatic path for a competitive market economy to reach full employment. They criticise the view held by new Keynesian economics that market failure can be explained by sticky prices. Piero Sraffa was closely associated with post-Keynesian economics but was also the founder of neo-Ricardian economics.

A number of post-Keynesian economists point to the difficulty of deriving well-behaved aggregate production functions from micro-founded production functions (Felipe & Fisher, 2003). The so-called Cambridge controversy involved Joan Robinson and Piero Sraffa at the University of Cambridge in England against Paul Samuelson and Robert Solow at the Massachusetts Institute of Technology in Cambridge, Massachusetts (Cohen & Harcourt, 2003). Robinson and Sraffa were critical that capital can be aggregated. Most growth models comprise only one commodity. The critiques point out that there are different types of capital. Neoclassical economists argue that you only had to add monetary values. Sraffa contends that the financial measure of the amount of capital is determined partly by the rate of profit, and therefore there is a circular argument involved. Criticism was directed specifically against the Cobb–Douglas function. If the Cobb–Douglas function is applicable at micro-level the aggregated function is not necessary Cobb–Douglas.

The so-called Wicksell effect entails that valuations of capital stocks are more complicated in a multi-commodity economy. Interest rate affects the relative prices of commodities. The so-called reswitching, which was raised in the Cambridge controversy, entails that a specific technology may be adopted at a low interest rate, then switched to another technology with a rise in the rate, but when reaching a higher interest rate reswitched back to the old technology. The central feature of these problems is that market valuations and physical properties cannot easily be equated and that profit cannot be explained by technical relations alone. Social power and relations cannot be reduced to technical conditions, and technical relations are partly socially determined. For example, as pointed out by Keynes (1973, p. 141), a confusing aspect of the concept of the marginal productivity of capital is that the marginal productivity of capital is also prospective, but the future is undetermined and new technological development may lead to present capital being scrapped earlier.

Austrian and Schumpeterian economics

While Menger is considered one of the three founders of the neoclassical school, he deviated from the latter and also founded the Austrian school. Even if Austrian economists share methodological individualism and radical subjectivism with neoclassical economics, they criticise neoclassical economics for the use of mathematical and formal-mechanistic models, too rigid assumptions of maximisation, stable preferences, market equilibrium and positive assumptions of stable empirical laws that can be tested empirically (Backhouse, 2000). As von Mises (1949, p. 354) points out:

> Economics is not about goods and services, it is about the actions of living men. Its goal is not to dwell upon imaginary constructions such as equilibrium. These constructions are only tools of reasoning. The sole task of economics is analysis of the actions of men…

Even if Schumpeter generally is not considered to belong to the Austrian economic school and advocated the use of mathematics, there are similarities in the emphasis on uncertainty, the lack of equilibrium at the market and the role of the entrepreneur to act under uncertainty and in causing disequilibria (Simpson, 1983; Vaz-Curado & Mueller, 2019). Austrians and Schumpeterians emphasise the qualitative nature of the economy and share in methodological individualism. They tend to be sceptical of aggregate indicators such as GDP.

Austrians contend that understanding human action rests on a priori knowledge. The investigations should not start with empirical observations but with axioms that can be known for certainty. Von Mises used the term praxeology to describe this approach (Selgin, 1988).

According to Schumpeter (1975, p. 82), equilibrium is a static concept. He maintains that capitalism cannot exist as a static system and necessarily comprises an evolutionary process. He praises the dynamic aspects of Marx' theory but criticises the Marxist view that social antagonisms are a driving force behind historical change (Schumpeter, 1994, p. 437). The driving force is instead the entrepreneur.

The evolutionary perspective of Austrian and Schumpeterian economic deviates from the assumptions in various mathematical growth models, which rest on the predictability of the future. While endogenous growth models strive to take into account various factors, including knowledge, into one production function, Schumpeter (1982, pp. 84–87) defines innovation, carried out by entrepreneurs, as new combinations or as the setting up of new production functions. Schumpeter suggests there could be social and organisational innovations.

Some of the arguments of Austrian and Schumpeterian economics against aggregate indicators have similarities with Robinson's and Sraffa's criticism of the one-commodity growth model. In the Austrian tradition, capital is not regarded as homogenous. One type of capital cannot be substituted against another, a condition that can generate malinvestment. The qualitative structure of both production and consumption is important, and each is viewed subjectively by different agents. In emphasising that capital is time, and indirectly arguing against the one-commodity model, von Hayek (2008, pp. 150–151) admits that:

> All attempts to reduce the complex structure of waiting periods, which is described by the input function and the output functions, to a single aggregate or average investment period, which could be generally substituted for these functions in the discussion of the productivity of investment, are bound to fail, because the different waiting periods cannot be reduced to a common denominator in purely technical terms. This would only be possible provided we had to deal with only one homogeneous kind of input, and provided the value of the product were always directly proportional to the amount of this input that was used. Of course neither of these assumptions is true in reality.

Austrian economics criticises the neoclassical view that interest rates are determined by supply and demand. Instead, interest rates reflect time preferences. Therefore, the contribution of capital is mainly not its productivity but the waiting time for consumption, which aligns with the subjectivist view on valuation. Waiting time for consumption is a subjective construct without any real objective foundation. von Hayek (1942, p. 281) writes that "the objects of economic activity cannot be defined in objective terms but only with reference to human purpose". Henceforth, while both neoclassical and Austrian economics advocate a subjectivist understanding of economic relations, Austrian economists take subjectivism one step further. Neoclassical and much of today's mainstream economics are ambiguous about whether economics should be analysed as subjective relations or if objective conditions should be taken into consideration. National accounts retain the ambivalence by reducing everything to price while at the same time upholding the necessity of regarding production as physically measured in quantities and giving the impression that volume value is a physical entity.

Eugen Ritter von Böhm-Bawerk is well known for his criticism of Marx' theory of exploitation, which according to von Böhm-Bawerk ignores the issue of time in production (von Böhm-Bawerk, 1898; von Böhm-Bawerk, 1890). A redistribution of profit would undermine the role played by the interest rate in the economy.

Feminism and the third person criterion

Feminist economics has developed as a field that doubts various assumptions in mainstream economics that are presented as socially neutral but often have a male bias (Nelson, 1995). An example is the neoclassical concept of rationality, which can be counterposed to caring work with different rationality

(Waerness, 1987). Early on, feminist economics focused on women's traditional work that has been systematically undervalued and neglected by economists. As explained by Paddy Quick (2004, p. 22):

> [W]age goods serve as inputs into household production and are transformed by household labor into use values that can indeed sustain (and reproduce) life. The grains and root vegetables are cooked and the dishes washed in preparation for the next meal; clothes that have been worn and become dirty are washed and further processed (mended, folded/ironed and put away) so that they can be worn again. Household production is thus analogous to the process of commodity production, although it appears (as yet) to lack the finality of capitalist production in the use values produced to not have the form of exchange values. The analogy carries further, in that there are alternative combinations of commodity inputs and labor ('alternative organic compositions', in Marxist terminology) that can produce the same outputs.

Some feminist economists argue that unpaid domestic services should be considered as production, in accordance with the so-called "third person criterion", which was originally developed by Margaret Reid (1934, p. 11):

> Household production consists of those unpaid activities which are carried on, by and for the members, which activities might be replaced by market goods or paid services, if circumstances such as income, market conditions and personal inclinations permit the service being delegated to someone outside the household group.

Although Reid relates the criterion to the possibility of replacing the activity with market goods or services outside of the household group, it is possible to formulate the criterion more generally. As Goldschmidt-Clermont (1993, p. 420) puts it:

> Non-market productive time is distinguishable from personal time by means of the 'third person criterion'. According to this criterion, an activity is deemed productive if it might be performed by some one other than the person benefiting from it; or, in other words, if its performance can be delegated to some one else while achieving the desired result. I can delegate the preparation of my meal (a productive activity); nobody can eat it for me (a personal activity).

The third person criterion is narrower than Marshall's definition of production given that the latter would include, for example, studying and some personal activities with the view of some good not directly derived from the activity.

Although the third person criterion is probably the clearest conceptualisation of work and production in general, it is ambiguous. The criterion is an operational definition and does not state what production or work is about in the actual world. The third person criterion refers to states in an alternative reality whose characteristics are difficult to narrow down. What are the features of an activity that makes it possible to delegate? Why are these attributes important for the classification of various human activities? To what extent various activities fulfil the third person depends on the characteristics of the alternative reality during which an activity is delegated. Although the criterion is used to categorise personal activities and studying as unproductive, it is possible not to make such an interpretation (Studenski, 1958, pp. 177–178). Work and production are often equated, but they are not the same.

As Anita Nyberg (1997, p. 87) points out, what can be delegated can change due to technological development. For example, pregnancy can today be delegated to a surrogate mother (being pregnant, however, is not a consciously directed activity). Eating may be possible to delegate to another person if it would be somehow possible to separate the agent's mind from its system of digestion. That seems bizarre but it is not impossible according to the present physical laws. Studying might one day be replaced by downloading knowledge to an entity that could be separated from oneself. Even sleep may one day be possible to delegate. What seems impossible to delegate are activities whose purpose lies in the effect on the agent performing them, i.e., leisure.

The inclusion of non-market production is not incompatible with the neoclassical tradition. In a sense, both feminists and neoclassical economists belong to the utilitarian tradition, but some feminist economists criticise the third-party criterion. Himmelweit (1995) questions the dichotomy between work and non-work, which she argues has developed historically with the rise of capitalism and a shift of commodity production from the household to the factory. A differentiated working day, separated from leisure, had been enforced on a reluctant working class. As Himmelweit (1995) highlights:

> In surveys carried out of time use in domestic work, it is often noted how much easier it is to record and categorize activities such as cleaning and washing, than the more personal sorts of activities such as emotional care and support. In these latter activities, a relationship is involved and who performs the activity becomes part of the activity itself. Indeed, I suspect that the amount of care needed for older children in these surveys goes down so markedly for older children, not so much because they do not need care, but because what that care consists of is harder to define when it cannot be reduced to clearcut, separable activities such as feeding and bathing, or measured in terms of the hours of physical presence that are necessary to caring for small children and bedridden elderly parents...

Wood (1997) purports that the third-party criterion sets an implicit market standard for non-market production but presents no alternative. Some activities that should be considered as work, for example, emotional or parental caretaking, cannot be delegated without losing their characteristics of being provided by a particular person, or as Wood (1997) puts it:

> [I]f there is anything about a mother's care for her child (or any other personal service in the household) which cannot be marketed but which nevertheless results in utility, this would seem to be an argument against a third party criterion for defining the economic rather than a justification for the exclusion of the personal aspects of unpaid domestic activity from economic analysis. There may be other arguments for excluding certain household activities or aspects of those activities from our conceptualization of the economic, but they will have to be made on some stronger basis than that they are "personal" or "private." Nor can these arguments rely on the market to define economic activity, even indirectly, if they are not to beg the question of why the market should be used for such a purpose.

The problems raised by Himmelweit, Wood, Nyberg and other feminist economists are specifically addressed in chapter 4 in a reformulation of the third person criterion to move beyond an operational definition based on the possibility of delegating an activity and the standards of the market.

Institutionalism

Institutional economics encompasses quite diverse currents. A common theme is to emphasise the role of institutions and transaction costs, which is claimed to be lacking in neoclassical economics. Various thinkers recognise sound institutions for economic prosperity. Activities performed within specific institutional frameworks have some affinity to the Classical conception of unproductive labour.

According to institutionalists, economic behaviour cannot be reduced to individuals maximising their utility in a context-free environment; this behaviour is largely dependent on historical and institutional context. Institutions support certain vested interests and may not be of benefit to society at large.

Thorstein Veblen argues that humans are no homo economicus and are part of the institutional and cultural context. He criticises neoclassical theory for being static and not evolutionary. Human behaviour is determined by various habits. Institutions are established thought patterns that are common to most people. In *The Theory of the Leisure Class*, Veblen (1899) contends that the labour-free class engaged in conspicuous consumption and waste, a way of demonstrating their wealth and status. Veblen (1908) disputes the marginal productivity theory and points out that profit was grounded in the social power of capitalists, a standpoint that has some commonalities with Marxism.

A key contribution by the early institutionalists is to underline the difference between what is useful for the individual and for society at large, which standard neoclassical economics tend to reduce to one and the same. Veblen stresses the difference between productive activity that is gainful and work that is detrimental to the community. Although a proper articulation of a productive activity is lacking, his emphasis on what is gainful for the community at large puts him in the utilitarian tradition. This could be regarded as an operationalisation of Mill's definition of distributive activities. It is also close to Marx' concept of unproductive work in the general case. As Veblen (1904, p. ch 3) writes:

> Work that is, on the whole, useless or detrimental to the community at large may be as gainful to the business man and to the workmen whom he employs as work that contributes substantially to the aggregate livelihood. This seems to be peculiarly true of the bolder flights of business enterprise. In so far as its results are not detrimental to human life at large, such unproductive work directed to securing an income may seem to be an idle matter in which the rest of the community has no substantial interests. Such is not the case. In so far as the gains of these unproductive occupations are of a substantial character, they come out of the aggregate product of the other occupations in which the various classes of the community engage. The aggregate profits of the business, whatever its character, are drawn from the aggregate output of goods and services; and whatever goes to the maintenance of the profits of those who contribute nothing substantial to the output is, of course, deducted from the income of the others, whose work tells substantially.

> There are, therefore, limits to the growth of the industrially parasitic lines of business just spoken of. A disproportionate growth of parasitic industries, such as most advertising and much of the other efforts that go into competitive selling, as well as warlike expenditure and other industries directed to turning out goods for conspicuously wasteful consumption, would lower the effective vitality of the community to such a degree as to jeopardize its chances of advance or even its life. The limits which the circumstances of life impose in this respect are of a selective character, in the last resort. A persistent excess of parasitic and wasteful efforts over productive industry must bring on a decline. But owing to the very high productive efficiency of the modern mechanical industry, the margin available for wasteful occupations and wasteful expenditures is very great.

While traditional institutional economics such as Veblen and Commons criticise capitalist institutions, new institutional economics have a more favourable view of the latter. New institutional economics strives to integrate institutional and neoclassical economics but retains the emphasis on institutions. Douglas North, the founder of the new economic history, attempts to reinterpret history using some standard economic concepts. Institutions are, according to North (1991), humanly constructed constraints on human interaction and consist of formal laws and informal norms. The new institutionalism stresses the transaction costs. According to Ronald Coase, transaction costs explain why some institutional arrangements result in different results under dissimilar conditions (Coase, 1992; Coase, 1960). For example, firms exist because there are transaction costs on the market. Well-defined property rights are critical for an effective solution to externalities (Coase theorem).

The institutional economist Steven N. S. Cheung points out that transaction costs (although he would prefer the term "institution costs") can be defined as costs that would not exist in a Robinson Crusoe economy. In such an economy, there would be no humanely devised constraints imposed on the individual. Cheung (2005, pp. 103–104) claims that in today's world, it would be difficult to find a richer country where transaction costs stand for less than half of GDP.

Cheng's definition largely could be used to operationalise what Veblen meant with unproductive work and conspicuous consumption. Neither unproductive work nor consumption only for the sake of increasing one's own status could exist in a Robinson Crusoe economy. This idea is further explored in chapters 4 and 5.

Ecological economics

The constraints of the environment on the economy have been analysed both by pre-classical and classical economics, reflected in the difference between the labour and land theory of value. As discussed above, land represented the main natural resource in the pre-industrial period. William Petty (1662, p. 49) argued that the father of wealth is labour, while its mother is nature. Cantillon advocated a land theory of value. Both Malthus and Ricardo emphasised the restraints posed by land on production. Malthus inspired Darwin (Vorzimmer, 1969). The more negative view on long-term economic growth of Classical economists is today shared by ecological economists.

Ecological economics is distinguished from environmental economics, the latter belonging to mainstream economics, in emphasising that the economic system must be analysed as part of the ecological system and that natural resources cannot be substituted with human-made capital (van den Bergh, 2001). It is largely a multi-disciplinary field.

Environmental economics focuses on negative externalities, which are framed as relations between agents. The negative externalities outside the market are estimated using a shadow price mechanism as if the market system would have internalised them. In contrast, ecological economics more directly deals with the relation between people and the environment and favours non-economic indicators such as the ecological footprint and material intensity per unit of services. Ecological economics does not consider aggregate value as the sum of individual values, given that the latter may not take fully into account life support functions, non-instrumental existential values and the welfare of future generations (even when shadow prices of externalities are applied). While environmental economics favour utilitarianism, ecological economists prefer various alternatives, such as Rawls' principle of justice (Rawls, 1972), hypothetically decided by people blinded to all facts about themselves (which resembles the Kantian categorical imperative). Environmental economics tend to advocate weak sustainability, where natural capital can be substituted for economic capital. Ecological economics tend to support strong sustainability, striving for some minimum level of natural resources and biodiversity.

Schrödinger (1967) asks the crucial question of what constitutes life. He shows how evolution is related to the second law of thermodynamics, whereby the entropy of the organism is lowered by increasing the system's entropy. Georgesco-Roegen (1975, pp. 353–354) purports that the second law of thermodynamics explains the foundation of economics:

> ... as has long been observed-and more recently in an admirable exposition by Erwin Schrödinger ... -life seems to evade the entropic degradation to which inert matter is subject. The truth is that any living organism simply strives at all times to compensate for its own continuous entropic degradation by sucking low entropy (negentropy) and expelling high entropy. Clearly, this phenomenon is not precluded by the Entropy Law, which requires only that the entropy of the entire system (the environment and the organism) should increase. Everything is in order as long as the entropy of the environment increases by more than the compensated entropy of the organism ...

> Most important for the student of economics is the point that the Entropy Law is the taproot of economic scarcity. Were it not for this law, we could use the energy of a piece of coal over and over again, by transforming it into heat, the heat into work, and the work back into heat. Also, engines, homes, and even living organisms (if they could exist at all) would never wear out. There would be no economic difference between material goods and Ricardian land. In such an imaginary, purely mechanical world, there would be no true scarcity of energy and materials. A population as large as the space of our globe would allow could live indeed forever ...

> In the context of entropy, every action, of man or of an organism, nay, any process in nature, must result in a deficit for the entire system. Not only does the entropy of the environment increase by an additional amount for every gallon of gasoline in your tank, but also a substantial part of the free energy contained in that gasoline, instead of driving your car, will turn directly into an additional increase of entropy. As long as there are abundant, easily accessible resources around, we might not really care how large this additional loss is. Also, when we produce a copper sheet from some copper ore we decrease the entropy (the disorder) of the ore, but only at the cost of a much greater increase of the entropy in the rest of

the universe. If there were not this entropic deficit, we would be able to convert work into heat, and, by reversing the process, to recuperate the entire initial amount of work-as in the imaginary world of the preceding paragraph. In such a world, standard economics would reign supreme precisely because the Entropy Law would not work.

Through production, human beings increase the total disorder of the world, but the free energy of humans is increased. For example, one argument for a higher GDP per capita is that such is associated with a prolonged life expectancy, i.e., the decay of the human body is postponed. However, as pointed out by Georgesco-Roegen (1975, p. 353):

> Some organisms slow down the entropic degradation. Green plants store part of the solar radiation which in their absence would immediately go into dissipated heat, into high entropy. That is why we can burn now the solar energy saved from degradation millions of years ago in the form of coal or a few years ago in the form of a tree. All other organisms, on the contrary, speed up the march of entropy. Man occupies the highest position on this scale, and this is all that environmental issues are about.

A Comparison

Various views on what constitutes production and value largely reflect the level of technology, prevalent economic and social system, and various economic interests. Still, many ideas evolve by their inner logic.

Thinkers of the pre-capitalist economies generally were sceptical of surplus accumulation, especially interest rates, which would threaten the stability of the social system not driven by a growth imperative. They put emphasis on the satisfaction of basic human needs.

The surplus tradition arose at a time of nascent capitalism. The mercantilists stressed the centrality of activities that generate a trade surplus, which mirrored a standpoint of merchant capital supported by the mercantile state. When capital penetrated production, a change took place in economic thought towards considering activities that produced a surplus for capital as the only ones productive. Classical economics promoted the labour theory of value and the distinction between productive and unproductive labour. Interestingly, when capitalism had conquered the world, the surplus tradition and the labour value theory was abandoned by mainstream economists and instead became a heterodox tradition. Within Marxist economics, these categorisations are still regarded as a cornerstone of political economy.

The neoclassical revolution in the 1870s de facto redefined all work as productive, corresponding to the growing importance of various services in the development of modern capitalism. Implicitly, this would implicate that unpaid domestic services should be included in the concept of production, but mainstream economics abandoned that idea in favour of a market principle concept. The Keynesian system entails that production is narrowed to the market economy, reflecting the point of view of the state acting to counteract deficiencies of the capitalist system.

The rise of the service economy and the expansion of higher education blurred the division between the market and non-market sector, giving rise to feminist economics and growth models that included human capital and knowledge.

The distinction between productive and unproductive labour is seemingly related to the dissimilarity between the material and the immaterial. Classical economists' physicalist notion of materiality implicitly made such associations. Ecological economics instead strives to explain human behaviour with our place in the natural system, underscoring how life tends to decrease its entropy by increasing the environment's entropy. Although this represents a materialist standpoint, it tends towards reductionist materialism. The laws of the mind cannot be reduced to the laws of physics. Is it possible to formulate a materialist conception that is neither dualist nor reductionist? One solution is to view the world as having different ontological levels. Even if we may consider higher levels, such as the social system, being enabled by lower levels, for example, the biological system, the higher levels can only partially be explained in terms of the lower levels (which would entail a reductionist position), not least because of our limited knowledge of the physical world.

Explaining prices in terms of labour value, i.e., subjective valuations on the market with human effort, and utility and disutility with the relation of entropy of various systems is to strive to find explanations of the laws of the mind in terms of the laws of physics. Neoclassical economics instead tends to delimit the analysis to one level, the ontology of revealed preferences, not how these preferences are formed. The preferences are for simplicity regarded as static, despite that the actions of agents are constantly changing.

A powerful argument of standard neoclassical theory is that price is all that exists as value. What we see at the market, or possibly shadow markets, is what is interesting for the economists – there is no underlying value behind prices. Labour is, therefore, paid its worth, capitalists are remunerated for their contribution, and goods are sold for what buyers are prepared to pay. Men are paid more than women because their marginal productivity at the market is higher. Speaking of bubbles in the real estate market is meaningless; properties cost what they cost because people are prepared to pay their price given the information they have. If property prices crash, it is only because new information arises. Such a viewpoint reduces economics to a theory of agency. Anything else is redundant. However, a social theory may also have the ambition to explain economic agency by the underlying material conditions.

3 National accounts

Introduction

National accounts provide a technique for describing and measuring the economic activity of a nation as flows and stocks. National accounts data often deviate from the underlying primary sources since various corrections have to be made to measure everything in the same manner. Usually, additions are made to economic activities where the reported production numbers are underestimations.

This chapter deliberates various approaches to national accounting. First, the *System of National Accounts 2008* is inspected, followed by a discussion of the index problem and historical national accounts. The central part of the chapter explores various alternatives to the mainstream tradition: welfare indicators, satellite accounts that take into account unpaid domestic services, human capital formation and natural degradation and accounts based on Classical economics. The chapter ends with a discussion of the paradoxes of national accounting in mainstream and heterodox traditions and possible avenues to move forward. The challenges raised in this chapter are further addressed in chapters 4 and 5.

The system of national accounts

Although a few countries reconstructed national accounts before the 1930s, it was in the 1930s and the 1940s that substantial progress took place. In 1953, *A System of National Accounts and Supporting Tables* (United Nations, 1953) was published, the first SNA. It was likewise to be used for developing countries. It, therefore, included some types of non-market output. In 1968, SNA was entirely revised (United Nations, 1968). The SNA 1993 (Inter-Secretariat Working Group on National Accounts, 1993) expanded the production boundary, for example, by including black markets, prostitution, drug trade and non-market goods production. It proposes satellite accounts for unpaid domestic services and environmental effects. *System of National Accounts 2008* (2008 SNA) is the most recent international systematisation (United Nations et al., 2009). Earlier Soviet Union applied the so-called

DOI: 10.4324/9781003057017-3

Material Product System (United Nations, 1971), but today the 2008 SNA has no real competition.

The starting point of national accounts is to delineate the production boundary, which determines how the various flows are recorded and measured, or as stated in the 2008 SNA (United Nations et al., 2009, p. 6):

> The activity of production is fundamental. In the SNA, production is understood to be a physical process, carried out under the responsibility, control and management of an institutional unit, in which labour and assets are used to transform inputs of goods and services into outputs of other goods and services. All goods and services produced as outputs must be such that they can be sold on markets or at least be capable of being provided by one unit to another, with or without charge. The SNA includes within the production boundary all production actually destined for the market, whether for sale or barter. It also includes all goods or services provided free to individual households or collectively to the community by government units or NPISHs.

What kind of agency is involved in an institutional unit is not further elaborated. This definition is historically contingent as it is based on products that can potentially be sold at the market.

The Gross Domestic Product is the central measure of economic activity. The GDP can be calculated in three ways: by economic activity (or from the production side), expenditure, and factor income (United Nations et al., 2009).

In national accounts, gross output (GO) is the total value of goods and services produced, which means that intermediate consumption (IC) is not deducted. Intermediate consumption consists of the goods and services used up in the production process, except for consumption of fixed capital that represents the reduction in the value of fixed assets used in production. Final consumption, which does enter into further production cycles, is distinguished from intermediate consumption and consumption of fixed capital. When intermediate consumption is deducted from the gross output, we are left with gross value added. In the SNA, the term "consumption of fixed capital" is distinguished from the depreciation of capital as measured in business accounts. Gross value added includes consumption of fixed capital, while in net value added, it is excluded (Inter-Secretariat Working Group on National Accounts, 1993, pp. 11, 153). GDP by economic activity (or from the production side) is directly computed as the sum of gross values added:

$$\text{GDP by economic activity} = \sum (\text{GO} - \text{IC})$$

Intermediate consumption is deducted to avoid double counting, which is a central principle in national accounting. The Net Domestic Product

(NDP) is the sum of net values added. However, wages are not deducted from the value added. If wages are deducted from value added, we are left with the gross surplus (or net surplus if consumption of fixed capital is also deducted). Today's concept of measuring production, of value added and not of surplus, belongs in this sense to the utilitarian tradition rather than the surplus tradition.

The NDP is a more accurate measure of economic activity, given that it takes into account changes in wealth due to the production process. Therefore, it is a kind of measure of sustainable production (Nordhaus & Tobin, 1973). However, given that depreciation can be computed in different ways, it is considered that GDP is more reliable than NDP. Another reason why GDP is preferred is related to the neoclassical assumption that the contribution of capital and labour is on equal footing, reflecting the marginal productivity of these two production factors. Deducting only the depreciation of capital would give the impression that the contribution of capital is only this depreciation and that present labour contributes to the whole net value added, i.e., what was argued by Marx.

GDP by expenditure is calculated as the sum of different uses: private final consumption (C), government final consumption (G), investment (I) and net export (NX, export, X, less import, IM), in equation form as:

$$GDP \text{ by expenditure} = C + G + I + X - IM$$

The third method is to calculate GDP by factor income, if applying the definitions of 2008 SNA as the sum of wages and salaries including social benefits (W), operating surplus (OS) and mixed income (MI):

$$GDP \text{ by factor income} = W + OS + MI$$

Operating surplus is defined as value added less wages and social benefits for all enterprises except unincorporated enterprises; it is the surplus or deficit accruing from production before taking account of any interests, rents or similar charges paid or received on financial or non-produced assets. Mixed income is a similar measure but for unincorporated enterprises owned by households and contains an element of remuneration for work performed by the owner or other members of the household, which cannot be separated from the income on capital invested (Inter-Secretariat Working Group on National Accounts, 1993, pp. 162, 174–175). In practice, the third method to calculate GDP is dependent on the calculation by economic activity or by expenditure.

Although all three methods are used to estimate GDP, GDP by activity directly measures productive activities. The equalities display that production is destined for consumption, including accumulation of capital that is consumed in subsequent cycles and net export that is consumed in other countries, and the added value of production provides the factor incomes. However, consumption and income are different concepts.

The three methods to estimate GDP reflect different aspects of the production process. GDP by activity estimates production from its characteristics as physical change. Calculating GDP by income recognises that the production process involves a disutility, either to workers (loss of free time) or capitalists (lost immediate consumption and capital depreciation). Estimating GDP by expenditure recognises that production must be useful. National accounts assume that all three methods yield the same result, reflecting the neoclassical conception that there is only one price and no underlying value. However, this is only an accounting equality as national accounts use basic and producers' prices by activity, but purchasers' prices by expenditure, the difference consisting of which taxes and subsidies are to be included (United Nations et al., 2009, p. 103):

Basic prices+

+ Tax on products excluding invoiced VAT − Subsidies on products

= Producers' prices +

+ VAT not deductible by the purchaser + Separately invoiced transport charges + Wholesalers' and retailers' margins = Purchasers' prices

Environmental depletion and degradation are not deducted from the GDP. Unpaid domestic services are not included. However, under a perfect market, there would be no externalities, and everything would be priced. Satellite national accounts complement the official national accounts by widening or narrowing the production boundary or introducing other measures or definitions. They are closely linked to the SNA, but since the latter applies definitions and measures that easily can be modified, it is a suitable framework also for various alternatives. Other alternative national accounts have been developed that are not official satellite accounts to the SNA but share many commonalities with the latter.

One oddity in national accounts is that some activities can register negative value added. For example, if the metal to produce a car is valued more than the car itself, the value added is negative. Such activity is value-destroying. One question is whether activities that record a negative value added, but have positive output, could be regarded as unproductive. The quandary with negative values added is that calculating such heavily depends on the value system. For example, at current prices, the production of a car may record a positive value added, but if last year's metal prices were much higher than current metal prices, the value added of a car in last year's prices may be negative. Environmental national accounts mostly do not apply an alternative production boundary. However, deducting environmental costs entails that some activities can have a negative value added.

The index problem

Qualitatively different items cannot be measured in a single homogenous unit. Hence, it is necessary to employ an index, but all indices are quite subjective and eclectic constructions. Even if prices are not actual properties of the physical entities they refer to, prices are used to estimate the size of the "real" economy. That is, in fact, implicitly practised when economists distinguish between the nominal and the real economy. For example, if we first recognise that the economy has increased eight times in nominal terms during a century and then calculate that the price level has doubled, we say that the real economy has increased four times (8/2 = 4). This is the procedure of deflating nominal values to arrive at volume values, i.e., the inflation (or deflation) component is eliminated from the nominal value. A value in constant prices is a type of volume value, but the latter can also involve more complicated procedures. Volume indices are not direct measurements of physical entities, such as the length of a human being or the number of apples produced in one year.

Neoclassical growth models often include only one commodity, making it easy to analyse various processes. In reality, the economy consists of several activities. Therefore, weighting is necessary. The challenge is how this weighting should be made, the classical index problem. Although neoclassical economics strives to dismantle the distinction between exchange and use value through the concept of marginal utility, the concepts still live on in contemporary national accounts through the distinctions between quantity, related to the material properties of the object that generate specific useful effects, and price, related to the concept of exchange value (United Nations et al., 2009, p. 296). Marginal utility cannot be directly measured. Estimates of volume values heavily depend on which period's prices are to be used and on the deflation technique.

A price index, or deflator, measures the level of prices in the compared year to the level in the base year. The volume index is then derived by dividing the ratio between nominal values in two years with the price index. Different deflation techniques can display quite divergent results. An example can illustrate this. Take an economy that produces 10 bananas and 10 apples in one year and in the next year 15 bananas and 5 apples. Have such an economy experienced a positive, negative or zero growth rate in real terms? It depends on how bananas are valued compared to apples, i.e., on the relative prices. If bananas, at constant prices, are valued more than apples, then the economy has experienced positive growth. If bananas are valued less than apples, then the economy has experienced negative growth. If apples and bananas are valued equally, the economy has experienced zero growth. Different volume indices can, henceforth, be constructed with different results. A similar difficulty arises when the economies of two countries, having different price levels and relative prices, are compared.

The question of which deflation technique to use and how to weigh the individual prices is of crucial importance for how to judge the economic development. The Laspeyres price index measures the level of prices in year *t* in relation to year *b* expressed in the quantities of the base year. The Paasche price index measures the level of prices in year *t* in relation to year *b* expressed in the quantities of the compared year *t*. The Fisher price index is the geometric average of the Laspeyres and Paasche price indices. The most commonly used volume indices are the Laspeyres and Paasche indices (United Nations et al., 2009, p. 297). The Laspeyres volume index expresses the change in the quantities of a bunch of items in the prices of the base year (if the accounting period is a year). The nominal value is then deflated by the Paasche price index (which may seem peculiar but can easily be proved mathematically). The Paasche volume index expresses the change in the quantities of a bunch of items in the prices of the compared year, *t*. The nominal value is then deflated by the Laspeyres price index. The Fisher volume index is a geometric average of the Laspeyres and Paasche volume indices. The Fisher volume index is more difficult to interpret than the Laspeyres and Paasche volume indices, but has the advantage of being more stable and represents a middle ground between the Laspeyres and Paasche volume indices. There are other types of indices, for example, geometric indices, which are less intuitive.

Usually, the Laspeyres and Paasche volume indices roughly equal each other, but when relative prices change dramatically, the two indices could diverge. If relative prices would be the same over time the deflation problem would be non-existent, but especially when the studied period is very long, relative prices change dramatically.

There is a systematic difference between the two volume indices. Over longer periods a Laspeyres volume index tends to display a higher growth rate than a Paasche volume index (if the base year is located earlier than the compared year), the so-called Gerschenkron effect (Gerschenkron, 1947; Jonas, 1970). This is the case when the increases of productivity of some items tend to be larger than those of other items. Mathematically this could be explained by the fact that Laspeyres volume index can be rewritten as a weighted arithmetic average of the growth relatives of the different items, while Paasche volume index can be rewritten as the weighted harmonic average of the growth relatives of the different items (although with different weights). Since the arithmetic average is more sensitive to large numbers and harmonic average more sensitive to small numbers, it implies that the Paasche volume index in most cases has a lower aggregate volume growth than the Laspeyres volume index. Sometimes, there is also an opposite Gerschenkron effect, when the Laspeyres volume index displays a lower growth rate than the Paasche volume index.

For an index not to be biased by an arbitrary choice of base year, chain indices are often recommended, whereas the base year is changed every year.

Still, when constructing a chain index, new problems arise. While quantities cannot be infinite due to physical restraints, nominal and volume values are not limited by such constraints. Consider, for example, that in one year blue hats are cheaper and therefore sold in larger quantities and in the following year yellow hats are cheaper and sold in larger quantities. Using a Laspeyres volume index, the economy can move back to its returning point every two years, but the volume value, calculated using a chain index, displays perpetual growth, while a Paasche volume index displays perpetual decline (i.e., there is a Gerschenkron effect). Neither of the two indices satisfies the so-called time-reversal test (International Monetary Fund et al., 2004, p. 12). Taking the geometric average of the two, a so-called Fisher volume index, seemingly satisfies the time-reversal test, but then we can instead construct a model of three commodities, where returning to the same point does not implicate zero growth in the volume value, whichever chain index is used. The example in Table 3.1 (displaying an opposite Gerschenkron effect) shows that such an index can grow towards infinity despite returning to the same state every third year. The point is that a volume index cannot represent material conditions in the same way as physical quantities. To this background, the *Producer Price Index Manual* (International Monetary Fund et al., 2004, p. 12) remarks that when prices fluctuate, chaining is not recommended. Using constant prices cannot generate infinite growth, but constant prices can only be used during shorter periods, but then these periods need to be chained to each other, and the problem returns.

The pervasive use of neoclassical growth models that the whole economy can be represented by one commodity, despite early formulations of a

Table 3.1 An example of production of three types of hats and how various index construction may give the impression of infinite volume growth despite that the production of hats every three years returns to its original level.

	Year 1	Year 2	Year 3	Year 4	Year 5	Year 6	Year 7
Quantity of yellow hats	10	1	2	10	1	2	10
Quantity of blue hats	2	10	1	2	10	1	2
Quantity of red hats	1	2	10	1	2	10	1
Price of yellow hats	5	1	2	5	1	2	5
Price of blue hats	2	5	1	2	5	1	2
Price of red hats	1	2	5	1	2	5	1
Nominal value	55	55	55	55	55	55	55
Laspeyres volume chain index, Year 1 = 100	100	49	24	12	6	3	1
Paasche volume chain index, Year 1 = 100	100	250	625	1563	3906	9766	24414
Fisher volume chain index, Year 1 = 100	100	111	123	136	151	167	185
Volume index, prices of Year 1, Year 1 = 100	100	49	40	100	49	40	100

neoclassical two-sector growth model (Uzawa, 1961), can be counterposed to these index problems. A one commodity model fits well with the market perspective of neoclassical economics. The law of one price states that the price of one good or asset should be the same globally. Money is the common unit of measure for everything. If relative prices are the same universally, everything can be reduced to just one commodity. The dilemma is that markets are not perfect, and there is no direct trade between economies at different periods; relative prices can change.

Another dilemma is that goods and services undergo qualitative changes. The main method is to classify a commodity undergoing such change as two different commodities. In the hedonic regression, the value contribution of each characteristic of a commodity is estimated. A hedonic price index uses a hedonic regression, which explains the product's price by its physical characteristics (ILO et al., 2004, pp. 116–122). According to hedonic pricing theory, the price of a product is the aggregate of all the objectively measured characteristics this product has (Sherwin, 1974). However, at the empirical level, the quantitative relation between price and quality is still not fully comprehended (Hoefman et al., 2018). The qualitative changes are quantified based on how the characteristics of a new product are valued by customers compared to an old version of the commodity. The trouble is that these differences are then accumulated. Chapter 5 further demonstrates the difficulties of using hedonic volume indices, based on subjective valuations, as indicators of physical properties.

Historical national accounts

In economic history, major contributions have been made in reconstructing historical national accounts. Historical national accounts are the endeavour to reconstruct national accounts for various countries to the period before statistical offices presented such data. New series have shown that there is no regular long cycle, that economic growth during the earlier stages of the industrial revolution was lower than previously thought and that Asia was not far behind Europe economically in the 18th century (Broadberry et al., 2015; Ma & de Jong, 2017; Grytten, 2021; Edvinsson, 2013; Edvinsson, 2013). The main pioneering work in this field was carried out by Angus Maddison (2010). In his database, he has extended the GDP series for all countries back to 1 AD. A project exists to continue his work (Bolt & van Zanden, 2014). Despite the progress made, there are several problems with estimates concerning various countries.

Even if historical national accounts often deviate from the most recent one used by the *System of National Accounts*, due to the continual changes in the latter, a major predicament is the use of modern concepts that are less suited to analyse the past. Reconstructing historical national accounts is not an exact science. Some assumptions must be made and accepted. Using the same definitions to construct macroeconomic series backwards introduces anachronistic elements. Although it is desirable for a historical series to apply the same conceptual framework for the whole period studied, societies undergo substantial alterations.

One question that could be asked is whether the concept of GDP is suitable to apply to the pre-industrial and pre-capitalist periods at all. GDP is based on price estimates, but in the pre-industrial society, most of the production was for self-use and not for the market. Take Pigou's example of a widower farmer marrying his housekeeper, mentioned in chapter 2. As a housekeeper, all her paid services should be included in GDP, but as a wife, her unpaid services should be considered outside of the production boundary. The dilemma is that the services performed may have been the same as a servant and as a wife. Some attempts have been made to include unpaid domestic services in historical series services (Jonsson, 1997; Edvinsson & Nordlund Edvinsson, 2017), but generally, the endeavour of historical national accounts lies in applying the framework of SNA. There is, therefore, a need to develop new alternative measures applied to history that are not based on valuations using market prices.

A critical aspect with indices is that even if they have low validity or even if they measure the level of aggregate production inaccurately if they are measured consistently, they could still be quite good indicators of the change in aggregate production. However, economies with no market activity, such as hunters and gatherers, cannot be valued at current prices at all as no prices are known from there. During some periods prices were quite distorted due to regulations, for example, in the Soviet Union (Kudrov, 1995).

Welfare indicators

In recent decades there has been considerable development to construct welfare indices as alternatives to GDP (Schepelmann et al., 2010). In neo-classical theory, consumers would be prepared to pay more than the asking price and stop buying the product when the marginal utility equals the price. The difference in total utility and price is the consumer surplus. As pointed out in 1993 SNA production is measured in physical units, which is "quite in-dependent of any utility that the households may, or may not, derive from consuming it" (Inter-Secretariat Working Group on National Accounts, 1993, p. 14).

Although welfare and production should be analytically separated, the two are closely related. The purpose of production is eventually final consumption. For example, the production of waste is not included in GDP given that waste will not be consumed and has no utility. Waste production is not placed within the production boundary. GDP only includes products that have a utility for somebody. Products of higher (marginal) utility will fetch a higher price – in this way, the level of utility affects the level of production. Production of a better mobile phone fetching a higher price than other mo-biles, being of more use to the consumers, will increase GDP.

At the same time, a production measure should abstract from whether a poorer person buying a mobile phone has higher utility from the phone than a rich person buying the same product. Welfare can be increased by relocating existing production more efficiently among consumers. If health care is distributed more equally and rationally, the average life span may increase, even when the total volume of health care services provided stays constant. In neoclassical theory, prices reflect marginal utilities and marginal productivities, but valuations in price terms do not capture the consumer surplus. A production measure and a consumer price index using prices as weights may underestimate the welfare gains in the consumer surplus (Shapiro & Wilco, 1996). Companies can price discriminate between various buyers and turn some of this surplus into profit, but then there is no longer one price. The increased variety of products increases the consumer surplus (Brynjolfsson et al., 2003), which is not captured by applying the methods of national accounting. Leisure increases utility, but the marginal utility of leisure, which is the opportunity cost that can be set equal to the wage rate, can be assumed to decrease with more leisure.

Various indicators have been developed to measure subjective and objective quality of life (Stiglitz et al., 2009). One set of indicators are measures of well-being in price terms, involving rearranging items in the national accounts and subtracting and adding others using shadow prices (Stiglitz et al., 2009; Schepelmann et al., 2010):

Nordhaus and Tobin (1973) propose a Measure of Economic Welfare (MEW). The largest change is the addition of unpaid domestic work and leisure. They deduct the disamenity of living in an urban area, a type of negative externality. The services of consumer capital formation are directly measured, which entails that investments of households have to be deducted. They raise the crucial question of deducting so-called "instrumental expenditures", regrettables or defensive spending, that are final expenditures that do not directly increase the welfare of households, for example, commuting and legal services. Military spending is a government final expenditure regrettable. The concept of regrettables has some affinity with the Classical notion of unproductive labour. Nordhaus and Tobin (1973) also distinguish between actual and sustainable welfare. Sustainable welfare is the consumption level that is consistent with sustained per capita steady-state growth, i.e., a stable capital-output ratio.

The Index of Sustainable Economic Welfare (ISEW) was developed in the early 1980s. Similarly, to the MEW, it adjusts personal consumption for the value of unpaid domestic services and defensive spending but likewise corrects for income inequality and depreciation of the natural capital stock. ISEW does not take leisure into account as MEW.

The Genuine Progress Indicator (GPI) calculates personal consumption similarly to ISEW but adjusts for leisure, crime, unemployment and divorce.

Some of the calculations of these indicators could also be used to modify a production measure. However, while for a production measure household work should be added, leisure should not.

Many non-conceptual indices of well-being have been developed that are not presented in price terms (Hoekstra, 2019, p. 93). The most well-known is the Human Development Index, which assumes values between 0 and 1, although it includes GDP per capita as one of three main components, alongside education and life expectancy. The inequality-adjusted HDI (IHDI) adjust downwards for inequality, while the planetary pressures-adjusted HDI (PHDI) adjusts for planetary pressures, which thus takes into account inter-generational inequality (United Nations, 2020, p. 235).

Satellite accounts including unpaid services

Satellite accounts that include unpaid domestic services widen the production boundary. In time use studies, sometimes a distinction is made between five types of different activities: paid work, unpaid work, studying, personal activities and free time (Gershuny, 2011).

SNA 2008 defines the production boundary in general, implicitly based on the third-party criterion, although it next states that the definition has to be narrowed (United Nations et al., 2009, p. 98):

> While production processes that produce goods can be identified without difficulty, it is not always so easy to distinguish the production of services from other activities that may be both important and beneficial. Activities that are not productive in an economic sense include basic human activities such as eating, drinking, sleeping, taking exercise, etc., that it is impossible for one person to employ another person to perform instead. Paying someone else to take exercise is no way to keep fit. On the other hand, activities such as washing, preparing meals, caring for children, the sick or aged are all activities that can be provided by other units and, therefore, fall within the general production boundary. Many households employ paid domestic staff to carry out these activities for them…
>
> The production boundary in the SNA is more restricted than the general production boundary… activities undertaken by households that produce services for their own use are excluded from the concept of production in the SNA, except for services provided by owner-occupied dwellings and services produced by employing paid domestic staff. Otherwise, the production boundary in the SNA is the same as the more general one…

If the 2008 SNA recognises that unpaid household services are "productive in an economic sense", it is argued that the "inclusion of large non-monetary flows of this kind in the accounts together with monetary flows can obscure what is happening on markets and reduce the analytic usefulness of the data" (United Nations et al., 2009, p. 6) and that "there are typically no suitable market prices that can be used to value such services" (United Nations et al., 2009, p. 99).

A major weakness with national accounts is that they are bound to measure production in price, which is even reflected in the formulation of production in SNA 2008. The production boundary is not set independently from the valuation of production, which becomes problematic when dealing with products and services that are not priced, i.e., performed outside the market economy.

Monetary estimates of the value of unpaid household work in developed countries vary substantially depending on the employed method (Goldschmidt-Clermont, 1993). One conduct is to use the wage of paid domestic labour as an indicator for the value added (Lindahl et al., 1937, p. 213–215; Krantz, 1987). This method may underestimate the contribution of women's labour and take the structural discrimination of women in society as an objective measurement of their actual contribution. Another procedure is to calculate the market output of these services (Nyberg, 1995), which yields higher values. A solution could be to equal the value added per unpaid household worked hour to the average value added per worked hour within the market sector (Folbre & Wagman, 1993). However, such a measure has little to do with how such services would be actually valued on the market and, henceforth, add no new information than already provided by the worked hours. Another quandary is that national accounts usually measure GDP in purchasers' prices, which, for example, add VAT, while no VAT is paid on unpaid work. The question of the labour productivity of unpaid household work relative market activities should be empirically investigated, not assumed.

Satellite accounts including human capital formation

Time use studies provide information on how many hours various age groups devote to studying activities, which permits the estimation of the value of human capital formation. Measures of years of schooling are part of the human development index. Despite the recognised importance of education, not least in various extensions of the Solow growth model, very few satellite accounts have been developed that include human capital formation (Riccardini, 2015). OECD calculates human capital in accordance with the lifetime income approach, which entails that the human capital of a retiree is set to zero, a conduct that disregards the non–economic effects of human capital (Hoekstra, 2019, p. 216). There are many similarities with satellite accounting including unpaid domestic services, given that pupils and students generally do not receive any wage. In many ways, learning can be considered more similar to work than leisure. Becker (1980, p. 10) points out that similarly to market and household production, human capital formation involves both the intermediate consumption of goods and time spent on the investment. However, in the SNA 2008 formation of human capital is not counted as an investment and is not included in the production boundary. The main argument is implicitly based on the third person criterion (United Nations et al., 2009, p. 9):

It is often proposed that expenditures on staff training and education should be classified as gross fixed capital formation as a form of investment in human capital. The acquisition of knowledge, skills and qualifications increases the productive potential of the individuals concerned and is a source of future economic benefit to them. However, while knowledge, skills and qualifications are clearly assets in a broad sense of the term, they cannot be equated with fixed assets as understood in the SNA. They are acquired through learning, studying and practising, activities that cannot be undertaken by anyone else on behalf of the student and thus the acquisition of knowledge is not a process of production even though the instruction conveyed by education services is. The education services produced by schools, colleges, universities, etc. are thus treated as being consumed by students in the process of their acquiring knowledge and skills. This type of education is treated as final consumption. When training is given by an employer to enhance the effectiveness of staff, the costs are treated as intermediate consumption.

Like learning, many activities that may be considered production at some stage involve transforming the agent. For example, going to fetch a pile of water first consists of the transportation of oneself to the location of the water. The transportation of a specific person to fetch a pile of water cannot be delegated to a third person, but somebody else can transport oneself in the place of another person to fetch a pile of water. Education and training at workplaces are not essentially different. Somebody can learn how a computer works to fix a computer later. Studying to become a computer scientist to later perform scientific research can be delegated if we are not interested in the teaching of a specific person. There is a difference between delegating the task of studying on behalf of somebody else, which is impossible, and delegating the task of studying, in general, to perform a type of work at a later stage.

Riccardini (2015) suggests that satellite accounts including human capital formation should approximate human capital stocks and outputs. Human capital formation is not only affected by formal education, but also by parenting, on-the-job training, informal learning, health and migration. Human capital is decreased by lack of use, knowledge obsolescence and population ageing. The World Bank estimates the human capital stock to be more than twice as large as produced capital (World Bank Group, 2018, p. 47). A similar conclusion was drawn more than 150 years earlier by Nassau Senior (1850, p. 11), who purports that the amount of revenue derived from the exercise of natural and acquired powers of the body and mind "in England far exceeds the rental of all the lands in Great Britain".

National accounts and ecology

There is a difference between utilities generated consciously through human activity and utilities that comes from nature. Many natural processes can cause the emergence of matters that serve human needs or lead to destruction. For example, photosynthesis generates the oxygen that human breeds, while natural disaster can cause loss of goods and human lives. These natural processes are outside human agency, although humans can promote or hinder those, for example, when crops are grown. SNA 2008 distinguishes between natural processes and production (United Nations et al., 2009, p. 98):

> A purely natural process without any human involvement or direction is not production in an economic sense. For example, the unmanaged growth of fish stocks in international waters is not production, whereas the activity of fish farming is production.

Environmental accounts provide a conceptual framework linking the economy with the environment, which usually does not require a production boundary change. The main problem with those accounts is that while the official national accounts focus on human activity, environmental accounts partly consider what is not consciously directed by humans.

System of Environmental-Economic Accounting Central Framework 2012 (SEEA-CF 2012) is a satellite account to the SNA 2008 (United Nations et al., 2009, pp. 534–538; United Nations et al., 2014) and contains several approaches to measure environmental stocks and flow. The World Bank presents the measure of Adjusted Net (Genuine) Savings by accounting for capital depreciation, depletion of natural resources, the damage of pollution to human health and investment in human capital (World Bank Group, 2018).

The measurement of physical and monetary flows contains natural input, output and residuals, surveyed within the ordinary framework of SNA, but this is limited to flows that have economic value. The framework of environment assets covers all natural resources and land areas that may be useful for economic activity, for example, mineral resources, land, soil resources, timber resources, aquatic resources, water resources and other biological resources. Depletion is defined as the decrease in the physical quantity of a natural asset beyond regeneration due to economic activity. Natural assets are treated similarly to capital stocks. In SEEA-CF 2012 both the natural assets and depletion are assigned a monetary value, based on market price. The monetary value of depletion is deducted from the net domestic product as calculated in the SNA, in addition to subtracting capital depreciation from the Gross Domestic Product, to arrive at a measure of depletion adjusted net domestic product. One challenge is how to deal with discoveries of subsoil assets, of which there are divided opinions, given that such assets are not renewable.

The concept of natural degradation, which consists of all effects on nature that are perceived as negative, is broader than depletion. For example, deterioration of the quality of air and water is natural degradation, but not natural depletion. There are two main methods to value natural degradation (United Nations et al., 2003, pp. 62–64), the cost- and damage-based options.

One cost-based option applies maintenance costing techniques by calculating the level of net domestic product if all environmental degradations would have been incurred and internalised at a market price, which yields the Environmentally Adjusted Net Domestic Product. The approach is criticised for combining actual transactions and hypothetical values, while in fact, the relative prices of the economy would change if all environmental degradations would be accounted for. An alternative cost-based method is greened economy modelling that approximates the Gross Domestic Product that would be sustainable in the long run and requires complex modelling. Different assumptions, for example, whether current conditions are taken for granted or if future possibilities with a broader range of technological possibilities are considered, yield quite different results.

Damage-adjusted income involves estimating the impact on natural and produced capital and human health. It is furthest removed from the SNA as it is more akin to a welfare measure.

Given the large disagreements on how to construct adequate market prices, SEEA-CF 2012 refrains from providing international guidelines to value natural degradation. It is difficult to consider an economy that would not damage the environment. Degradation involves externalities, but such could be perceived differently by various agents. There could be both positive and negative externalities. Some of the nature destroyed is not replaceable, but what is the value of, for example, saving an endangered species? Magnus Lindmark (2019) exemplifies the conundrum of valuing wild wolves. Up to 1965, the Swedish government paid a bounty for a killed wolf, while today substantial economic efforts are made to protect wolves, i.e., the shadow price of preserving a wolf has been changed from being highly negative to highly positive. The valuation of the wolf may be different among various layers of the population. A sheep farmer killing a wolf may be considered to cause positive externalities for other sheep farmers, but negative externalities for environmental activities. Cultivation may degrade the quality of the soil, but if cultivation stops, natural processes may restore the quality allowing renewed cultivation after some time. How to account for, and put a market price on, this process is problematic. Clean air and water are supplied by nature. Given that there is abundant supply, the marginal utility, and therefore also market price, is zero. Only when clean air and water become rare may there arise some kind of market price on these utilities.

Despite damage-adjusted income being more of a welfare measure, directly valuing damages on human health and physical properties is more objective, although difficult to measure. Those costs can be assigned a value at par with the marginal cost of health services of saving a human life or the price of comparable physical properties. However, how to value future negative damages poses several challenges. Neoclassical economics value the future by its present value assuming time preferences. This may do for the near future, but for a longer period, negative externalities approach zero − a paradox of the utilitarian approach. For example, with a discount rate of 3 per cent per year, saving one life today would be 1691 times more worth than saving 10 billion lives 1000 years from now. In contrast, in regular national accounts, capital stocks and their depreciation are not valued by discounted future income streams, but by the replacement value. In a perfect market economy, the replacement value of the stock will be equal to its discounted future incomes, but for an actual market, such equivalence cannot be assumed. Neoclassical economics is, in a narrow sense, a theory about human behaviour under specific assumptions that only partly correspond to actual behaviour.

From this background, it could be asked whether it is meaningful to put a price tag on natural degradation at all. Many physical indicators exist not based on prices, such as CO_2 emissions, ecological footprint and the state of endangered species.

National accounts and classical economics

The Classical distinction between productive and unproductive work, and the use of labour values by Marxists, could be integrated with modern national accounting in the same way as the inclusion of natural degradation and unpaid domestic services. No such satellite accounts are promoted in the SNA, although the treatment of regrettables advocated by Nordhaus and Tobin (1973) has some affinity to the Classical analysis.

Production generates a utility for society at large, not necessarily a utility only for the individual. Productive activity must be productive of something – national accounts rest on the concept that there is an output. An activity that does not result in an output that potentially can be consumed by somebody else may not be considered productive. Equating work with production presupposes that there is perfect information and that the agent acts in a perfectly rational way. Furthermore, it implicitly rests on the assumption that what is individually rational is collectively rational, i.e., there are no market failures or Prisoner's dilemmas.

SNA 2008 considers illegal activities such as prostitution and the manu- facture and distribution of narcotics as productive in an economic sense, but not so when it comes to theft, even if theft provides an income to the thief (United Nations et al., 2009, p. 48):

> For example, theft can scarcely be described as an action into which two units enter by mutual agreement. Conceptually, theft or violence is an extreme form of externality in which damage is inflicted on another institutional unit deliberately and not merely accidentally or casually. Thus, thefts of goods from households, for example, are not treated as transactions and estimated values are not recorded for them under household expenditures.

The perplexity is that if states kill persons or collect taxes against a person's will, or when private companies legally employ guarding services, these are not treated as zero-sum games by SNA 2008. Although there is a difference between legal and illegal activities, one of the reasons to consider prostitution and drug trade productive is that the production boundary should not depend on whether an activity is legal or not. There is a thin line between legitimate and illegitimate use of force. As Charles Tilly (1985) points out, from a historical point of view, war-making and state-making can be seen as organised crime:

> Apologists for particular governments and for government in general commonly argue, precisely, that they offer protection from local and external violence. They claim that the prices they charge barely cover the costs of protection. They call people who complain about the price of protection "anarchists," "subversives," or both at once. But consider the definition of a racketeer as someone who creates a threat and then charges for its reduction. Governments' provision of protection, by this standard, often qualifies as racketeering. To the extent that the threats against which a given government protects its citizens are imaginary or are consequences of its own activities, the government has organized a protection racket. Since governments themselves commonly simulate, stimulate, or even fabricate threats of external war and since the repressive and extractive activities of governments often constitute the largest current threats to the livelihoods of their own citizens, many governments operate in essentially the same ways as racketeers. There is, of course, a difference: Racketeers, by the conventional definition, operate without the sanctity of governments.

In the 2008 SNA, transfers of income are not classified as production. Counting a transfer as a produced value added is considered double counting. Although national accounts distinguish between production and transfer, there are several examples where transfers are classified as a payment for a productive output. According to the 2008 SNA, the payment of interest in itself does not add anything to GDP, while the difference between the receipt and payment of interest in the banking sector is classified as a "service" and is included in GDP (United Nations et al., 2009, p. 45). The financial crisis in 2008 has raised questions concerning financial intermediation as a productive activity. As argued by Coyle (2014, p. 101):

> So, is finance being properly accounted for in the economic statistics? No.

> A reason to be suspicious can be found in the United Kingdom's GDP statistics for the final quarter of 2008, the period during which Lehman Brothers went bankrupt and the global money markets were on the verge of ceasing to function. In that quarter, the statistics showed the fastest growth in the United Kingdom's financial sector on record. The figures suggested finance was making roughly the same contribution as manufacturing to the economy.

Another challenge discussed by Coyle (2014, p. 102) is the following:

> UN System of National Accounts introduced the concept of "financial intermediation services indirectly measured," or FISIM. This current measure compares banks' borrowing and lending rates on their loan and deposit portfolios to a risk-free "reference rate" such as the central bank's policy rate, and multiplies the difference by the stock of outstanding balances in each case.

Measuring the value added of insurance poses similar problems (Hoekstra, 2019, p. 58).

Another example of double counting is when a person builds a house for own uses. First, the activity is recorded in GDP as finished construction. Then it is recorded a second time, as the stream of rental services it provides to its owner. The "services" of self-use of owner-occupied apartments are equalled to a fictitious rent. However, this is rather a consumption than a production. Interestingly the self-use of owner-occupied apartments does not even involve transferring any money. A family owning the house they live in would thus be considered to pay a substantial rent to themselves, which would substantially raise the estimated income of the family. This is called imputation. The main reason is to accomplish comparability between countries, given that in some countries more persons are owning the houses they live in. In contrast, the consumption of durable goods (as cars and household machinery) is excluded from the production boundary and considered a pure "consumption activity" (Inter-Secretariat Working Group on National Accounts, 1993, pp. 126, 134). Theoretically, if everybody owns a house that is worth 20 trillion dollars, and if rent is 5 per cent of the value per year, then everybody would produce one trillion dollars in real estate services that everybody consumes each year by renting out the property to oneself. In practice, such an economy could not exist because somebody owning a house would be prepared to sell it for some perishable consumer goods. However, theoretically, it could exist if nobody would have more preferences for perishable consumer goods than for owning landed property. With such imputations of fictitious values, there is no theoretical upper limit to the increase in GDP following an increase in property prices.

By trade, we can mean different processes. SNA 2008 describes wholesale and retail trade as productive activities that must be separated from the good (United Nations et al., 2009, p. 45):

> The recording in the SNA of transactions for wholesalers and retailers does not mirror the way in which those involved view them. The purchases of goods for resale by wholesalers and retailers are not recorded by these units explicitly, and they are viewed as selling, not the goods, but

the services of storing and displaying a selection of goods in convenient locations and making them easily available for customers.

However, the main purpose of trade is to change ownership rights (O'Connor, 1975, p. 301), not to make goods easily available to customers. Consumers are not paying for the trade as such, but for the objects, they want to consume. Ownership rights are mental constructions that do not exist physically, while production must involve a physical process according to SNA 2008. The treatment of SNA 2008 of trade is de facto double counting, registering first the production of a good and then the good again as traded.

While transport and storage of a good physically transform the spatial and temporal location of the good, a change in ownership rights of a good does not in itself transform the good in any physical sense (Shaikh & Tonak, 1994, pp. 23–34). Inventories are one type of capital, but an increase in this type of capital does not increase total output as assumed in the neoclassical theory of the production function with a continuous decreasing marginal productivity of capital. Inventories instead contribute to a better distribution of products over time. If the price of corn is higher during famine than in the fruitful years, it is because corn sold during a famine is a different type of good than the one sold during fruitful years because they have different time locations. The intrinsic properties of the corn are changed during storage. The gross output of storage could be measured by the price difference of two different goods, for example, corn during famine and corn during fruitful years. Similarly, if the price of corn is higher in Egypt than in Italy, corn sold in Egypt is a different type of good than corn sold in Italy, because they have different locations. The intrinsic properties of the corn are changed during transport. The gross output of the "service" of trade is similarly equalled to the trade margin, i.e., as the price at which a good is sold less the price that would have to be paid by the distributor to replace the good. The difference between storage and transport is that the good before and after the trade is precisely the same. The price margin is therefore not estimated as the difference between the price of two goods of different intrinsic properties, but national accounts invent two types of prices for the same good of the same intrinsic properties. The only difference is the extrinsic properties of a sold and unsold good, i.e., a relation of social power.

In the Soviet Union and its satellites, a competing system of national accounts was used termed the Material Product System, MPS (World Bank, 1993). At the heart of the MPS is the National Material Product (NMP), which consists of physical goods and material services. It is the equivalent of the net domestic product. However, a difference is that non-material services are excluded. Material services include transport, trade, maintenance and repairs, while non-material services include education, health and personal services. The relation can be stated as:

GDP = NMP+

+ depreciation + value added of material services − non-material
  inputs in material production

The "physicalist" notion of the MPS has been claimed to be derived from Marx, but its roots can instead be traced back to Adam Smith (Shaikh & Tonak, 1994, p. 4). Marx considered productive labour productive of surplus value, i.e., of profit, while the Soviet Union had abolished capitalism. Marx (1965) did not consider trade a productive activity, while he categorised teaching for profit as productive, i.e., opposite the MPS.

Various Marxist economists, most notably Shaikh and Tonak (1994), have developed complicated frameworks of how to construct national accounts based on Marxist concepts of labour values and the distinction between productive and unproductive labour. To estimate labour values, i.e., hours worked, it is necessary to know hours worked per unit of production. However, industries producing output used for intermediate consumption are using up labour input and intermediate consumption, and so on. To solve this conundrum, labour values can be estimated using Leontief's input-output analysis, which involves matrix algebra (Screpanti, 2019, pp. 65–70).

For example, assume that to produce 1 kg of iron, it takes 1 hour of labour and the intermediate consumption of 0.5 kg of iron and 0.8 barrels of oil, and to produce 1 barrel of oil, it takes 3 hours of labour and the intermediate consumption of 0.1 kg of iron and 0.2 barrels of oil. In matrix form, with no fixed capital or other intermediate consumptions:

$$
\begin{bmatrix} L_{one\ kg\ iron} \\ L_{one\ barrel\ oil} \end{bmatrix} = \begin{bmatrix} 1 \\ 3 \end{bmatrix} + \begin{bmatrix} 0.5 & 0.8 \\ 0.1 & 0.2 \end{bmatrix} \begin{bmatrix} L_{one\ kg\ iron} \\ L_{one\ barrel\ oil} \end{bmatrix} = \left(I - \begin{bmatrix} 0.5 & 0.8 \\ 0.1 & 0.2 \end{bmatrix} \right)^{-1} \begin{bmatrix} 1 \\ 3 \end{bmatrix} = \begin{bmatrix} 10 \\ 5 \end{bmatrix}
$$

In other words, 1 kg of iron embodies 10 hours of labour, while 1 barrel of oil only embodies 5 hours, despite that more labour is used in the actual production process of 1 barrel of oil. The difference depends on more intermediate consumption used up in the iron industry. The matrix $\begin{bmatrix} 0.5 & 0.8 \\ 0.1 & 0.2 \end{bmatrix}$ consists of the technical coefficients a_{ij}, i.e., intermediate consumption of jth commodity in the production of one unit of the ith commodity, where *i* stands for row number and *j* stands for the column number.

The same type of analysis can be used in environmental accounts. For example, assume that producing 1 kg of iron causes 1 ton of CO_2 emissions and that production of 1 barrel of oil causes 2 tons of CO_2 emissions. With the same technical coefficients, 1 kg of iron embodies 7.5 tons of CO_2 emission, and 1 barrel of oil embodies just 3.4375 tons of CO_2 emissions, the high value for iron being again explained by more intermediate consumption used up in iron production. Despite this, 1 hour of work embodied in iron production causes 0.75 tons of CO_2 emissions and 1 hour embodied in oil production causes 0.6875 tons of CO_2 emissions, not so large difference. Impact on life expectancy could be used as objective "value" as well, although such impact is very difficult to estimate for various sectors.

The terms value or labour value obscure that the analysis is based on objective conditions, i.e., hours worked, similar to the objective condition of CO_2 emissions. It is official national accounts based on prices that are using subjective measures, although the advantage with prices is that they relate to how production is actually valued in society (while labour value is not a value in this sense). To continue with the same example, for simplicity, assume that a profit rate of 10 per cent is made on capital accumulated from inventories of intermediate consumption, with 1-year turnover time, and not on wage (by model assumption, not to be confused with the discussion on whether the surplus is generated by labour or capital), which is paid post-factum (Screpanti, 2019, pp. 67–70). The price could be set to one dollar for 1 hour's work. The production prices can then be calculated:

$$
\begin{bmatrix} P_{one\ kg\ iron} \\ P_{one\ barrel\ oil} \end{bmatrix} = \begin{bmatrix} 1 \\ 3 \end{bmatrix} + (1 + 0.1) \begin{bmatrix} 0.5 & 0.8 \\ 0.1 & 0.2 \end{bmatrix} \begin{bmatrix} P_{one\ kg\ iron} \\ P_{one\ barrel\ oil} \end{bmatrix}
$$

$$
= \left(I - (1 + 0.1) \begin{bmatrix} 0.5 & 0.8 \\ 0.1 & 0.2 \end{bmatrix} \right)^{-1} \begin{bmatrix} 1 \\ 3 \end{bmatrix} = \begin{bmatrix} 13.45 \\ 5.74 \end{bmatrix}
$$

In the example, the price of 1 kg of iron is 13.45 dollars and 1 barrel of oil is 5.74 dollars. The rate of exploitation in price terms is 35 per cent in the whole economy, but much higher in the iron industry, at 113 per cent, than in the oil industry, at 8 per cent. The value added per hour worked is 2.1 dollars in the iron industry, but only 1.1 dollars in the oil industry, which shows how production prices deviate from labour values. Marx describes this as a transfer of value from the industry with low to high organic composition. Under the assumption of a zero profit rate, the price would be the same as the labour value. With an increase from 0 to 10 per cent profit rate, the ratio of the price of iron to the price of oil is increased from 2 to 2.34, and with a 40 per cent profit rate to 3.92, under the same technical conditions. As pointed out by Screpanti (2019, p. 69):

> The fundamental reason why labour values and production prices are different is not so much because the profit rate is uniform, but rather because it exists.

Given that the rate of profit could be the result of, for example, class struggle or just monetary policy, prices do not only reflect technical conditions of the production process but are also socially determined. Using hours worked, or even emissions of CO_2, as weights in national accounts, have the clear advantage of abstracting from social power or subjective valuations.

Neoclassical theory attempts to justify the prevalent profit and wage rates by technical conditions and the marginal productivities of labour and capital. However, the Solow model does not tell us what is the cause and effect: the marginal productivities of labour and capital can be adjusted to a specific profit rate so that high profit rates are associated with a lower capital-output ratio. When the profit rate is zero, the capital-output ratio is so high that the marginal productivity of capital equals depreciation, which would not occur due to time preferences.

Counterposing productive to unproductive labour complicates the analysis. Some of the surplus is then used to support unproductive workers and the intermediate consumption of unproductive activities (Shaikh & Tonak, 1994, p. 50). For example, assume that the productive sector involves 100 hours worked, divided between necessary labour of 50 hours to support the consumption of the worker and surplus labour of 50 hours, while the unproductive sector involves 100 hours worked as well, with 50 hours to support the consumption of the unproductive worker. The rate of exploitation estimated without considering the distinction between productive and unproductive labour is 100 per cent $[(50 + 50)/(50 + 50)]$, while the rate of exploitation when the distinction is made is much higher, at 300 per cent $[(50 + 50 + 50)/50]$. Shaikh and Tonak, therefore, argue that it is not enough to deduct the value added of unproductive activities from GDP. In addition, all the intermediate consumption, produced by productive labour, into the unproductive activities should be deducted. This involves matrix algebra. The trouble with the analysis of Shaikh and Tonak is that the estimates of rate of exploitation deviate substantially from the estimate of actual ratio of profit to wage. This is an interesting analysis of how the surplus generated in the production process is used up both as unproductive activities and profits.

Circularity, self-reference and infinite regress of national accounting

Many of the oddities of mainstream national accounting and various alternatives have similarities with classical paradoxes, i.e., seemingly valid reasonings from true premises that lead to unacceptable conclusions.

Some of the standard concepts of mainstream and heterodox economics are defined circularly. Joan Robinson (1962, p. 47) asserts that the neoclassical definition of utility, which is also foundational for national accounting, growth models and distribution theory, is circular:

> Utility is the quality in commodities that makes individuals want to buy them, and the fact that individuals want to buy commodities shows that they have utility.

The definition of the production boundary in SNA quoted at the beginning of this chapter is circular since the concepts of goods and services are used to delineate production, while the definition of production is a condition in order to recognise goods and services. The Marxist definition of productive and unproductive labour is also circular. Productive labour is defined as productive of surplus value, while surplus value is defined as the surplus generated by productive labour above the wage. Unproductive labour is assumed to not generate any surplus value for this reason.

The classical example of self-reference, is the liar's paradox, stating that "I am lying now", which is neither true nor false (Beall et al., 2020). Another example is the barber's paradox (an exemplification of Russel's paradox). There is a barber in a town who shaves all those, and those only, who do not shave themselves. Then who shaves the barber? Tarski proposes that the solution to this type of self-references is a hierarchy between languages, i.e., to distinguish between object language and the metalanguage of the latter (Bolander, 2017). The metalanguage describes the object language, but the object language cannot describe itself. The metalanguage cannot describe itself either. To describe it, there is a need for a meta-meta-language, and so on. Since the 1970s, this solution has been criticised. There could be instances where self-reference could be meaningful. Self-reference is a distinguishing characteristic of human self-awareness (Morin, 2006).

This book does not argue for the ontological duality between reality and ideas. There is only one type of reality and ideas are also part of reality – this is the standpoint of monism-materialism (Plekhanov, 1947). However, there is a need for epistemological duality between reality and descriptions of reality. Mixing up the language about physical objects and the metalanguage may generate self-referential paradoxes (Bolander, 2017) and infinite regresses (Cameron, 2018). The concept of material product is confusing, given that so-called non-material products also exist materially, as pointed out by Marshall (see chapter 2) concerning the materiality of services. A drawback with Mill's distinction between production and distribution is that it could be questioned whether distribution does not change any material conditions. Mill's distinction between the laws of physics and the mind, as generally of any distinction between materiality and immateriality, opens up for philosophical dualism regarding the world of ideas as separate from the material world. However, while neoclassical economics correctly questioned the separation of the laws of physics and the laws of the mind, it tends to mix them up as analytical distinctions.

Double counting of transactional activities, when transfers are mixed up with production, may generate self-reference and infinite regress. The problem of Irish GDP arises because the production of knowledge enters twice in modern national accounts after the reclassification of R&D as investment, firstly as research and secondly as capital income streams from copyrights. Similarly, production of homes also enters twice, firstly as the construction of buildings and secondly as the renting out of these buildings. The printing of one trillion dollars would usually not be considered real production. However, banks that earn income from borrowing such money from central banks and lending it out at a higher interest rate would be considered to contribute to value added. As Aristotle points out, charging an interest rate embodies the potential for infinite economic growth, while the physical world is limited.

The inclusion of transactions in the production boundary potentially generates an infinite regress. Similarly to an object language referring to itself, treating mental objects, such as ownership rights, as physical objects can generate self-reference. If trade is considered a service that is separable from the goods or services traded, then it should be possible to trade the trade, trade the trade that trades the trade, and so on, in an infinite regress. This becomes problematic if shadow transactions are included in the national accounts, such as the renting out of owner-occupied buildings. Trade consists of a material change. Even if it is a material change in social relations, social relations belong to the material world. We should distinguish between self-reference that exists in the economy, often studied as a real endogenous phenomenon where causality runs both ways, but in sequence, each time changing objects physically, and the static self-reference introduced in national accounting based on the implicit assumption that the mental object of a transaction is an actual physical object. Transactions that cancel each other can theoretically approach infinity, as in the example of eating dog shit in chapter 1, precisely because they are mental constructs and not physical phenomena.

The distinction between use value and exchange value, and also between quantity and price, is related to the distinction between productive and unproductive labour (or more precisely the part of unproductive labour involved in voluntary transactions). The use value of a good or service is determined by its objective properties that potentially have useful effects on a consumer. The exchange value is a concept of a metalanguage referring to a use value at the market. The exchange value has no equivalence in the real world, it only exists in the heads of agents. Abandoning the distinction between use and exchange values can generate peculiarities. Normally, we consider prices to be determined by the market, which are then observed independently without influencing these prices. The use of shadow prices for non-market activities introduces a potential for self-reference. A paradox of shadow pricing is that if we assign a price for activities that are not assigned a price, then the latter are assigned a price, which contradicts the statement that they are not assigned a price. Furthermore, if we only include activities in GDP that are assigned a price, that in turn depends on whether the accounts choose to assign a price or not – which makes the production boundary indeterminate.

Standard neoclassical models assume that there is only one price for an object of specific properties. In reality, markets set the price for an object differently. The construction of volume values entails that a physical quantity is assigned at least two prices, one is the actual price but the other is the assigned price of another time period that is not the actual price of the market. The use of assigned prices, instead of actual prices, also has the potential to introduce infinite economic growth for an economy that just returns to its original state, as discussed in this chapter in the example of hats. The price is a social construction referring to a physical object or process. The price cannot exist outside of those who think about this price. They are not more real than characters in a fictional novel or gods in mythologies. That does not mean the price is outside of reality since the persons thinking about prices are physical beings, but the mental object of price is not the same as those thinking about the price. Prices can have real causes and real consequences. For example, in pre-industrial society, harvest failure caused increases in grain prices, which caused increases in death rates and even starvation. Stories in novels and mythologies can have real consequences without making the characters and gods of the stories more real. When we say that an object has a price, we do not say anything about the object as a physical entity. Prices can therefore not be wrong descriptions of an object. If an object is sold for a price or assigned such, that is the price. In contrast, when we measure the weight of an object, such measurement can be wrong. The weight is a property of the object, existing independently of how we measure it. Prices make qualitatively different physical objects and processes comparable, but only as mental objects detached from the physical characteristics of these objects.

Criteria for the reconceptualisation

One of the purposes of national accounts is to account for the production process abstracted from specific social and subjective perceptions. The objective technical conditions of production should be distinguished from the subjective perception and social power relations of this process. However, present aggregates do not completely accomplish that. A GDP concept that mixes up transfers and actual productive activities, while a large part of activities that could be considered productive are excluded, may yield spurious measures of what we mean by economic growth. As discussed in chapter 2, theories of what activities are productive and unproductive have changed substantially over time. These changes sometimes reflect shifts in ideological standpoints of different groups within a contemporary social and economic system and not always genuine scientific progress.

The purpose of this book is to discuss various frameworks to clarify how those may suit different analytical purposes. Concepts do not have a real existence in a Platonian world of ideas but are social constructions. There is no "true" way to draw the production boundary. Nevertheless, reality limits what can be accomplished with different definitions. Statistical offices should promote the proliferation of various satellite accounts and provide the raw data to enable scientists to construct their own measures that best suit their analytical purpose. In this way, scientists from different disciplines would not be limited to just one measure in their analysis.

As discussed in this and previous chapters, although there are many different views on how to draw the production boundary in national accounts, there are some agreements on what conditions should be met. Some of the paradoxes of national accounting are well-known. The following criteria have guided the conceptual framework in the next chapter:

Consistency

The production boundary should be set according to certain criteria used consistently. The same criteria should be used for one activity as for another. The *System of national accounts* violates many of these conditions, for example, by excluding unpaid domestic services, but including some non-market activities, such as non-market goods production. In contrast, the third-party criterion used in feminist economics is consistent.

Parsimony

A simpler articulation should be preferred if the same purpose with the definition can be accomplished. For example, formulations should not include statements already covered by other statements.

Non-operational definition

A theoretical definition should not be operational. It should state what production is in the present world. The third-party criterion violates this criterion, but as discussed in the next chapter, some reference to an alternative world cannot be completely avoided.

Trans-historicity

The production boundary should be set in such a way as to be adequate for all societies that hitherto has existed. An advantage of the third-party criterion is that it is relevant to all societies. In contrast, the SNA definitions have been formulated to address current economic and political problems, not the problems of a hunter and gatherer society or a future economy dominated by artificial intelligence.

Non-circularity

The production boundary should not be defined circularly and avoid self-references.

Reduction to non-economic conceptualisation

The definitions should as far as possible only contain non-economic properties and relations.

Independence from legal framework

The production boundary should be set independently from the legal frameworks or how various agents view the production process. This criterion is related to trans-historicity.

Valuation independence

The production boundary should be set independently of the valuation of the production process, i.e., of the valuation of inputs and outputs.

Quantification

It should be possible to quantify the object transformed during a productive activity irrespective of any valuation system. More specifically, it should not be possible to infinitely increase any positive quantity produced, a type of infinite regress.

Time frame independence

The production boundary should be set independent of the time frame of the production process, i.e., it should be independently of how long time an activity is conducted. Learning poses a specific challenge as the output that may be resulted occurs much later.

The non-time reversal criterion

The production boundary should be defined entirely by the objective conditions up to the end of the production process. What happens after the end of the production process must not be allowed to define whether an activity is classified as productive or not. More generally, no causation should run backwards. Unfortunately, this criterion stands in contradiction with the time frame independence conditions.

Utility independence criterion

Production, and its measure, should be defined separately from the utility it generates when consumed, even if productive activities have the purpose of generating useful objects or effects.

Separation of production and consumption

It should be possible to separate production from consumption, at least at an analytical level, which is related to utility independence.

Separation of production from transfer and distribution

All national accounts usually consider transfers as something different from productive activities. Distinguishing the two is not always crystal clear. Why should, for example, interest rate payment and taxation be profoundly distinct from payment for the use of intellectual property?

No double counting

The production boundary should be such as to avoid double counting, i.e., two separate activities should not both be counted as productive if they both are considered to end with the same output. This is related to the criterion of separating production and transfer, given that the inability to make such distinction generates double counting and self-reference.

4 Formalising the definitions of production, work and consumption

Four conditions of production

This chapter constitutes the cardinal contribution of the book, describing a possible trans-historical formal framework of basic national account constructs. First, some more elementary concepts are deliberated, such as causation, intentionality, purposefulness and exteriority, which are part of various non-economic sentences presented in Table 4.3. These sentences, in turn, are used to specify production, work and consumption as relations between events, the subject matter of transformation and the agent. First-order logic is applied, complemented with modal operators for some of the sentences. Next follows a presentation of the distinction between consumption in general and final consumption, followed by an examination of various alternative notions of the production boundary. Through the use of formal logic, it is shown that various perceptions of production can be seen as alterations of common themes. Finally, work and leisure are counterposed and the possibility of unproductive work and leisure production is introduced.

To synthesise the previous discussions, production fulfils four main conditions:

1 **The physical transformation condition:** There must be a subject matter that undergoes transformation, whereby it loses some of its intrinsic properties and gains others. The set of properties of the subject matter has to change to another set of properties, or to a series of various properties at different periods. The condition is implicitly recognised, for example, in SNA 2008. This aspect is shared with many natural processes, which may satisfy human needs. One of the properties is always time. For example, the purpose of an activity can be not to change any other properties than time, which is the intention of storage.

2 **The intentionality condition:** An agent must intentionally cause the transformation of the subject matter. Natural processes do not fulfil this condition and neither are collective agents. The condition is theoretically related to methodological individualism and the concept of praxeology. Institutions cannot be agents; only individuals are. Animals are here not

DOI: 10.4324/9781003057017-4

considered to produce or work as they lack consciousness at the level of humans. Neither does a small child produce. In the same way, some human activities, such as sleeping or digesting food, are not conscious even if they are highly useful.

3   **The exteriority conditions:** What generates the possibility of delegating a task to a third person is an exteriority criterion, in this special case that the subject matter is separate from the agent. The condition is related to the view held in ecological economics that human activity involves a relation between the agent and exterior nature. Other types of exteriorities can also be recognised.

4   **The final utility condition:** Production must result in changes in the physical world that actually or potentially can contribute to the satisfaction of human needs, of final consumption, in accordance with the utilitarian tradition of setting the production boundary.

Different definitions of production share all four points but vary in restricting or expanding the exact meaning. Definitions of work and consumption rest on the first three points, In the case of leisure there is a purpose internality condition.

Causation

Production, work and consumption are causal processes. Causation is a complex phenomenon and can be further differentiated, for example, between intentional and non-intentional causation. In this study, it is argued that an essential attribute of what distinguishes productive from unproductive work, is not that the latter fails to change any material properties, but how the chain of causation runs, what type of matter is transformed and how this transformation is perceived by the agent. Table 4.2 lists several types of causation, which are specifically designed for the objectives of this book.

The standard view is that causation is a relation between two events (Kim, 1973). An event is concrete, occurring at a specific spatiotemporal location. One of the events cannot be constitutive, or part, of the other. Stating that event e_1 causes event e_2, must be distinguished from stating that event e_2 is part of event e_1, which is an ontological relation rather than a causal one. If event e_2 is part of event e_1 then e_2 follows from e_1 by logical necessity, which is not the case for a causal relation. Stating that event e_1 causes e_2 is here defined in the counterfactual tradition (Lewis, 1973; Hoover, 1990). Counter-factuality entails that if event e_1 would not occur, and all else would stay the same (including outcomes of purely random events) except for the causal mechanism (the chain of causations), event e_2 would not occur. No further elaboration is made here to determine what stays the same and what the causal mechanism is.

Picking an orange by *Maria* could be considered to cause the final con-sumption of orange juice manufactured from the specific orange. Imagine that another person, *Anna*, picks the orange if *Maria* does not pick it up, which enables the consumption of the same orange juice, but this would not entail that *Maria* did not cause the final consumption of the orange juice if she was the one that picked the specific orange. Given no other than *Maria* picked the orange, i.e., the world except for the causal mechanism is assumed to be the same, for the consumption of orange juice made from this specific orange to occur, it is necessary that *Maria* has picked the orange.

To what extent a causal relation can be established depends on how the specific events are defined. A doctor that saves a child's life so the child can live into adulthood is at the same time causing a future death of an adult, but the doctor is not causing the future non-existence of that person, given that the child would not have existed as an adult without the doctor's efforts.

Intentional causation

The notion of intentional causation is central in the history of ideas, from religious myths to modern perceptions of economic agency and account-ability. It can be epitomised by the well-known passage of the *Book of Genesis* (Douy-Rheims_version, 1609, p. 3):

> And God said: Be light made. And light was made.

The andromorphic God causes light to be made, but he does that intentionally by first having a mental image of the light. Intentional causation entails that intentional states act causally (Searle, 1983, p. 112). Agency can be described as changes in the mental state of the agent that causes the bodily movement of the agent (Davidson, 1980; Dretske, 1988). In this book, an agent intentionally causes an event if

1   the agent undergoes a self-directed transformation, which causes the event (God first speaks of light and thus self-transforms, which in turn causes the light);
2   the agent believes that this self-direct transformation causes the event (God believes in his acts and its causal power); and
3   if everything else except for the causal mechanism stays the same, it is necessary that the event would not occur if the agent would not exist (without God, there would not have been any light all else staying the same, for example, no other supernatural being is intervening).

This formulation is solely constructed for the purpose of defining production, consumption and work. It is not an attempt to describe what intentional causality entails in general. In this book, intentional causation necessitates an active role for the agent, which must be a person. The praxeology of Austrian economists (Selgin, 1988) attempts to be value-free by not judging actions. It avoids describing any action as irrational. However, even if assuming that the agent is a consistent reasoner is more straightforward, it would be unfortunate if the definitions would rule out the possibility of an inconsistent or irrational agent.

One issue is how to define the agent. It is essential to distinguish between persons and non-persons and between two distinct persons. Production, work and consumption are classified as human activities. Human activity is affected by the surrounding environment. What we consider as uniquely human can be further problematised. The *System of National Accounts* assumes that animals neither work nor produce, a consensus shared by various economic theories – from neoclassical theory to Marxist and Feminist economics. Nevertheless, intentional causation is not a unique attribute of humans, even if humans distinguish themselves by their possession of shared intentionality through the use of language. Humans have evolved from animals. Some qualities that previously were considered uniquely human have been shown to be shared by some animals at a rudimentary level. Chimpanzees are known to use tools, learn from others how to handle these tools and engage in semi-coordinated violence (Fuentes, 2018). Chapter 5 further considers widening the production boundary to include some activities of animals.

The standpoint taken in this book is that agency is performed by a person, in accordance with methodological individualism, not a collective or institutional entity. Max Weber (1978, p. 13) argued for the following view, which in turn heavily influenced von Mises (Selgin, 1988):

> For still other cognitive purposes as, for instance, juristic, or for practical ends, it may on the other hand be convenient or even indispensable to treat social collectivities, such as states, associations, business corporations, foundations, as if they were individual persons. Thus they may be treated as the subjects of rights and duties or as the performers of legally significant actions. But for the subjective interpretation of action in sociological work these collectivities must be treated as solely the resultants and modes of organisation of the particular acts of individual persons, since these alone can be treated as agents in a course of subjectively understandable action. Nevertheless, the sociologist cannot for his purposes afford to ignore these collective concepts derived from other disciplines.

Theoretically, it is possible that an intelligent agent may be a collective. We can imagine that a bee-hive intelligence could evolve on another planet. In the near future, AI could develop that performs similar roles as human agents. However, such agents do not exist today on Earth and may therefore be disregarded for the time being.

The methodological individualist perspective on agency seemingly stands in contrast to Marxism that emphasises class action. Puzzlingly, such perspective can also underpin some of the Marxist ideas concerning exploitation and unproductive labour. Chapter 5 discusses what the marginal productivity of capital denotes, as is implicitly assumed in the neoclassical growth model. Is it the physical capital that "contributes" to production or is it the owner of this capital? The actual owner could be unconscious and therefore not be able to intentionally cause anything. The formulation of the production boundary in SNA entails that an institutional unit can act as the "agent" of production, which stands in contrast to Weber's view. Such a unit "contributes" to production through its ownership of capital. In contrast, the labourer must always be a person. The entrepreneur is, of course, actively involved in the production, but is in this sense also a labourer.

While institutional units can only act through individuals, ontological individualism does not necessitate epistemological individualism. To describe institutional agents, it can sometimes be convenient to treat them as individuals. The standard neoclassical model rests on methodological individualism, but the individual in this tradition is an abstract entity, not an empirical individual living in a social and historical context. The individual in the standard neoclassical model can easily be replaced by another entity, which may better behave according to the assumptions made. In Becker's (1980) model of households, the individual is replaced by the household, leading to the conclusion that the gendered division of labour, where women are relegated to the home, is actually a consequence of the maximisation of the utility of the household as a whole, not patriarchal power. Even the entrepreneur, which in Schumpeter is acting to find new ways, disappears in the standard neoclassical model under the assumption of rationality and perfect information.

To identify the agent of production, consumption or work, we have to distinguish between intentional causation and allowing. In this book, when agent s allows event e, where event e does not presuppose the existence of s, it entails that s has the power to prevent e, while s chooses not to prevent event e. For example, owning a factory empowers the owner to stop production. While the physical existence of a car worker, all else being equal, is necessary for the production of a car, the physical existence of the owner (if passive) is not necessary for the production since, all else being equal, without the owner, the production continues. For the owner to stop the production he/she has to act, which presupposes his/her existence.

Allowing is de facto the "contribution" of the owner of capital to production, for example, in the Austrian theory of capital as time. The owner allows the production to take place, given the owner chooses not to consume the current capital and waits for more benefits in the future. The "contribution" here does not necessarily involve physical causation (a passive owner is different from the entrepreneur). Austrian theory acknowledges the subjective nature of this relation, while neoclassical growth models somehow describe the contribution of capital as physical causation by using the terminology of capital productivity. The subjective understanding of why capital is remunerated is indispensable to understand the production process. Yet, the production process comprises of intentional causation, which is objective.

Purposefulness

Intentional causation is related to subjective utility and disutility. Utility that is generated in the production process can be understood in several ways, in accordance with various traditions of utilitarianism. Stanley Jevons (1871, pp. 69–70) distinguishes between three types of utilities:

> It is quite usual, and perhaps correct, to call iron or water or timber a useful substance; but we may mean by these words at least three distinct facts. We may mean that a particular piece of iron is at the present moment actually useful to some person; or that, although not actually useful, it is expected to be useful at a future time; or we may only mean that it would be useful if it were in the possession of some person needing it. The iron rails of a railway, the iron which composes the Britannia Bridge, or an ocean steamer, is actually useful; the iron lying in a merchant's store is not useful at present, though it is expected soon to be so; but there is a vast quantity of iron existing in the bowels of the earth, which has all the physical properties of iron, and might be useful if extracted, though it never will be. These are instances of actual, prospective, and potential utility.

To formulate the final utility condition, this study avoids the concept of utility, by focusing on the purpose of the activity for the agent of transformation, which, in turn, is related to the beliefs held by an agent.

The statement that the purpose for agent s of event e_1 lies in another event e_2 is used to distinguish, for example, work from final consumption and leisure. Purposefulness must at least entail that the agent allows an event. Here, an agent s has event e_2 as a purpose for allowing event e_1 if three conditions are satisfied:

1   s believes that event e_1 causes event e_2
2   s allows event e_1, and
3   it is necessary that if s believes that event e_1 does not cause event e_2, then s intentionally prevents event e_1 from happening.

For example, suppose the purpose for an owner of a factory to allow the introduction of a new computer system is to increase production. This, in turn, presupposes that (1) the factory owner believes that introducing a new computer system increases production, (2) the factory owner allows the introduction of a new computer system, and (3) it is necessary that if the owner believes that the introduction of a new computer system does not cause increased production, then the owner intentionally prevents the introduction of the computer system. The purposefulness lies in the factory owner's beliefs about the relationship between those events (which logically encompasses modal operators), but also in the capability of the agent, the factory owner, to be able to prevent the introduction of a new computer system.

We may consider that the purpose of an event lies in the event itself and not in other events. The statement that an agent has an event as a final purpose is used for the definitions of leisure and final consumption. Here it entails that the agent has no other imagined second event as a purpose for allowing the final purpose event. For example, hunting may be performed because the hunter imagines that the hunt will be turned into meat that can be eaten by the hunter or somebody else. The hunter then has not the hunting as a final purpose. However, hobby-hunting is a leisure activity. It would be performed even if not successful. Many activities involving social obligations, such as attending weddings and Christenings, are also satisfying in themselves to the agents (Lucassen, 2021, p. 3).

Actualised utility, as discussed by Jevons, could here be interpreted as the transformation of an object as part of an activity that is a final purpose for the agent. Jevon's concepts of prospective and potential utilities are more problematic as they rest on the judgement of possible future utilities for society at large. Work and production are in a sense generating prospective utility. Still, in this book, for work, it is stated that the purpose lies outside the activity itself, and for production that it possibly causes a transformation that is finally purposeful for some agent.

Social causation

Max Weber (1978, p. 4) defines action and social action as follows:

> We shall speak of "action" insofar as the acting individual attaches a subjective meaning to his behaviour – be it overt or covert, omission or acquiescence. Action is "social" insofar as its subjective meaning takes account of the behavior of others and is thereby oriented in its course.

The crucial aspect of social action is, per se, not that there are several different individuals that interact, but that the social action is oriented towards other individuals' subjective meanings, which is distinct from the agent's. A parent feeding an infant is in a sense not a social action given that the infant has not yet formed a subjective meaning to the process. Only when the child becomes elder, a social relation is formed.

In this book, one instance of intentional causation is labelled social causation, necessarily comprising the transformation of another person's actions or capacity for action. For example, we usually do not consider a person to have created artwork by paying somebody else to do all the labour. Although the person in question has intentionally caused the artwork through the payment, it has been executed by convincing somebody else to create the artwork. The intentional causation of the artwork occurs not by physical necessity, but by social necessity. In contrast, if the person in question first had made a sketch of the artwork, we could consider this person to share in the creation by physical necessity since making a sketch is a part of the physical process of producing the artwork.

As discussed in chapter 2, Steven N. S. Cheung (2005, pp. 103–104) claims that transaction, or institutional, costs can be defined as costs that would not exist in a Robinson Crusoe economy. For example, Robinson Crusoe would not have paid himself to create an artwork, but he may have made a sketch in the first stage of the art creation. Cheung's definition could be regarded as an operationalisation of Mill's notion of distributive activities and is close to the Marxist concept of unproductive work in the wider use value tradition.

Cheung presents an operational, not a theoretical, definition of transaction costs, but the device of imagining a counterfactual state to formulate sentences of the actual world is common in several theoretical traditions. The idea of possible worlds is used in modal logic (Menzel, 2021). Marxists point out that unproductive activities are only necessary due to the specific social form. Baran (1957, p. 33) suggests that unproductive work performed under capitalism would be unnecessary in a socialist society, while Shaikh and Tonak (1994, p. 20) purport that unproductive activities are necessary in a rational, socialist society as well. The third person criterion compares the activity with an imagined state where the activity would be executed in a different way and ask whether that is possible. Modern national accounts and economics often apply prices of an idealised version of the market, which deviate from actual pricing or business accounts. As discussed earlier, causation itself is commonly defined counterfactually, where an imagined world is considered where the cause would not have occurred. A quandary with applying these devices is that they deviate from the observed reality. There is uncertainty about how the alternative possible world is to be described.

The present study uses Cheung's definition of transaction costs as a criterion of social causation, which, in turn, is used to distinguish between productive and unproductive labour, but with some modifications.

To avoid describing all activities involving more than one person as instances of social causation, the Robinson Crusoe condition could be reformulated by imagining a society of individuals, with the same preferences for all types of combinations of actions of all agents at a time t if all agents have the same information. In such a society, for all pairs of agents i and j, and all possible combinations of actions, A_k, it is necessary that, if agents i and j have the same information, and if $A_k \succ_i \neg A_k$, then $A_k \succ_j \neg A_k$, all else being equal. Under these conditions, there would be no conflict over actions, no negotiations and therefore no transaction costs – all agents would de facto act as one. In this sense, there would not be any social relations between separate agents – a state that is neither possible nor desirable, but a purely theoretical construct. Such a society would de facto be composed of one (Crusoe) superindividual.

A utopian version is the biblical paradise, where everybody lives in harmony. Adam and Eve, constituting one flesh, do not know anything about good and evil simply because such knowledge is not necessary. After Adam and Eve had eaten from the tree of the knowledge of good and evil, a society of different wills and conflict is established. Similarly, according to Buddhism, nirvana is the realisation of the non-self.

A dystopian version can be exemplified by the Borg hive mind (called "the Collective") in the TV series *Star Trek*. There exist individuals in this alien civilisation, but there is no individuality. Carlos Santana (2021) describes the Borg society as a eusocial hive, i.e., comparable to an ant colony on Earth, although the latter lack intentional will at the level of intelligent beings. Kramer and Bressan (2015) liken the Borg collective to a superorganism. They argue that the human individual can be seen as a form of superorganism, a coexistence of various selfish entities, which entails that not even the individual is a fully unitary individual. Some dictatorships that have existed throughout history may have, to some very limited extent, approached the dystopian version, a state of one will, or as argued by von Hayek (2001, p. 157):

> The most effective way of making everybody serve the single system of ends towards which the social plan is directed is to make everybody believe in those ends. To make a totalitarian system function efficiently it is not enough that everybody should be forced to work for the same ends. It is essential that the people should come to regard them as their own ends. Although the beliefs must be chosen for the people and imposed upon them, they must become their beliefs, a generally accepted creed which makes the individuals as far as possible act spontaneously in the way the planner wants. If the feeling of oppression in totalitarian countries is in general much less acute than most people in liberal countries imagine, this is because the totalitarian governments succeed to a high degree in making people think they want them to.

Obviously, the Crusoe individuals that compose the superindividual could have different information and their collective intentions for action could change. Just passing information from one Crusoe to another could therefore occur in the Crusoe society. Even the lonely Crusoe can pass information to himself, for example, to remember something later. Informing per se does not involve social causation in this sense. It does not change a person's preferences for action. Accumulation of knowledge does not necessarily constitute social causation. Studies of ants show that they respond to environmental change, when memories become less reliable, strongly by upregulating pheromone deposition (Tomer & Jürgen, 2015). Even if this shows that individual ants act independently based on their individual cognitive capacities, such as memory, the action accords with the preferences of the whole colony, i.e., to maximise foraging of food for the colony to survive.

Nevertheless, passing off information can sometimes involve social causation. To take a classic mythological example, suppose that the serpent passes information to Eve that she would not die from eating from the tree in the midst of Paradise. Eve chooses to eat the fruit. If the serpent's intention would have been honest, to just pass information, then this action by the serpent does not constitute a social action. The serpent and Eve would have the same preferences for the action of Eve, given that both have the same information. This action is also possible at a Paradise with a lonely Eve if Eve passes off information to herself that she would not die from eating the fruits of a specific tree. However, assume that the objective of informing Eve could be to make her and Adam come into conflict with God, which she does not desire. Then, the action of the serpent involves social causation. The serpent represents social relations and conflicts.

A complicating circumstance is that the same individual may have conflicting wills, either at the same time or over time. For example, transaction costs could occur at Robinson Crusoe Island if Crusoe decides to burn a bunch of packets of cigarettes, which may involve work, so as to not be tempted in the future to smoke. In the *Odyssey*, Odysseus obliged his sailor to plug wax into their ears and to tie him tightly to the mast, so as to not be tempted by the Sirens. In both circumstances, there is an intentional action to change a person's intentional action. It is made logically possible as the individual existing at different times is partly different individuals. In this sense, it is not entirely inadequate to open to the possibility that a social relation can be formed by the individual to oneself, i.e., where the clash of wills could be possible. In fact, central attributes of human consciousness are perception of self in time and meta-self-awareness, the awareness of being self-aware (Morin, 2006), which also involves the capacity to question the choices that one is making. Such an intelligent being deviates from the ideal-type individual of Austrian and neoclassical economics with no conflicting purposes.

To formulate a theoretical definition, and not an operational one, of social causation, the starting point is that such causation involves the intentional change of other people's prospective intentional action or capacity for action in such a way that contradicts the latter's original intents. The essential aspect of social causation and a social relation is that there are two wills that have different intentions that at least potentially could clash with each other. This is the basis of social conflict, including class struggle.

Aristotle (*Ethics*, 5, 1130b32–1131a22, translated by J.A.K. Thomas) notes that:

> ... some transactions are voluntary and others involuntary. Voluntary transactions are, e.g., selling, buying, lending at interest, pledging, lending without interest, depositing, and letting (these are called voluntary because the initial stage of the transaction is voluntary). Involuntary transactions are either secret, such as theft, adultery, poisoning, procuring, enticement of slaves, killing by stealth, and testifying falsely; or violent, e.g., assault, forcible confinement, murder, robbery, maiming, defamation, and public insult.

Similarly, in this book, the two main types of social causation are labelled as coercive and non-coercive social causation (even if not exactly corresponding to Aristotle's examples). Agent s_1 may be said to coercively cause event e_1 if the causal mechanism necessarily involves the intentional transformation of an agent s_2, event e_1, against the will of s_2. Agent s_1 may be said to non-coercively socially cause event e_1 if the causal mechanism necessarily comprises of the intentional transformation of agent s_2 to perform an intentional action, event e_2, in such a way that s_2 would not have preferred event e_2 if event e_1 would not occur, even when being past the information contained in event e_1. Both financial services and gang wars involve social causation, but the difference is that financial services are based on some kind of mutual agreement, while those who are shot dead in gang wars have not agreed to the acts of the perpetrators.

Transformations of other persons do not necessarily encompass social causation, for example, if a transformation occurs in accordance with the will of the transformed person even if the latter would not receive anything in exchange. Social causation transforms an agent in the capacity of an agent. Transaction costs involve an externality both for those performing the transactional activity and those affected by the transactional activity, but not all externalities embody transaction costs. Some damage to a third party can occur without the intent of any consequences to the third party. Ronald Coase (1960) argues that negative externalities often occur reciprocally:

> The question is commonly thought of as one in which A inflicts harm on B and what has to be decided is: how should we restrain A? But this is wrong. We are dealing with a problem of a reciprocal nature. To avoid the harm to B would inflict harm on A. The real question that has to be decided is: should A be allowed to harm B or should B be allowed to harm A? The problem is to avoid the more serious harm. I instanced in my previous article the case of a confectioner the noise and vibrations from whose machinery disturbed a doctor in his work. To avoid harming the doctor would inflict harm on the confectioner. The problem posed by this case was essentially whether it was worth while, as a result of restricting the methods of production which could be used by the confectioner, to secure more doctoring at the cost of a reduced supply of confectionery products.

The activity of a confectioner whose noise disturbs a doctor does not involve any social causation given that the intent is not to transform another agent's intentional action or capacity for action. Although it could be argued that such activity would not take place at Robinson Crusoe Island if inflicting more harm than benefits, it is not excluded that it could occur, in contrast to financial services or waging gang war. Similarly, if a factory causes effects on the environment that are perceived as negative by other people, it is a negative externality in economics, but that is not a social causality according to the conceptual framework of this book if it is an unintended consequence. On the other hand, if a factory causes mayhem in the environment in order for people to move out so that the company can buy up the land, then there is social causation. There is a difference between negative externalities that are side-effects of the activity and those that are aimed intentionally.

The transformation of objects

While physiocrats regarded agriculture solely as productive, given that manufacturing merely reshapes raw materials, Adam Smith deemed services to be unproductive since there is no product from them. Modern natural science has changed the view of what is materiality, demonstrating that some physical processes exist that have been perceived as invisible to earlier thinkers. At the same time, we must still distinguish between how agents perceive a transformation and the actual physical transformation itself. Change in ownership, for example, is a change in an imagined object, although such change has a material foundation in the minds of agents. The law can recognise that a person has ownership over a property retroactively, but physical causation cannot run backwards in time. Emphasising that production and consumption involve physical transformations relates to the argument of ecological economics, which can be traced back to Aristotle, that there are limits to economic growth due to physical constraints.

Production, work and consumption consist of the intentional transformations of several objects, including intentional self-transformation:

1   The subject matters are here defined as the objects designated for transformation during an activity. An essential attribute of production is that it must encompass a change in the intrinsic properties of a subject matter and not just how this object is perceived by agents. It can be distinguished between a mental object (the thing for us) and the exteriorly existing object (the thing in itself), which is related to John Stuart Mill's distinction between transforming physical object (production) and transforming mental objects (distribution). Transforming a mental object involves a physical change, but that may not be the object of transformation. For example, financial services and trade comprise transformations of mental objects, i.e., the perceived ownership rights. Such ownership rights do not exist physically, they are mental constructions, but people recognising and defending these rights exist physically. During leisure, the subject matter of the activity is the agent itself. Studying requires that the subject matter of the activity is the agent of transformation. Sleep does not involve agency, given that the activity is not conscious (Morin, 2006).

2   Marx (1965, p. 179) distinguishes between instruments and subject matters of production. Human production is characterised by advanced use of tools. Darwin (1889, p. 51) in *Descent of Man* speculates that humans began walking on two legs in order to use their hands. In this study, an

instrument of the transformation of the subject matter can be seen as a physical object whose intended transformation causes the transformation of the subject matter. For the agent, the purpose of transforming the instrument lies in transforming the subject matter. During work, the agent in itself is an instrument of transformation as the transformation of the agent only serves the transformation of the subject matter. During leisure, the consumed object is usually an instrument of transformation since the intent typically is to transform the agent, although this is not always the case. As stated by Pigou (1920, p. 12): "Human beings are both 'ends in themselves', and instruments of production."

3   There are physical objects that cause the transformation of the subject matter, but that are neither subject matters nor instruments of transformation. For example, the sun may affect the growth of wheat. However, the agent of transformation does not cause any transformation of the sun. The change in the sun during the production process is not part of the production process, although the labourer can decide whether the sun causes the growth of wheat, either by planting the wheat seeds or not.

4   Production, work and consumption may involve transformations of objects not intended to be transformed, for example, consisting of negative environmental impacts or people killed by accident due to the production process.

In this book, the focus is on the object that is transformed intentionally by an agent. Such an object could be either a subject matter or an instrument for transforming the subject matter.

What is a transformation of an object? There is a material continuity in that the same physical entities are preserved, but their properties are changed. One way to express this is to use higher-order logic, for example, that the n-vector V of n properties of an object is transformed to the n-vector W of n properties of the same object. Still, the objective of some production processes may not consist of transforming an object to specific properties, but rather in the changes during the production process. For example, the purpose of theatre may not be to transform the audience from unsatisfied to satisfied, but in the play itself during the production process, or as a continuous series of changes in a vector of properties. When the theatrical performance is ended, the stage is cleaned up and returned to its original state. This is the nature of many services, which makes it problematic to describe and quantify them.

Exteriority

Logically, the third person criterion implicitly applies modal operators. Modal logic, which was developed in the 1960s, complements propositional and predicate logic to include modality (Garson, 2021). In contrast to propositional and predicate operators, modality communicates things or situations relative to what is actually, for example, what could or is believed to be. The third person criterion cannot be expressed using proposition and predicate logic alone. It states conditions not pertaining to the actual world. Expressing that an activity is taken over by a third person does not require any modality, given that the statement as such does not go beyond what is actual. However, expressing that it would be possible to delegate an activity to a third person declares something about a situation that does not occur. In addition, it must be specified what is delegated. If an activity is delegated to a third person, it loses some of its characteristics. Cutting my hair can be delegated. Being cut cannot even logically be delegated. Learning *myself* cannot be delegated to another person. Learning something to perform a future task can be delegated.

How can we know if an activity can be delegated to a third person when it is actually not delegated? One way to handle that in modal logic is to describe possible worlds (Menzel, 2021) – something can be true in a possible world without being true in the actual world. The drawback is that we then have to articulate the characteristics of the possible world. It may be possible to delegate an activity to another person, or it may not be possible. It depends on whether the possible world where a task is delegated is, for example, restricted by the present technology, if it follows the laws of physics, or if it is logically coherent. If Robinson Crusoe is fishing, it is not logically excluded that the activity can be passed to another person, even if Crusoe is the last person existing on Earth. Although it may be argued that logical consistency is a minimum requirement, in the actual world, according to quantum mechanics, a particle can be observed as A and not A at the same time, allowing the production of quantum computers (that in turn can be delegated), which at least superficially violates the law of non-contradiction.

There are types of work that could not be delegated even under very advanced technological conditions. For example, can Madonna delegate the task of performing at a concert, or Picasso the task of creating art, to a third person? Neither Madonna nor Picasso can hire somebody else at the market to be them. If they would, their audience would certainly feel cheated. When Madonna cannot perform, she does not delegate, she cancels the concert. When Picasso feels too ill to create art, he does not find a third person to do the work for him. He waits until he feels better. They can delegate to create art or to perform at a concert, but they cannot delegate being them. A similar argument can be made concerning parenthood. Although taking care of one's child can be delegated to a third person, being the parent cannot easily be delegated.

A reformulation of the third person criterion based on statements of the actual world is to consider work fulfilling two conditions: work is an activity and its intent is the transformation of an exterior object. The third person criterion rests on the assumption that there is a difference between the agent of work or production and the object that is transformed by the agent. Without such differentiation, it is not possible to delegate the task. Such distinctions between the self and the exterior world, and individuality, are social constructions and expressions of modern individualism distinct to earlier thought. Moldoveanua and Stevenson (2001) distinguish between two models of the self in social sciences: the mainstream Aristotelian tradition, presenting a view of a unitary self and the dissenting Heraclitan tradition – a stream of thought argued by among others Hegel, Marx, Nietzsche and Foucault – questioning such conception. Neoclassical economists and rational choice models often assume that human behaviour can be reduced to a maximisation model where individuals have a clear preference order. Stressing the fluid boundaries of individuality belongs to a long non-Western historical tradition (Ho, 1995). Confucianism does not deny a self, but considers it as an interrelational self – the individual can only exist in relation to others. Buddhism goes further and accepts the nonexistence of the enduring self (anātman) (Harris, 2011). The Taoist philosopher Zhuang Zhou (2013, p. 78) tells the following story:

> Once Zhuang Zhou dreamed he was a butterfly, a butterfly flitting and fluttering around, happy with himself and doing as he pleased. He didn't know he was Zhuang Zhou. Suddenly he woke up, and there he was, solid and unmistakable Zhuang Zhou. But he didn't know if he were Zhuang Zhou who had dreamed he was a butterfly or a butterfly dreaming he was Zhuang Zhou. Between Zhuang Zhou and a butterfly, there must be some distinction! This is called the Transformation of Things.

To this background, we may consider different exteriority conditions, depending on how the individual agent is defined:

1   The **agent exteriority** condition distinguishes between the agent and everything else. It presupposes continuity of the individual over time. Agent exteriority involves transformations that are outside of the individual agent. Productive activity involves the physical transformation of matters that are exterior to the agent. Individually interior changes comprise of changes of the individual agent. The reason human capital formation is not classified as production is due to such interiority.

2   We can decompose an individual into its active mind and body to move beyond the self as an absolute holistic entity. **Mind exteriority** entails that the object of transformation is an object that is not the mind of the agent, which may be the rest of the body of the agent or an object outside of the agent. It could be seen as an instance of agent exteriority if the agent is equated with its mind rather than with its body. The body could theoretically be delegated, but not the mind. For example, pregnancy could be delegated. An organ could be separated from the body and put back into the body. Cutting one's hair could be fully delegated if a person wears a wig and it is the wig that is cut. Even the human brain could theoretically be delegated to a third party, for example, if the active mind would be downloaded to a computer.

3   The future self could be a very different person from the current self and even consists of other atoms than the current self. The **current self-exteriority** necessitates that the object of transformation is not the current self, but may be the future self or an object exterior to the agent.

4   **Purpose exteriority** entails the final purpose does not lie in the current event. This condition is more of a defining characteristic of work than of productive activity. The current self-exteriority is strongly related to the purpose exteriority condition. The Marshallian articulation of work requires that the purpose lies outside the activity, i.e., the object of transformation is not the current self, for example, learning or bathing. If the purpose is to transform the current self, the purpose is not to accomplish a certain state of oneself after the activity has ended, but to realise the various states during the course of the activity.

5   **Social exteriority** involves transformations that are exterior to social relations, i.e., not comprising of social causation as a necessary part of the causal mechanism. One reason we may consider trade, finance and war as unproductive is that they presuppose social causation. What is rational at an individual level may not be rational at a societal level. The social exteriority condition avoids some of the problems of double counting by only considering transformations that do not involve transforming other persons as agents.

6   **Humanity exteriority** encompasses transformations of objects exterior to humanity, i.e., only matters that are not persons are transformed. Actions directed towards transforming human beings could, in turn, be termed reproductive.

7   In today's national accounts production for the household is regarded outside of the production boundary, except for produced goods that are assumed to be potentially sold at the market outside of the household relations, a kind of **household exteriority** condition. In the *Bible*, husband and wife are described as one flesh, which can be counterposed to modern individualism. It is perplexing that the mainstream Western concept of GDP rests on household exteriority, a non-liberal idea assuming that the household is a type of distinct individual agent.

In contrast to the third-party criterion, these exteriority conditions state something about the actual world, not about a world in an alternative reality, which is usually the attribute of an operational definition. Different definitions of the production boundary often reflect distinct conceptions of exteriority. There are reasons to exclude transformations that are not agent or socially exterior from the concept of production and the reasons are similar, although not identical.

The condition of exteriority is related to the concept of "negative entropy", or the process in which life preserves its order by increasing the disorder in the surrounding environment. This process presupposes a relationship between a life form and its exteriority, which is a modus operandi for production as well as consumption. In fact, self-reproduction involves such a process in relation to exteriority since self-reproduction is not possible without increasing the disorder of the exterior environment.

The concept of externalities in mainstream economics is related to the concept of exteriority presented in this book, but the two notions are not the same. Externality is a complex, subjective concept in the market tradition of neoclassical economics, quantitatively determined by whether there are persons who consider some activities as negative, while their costs are not internalised by the market. Agent exteriority can be determined objectively. If people do not care if the air they breathe is polluted by a company, there is no negative externality. If they enjoy smog, there could even be a positive externality, despite that the smog kills those who enjoy it. For a polluting profit-maximising company, it would be preferable for people to enjoy the pollution than to be unhappy with it and demand action from the state and may therefore try to persuade people into seeing the pollution in a positive way. Production involves transformation of exterior matters, but this is not in itself an externality as the negative and positive aspects of the transformation may be internalised by the agent or the company directing those agents.

The application of formal logic and natural language

To formalise the definitions, this chapter employs first-order logic and complements with modal operators for some of the sentences. Table 4.1 displays the logical symbols used. An individual constant denotes an object. It can be anything in the discourse of the domain but must denote only one object. Consumption, production and work are defined as relations between individual constants. The symbols for individual constants are here letters in the alphabet before x, with or without a subscript. Variables refer to objects as well, but not to specific ones, and are here denoted by the letters x, y, and z with or without a subscript. Three types of objects are considered: matters, persons (which are also matters) and events:

Table 4.1 The logical symbols used in this study

Logical symbol	Meaning
$\rightarrow$	if... then
$\neg$	it is not the case that
$\wedge$	and
$\vee$	or
$\forall$	for all... is the case that
$\exists$	there exists... such that
$\equiv$	if and only if
$=$	is the same as
$\Diamond$	it is possible that

- Matters that are individual constants are denoted by the letter q or any subscript of q. Matters that are variables are denoted by the letter x or any subscript of x.
- Persons that are individual constants are denoted by the letter s, or any subscript of s (but can also be denoted as matters). Persons that are variables are denoted by the letter y with or without a subscript.
- Events that are individual constants are denoted e with or without a subscript. Events that are variables are denoted by the letter z with or without a subscript.
- The letter a with or without a subscript is used to denote any individual constants, such as matters, persons or events.

For simplicity, an event can also be an event where another event does not occur. Although the subscript usually is a number, for pedagogical reasons, the subscripts in this book are mostly descriptive labels.

A property states a property of an object and has only one argument. A relation states the relation between objects, and can have an arbitrary number of arguments. Properties and relations are designated by capital letters and are either true or false:

- The letter K denotes causal relations between events.
- The letter O denotes ontological properties and relations between objects (matters, persons and/or events).
- The letter P denotes purposeful relations.
- The letter A denotes various relations of an activity, mainly relations of production, work or consumption.

Definitions are formulated by providing the necessary and sufficient conditions for the relations in terms of other predicates and relations of the same objects.

Table 4.2 displays the basic causal, ontological and other relations. Tables 4.3 and 4.4 present the sentences that are employed to define various activities. Relations of production, consumption and work are defined through the sentences in Tables 4.3 and 4.4 and the logical symbols in Table 4.1. All the sentences in Tables 4.3 and 4.4 are non-economic (except for market saleability). In this way, the basic economic concepts of production, consumption and work are reduced to non-economic notions. Even the expression of utility is shunned.

Production, work as well as consumption contain the transformation of matter intentionally caused by one or more agents. The definition of production, work and consumption can logically be expressed as a relation, which is either true or false, between three events, the agent of the transformation of the matter, s_{agent}, and the matter that is transformed, q_{matter}. The three events consist of the intentional causation of the transformation of the matter by the agent, event $e_{intentional\_causation}$, the transformation of the agent that causes the

Table 4.2 Statement on basic causal relations used in this study

Non-logical symbol	Label	Further description
$K^2_{\text{causes}}e_1e_2$	Event e_1 causes event e_2.	It is necessary that both events e_1 and e_2 occur, but if event e_1 would not happen and all else (including outcomes due to pure chance) would stay the same except for the causal mechanism, event e_2 would not occur.
$K^2_{\text{intentionally\_causes}}se$	s intentionally causes event e.	• s undergoes a self-directed transformation, which causes event e, • s believes that this self-direct transformation causes event e, and • if all else except for the causal mechanism would stay the same, it is necessary that event e would not occur if s would not exist.
$K^2_{\text{prevents}}se$	s intentionally prevents event e from happening.	• s undergoes a self-directed transformation, which causes event e to not happen, • s believes that this self-direct transformation causes event e to not happen, and • if all else except for the causal mechanism stays the same, it is necessary that event e would occur if s would not exist.
$K^2_{\text{power}}se$	s has the power to intentionally prevent event e from happening.	If s chooses to act to prevent event e from happening, s prevents event e from happening.
$K^2_{\text{allows}}se$	The person s allows event e.	• s has the power to prevent event e, • s believes s has the power to prevent event e from happening, and • s does not prevent event e from happening.
$K^2_{\text{socially\_causes}}s_1e_1$	Agent s_1 socially causes event e_1.	Agent s_1 socially causes event e_1 if the causal mechanism necessarily involves coercive or non-coercive social causation. Agent s_1 may be said to coercively cause event e_1 if the causal mechanism necessarily involves the intentional transformation of an agent s_2, against the will of s_2. Agent s_1 may be said to non-coercively socially cause event e_1 if the causal mechanism necessarily comprises of the intentional transformation of agent s_2 to perform an intentional action, event e_2, in such a way that s_2 would not have preferred event e_2 if event e_1 would not occur, even when being past the information contained in event e_1. [Alternative formulation: Social causation would not occur in a society of individuals with the same preferences for all types of combinations of actions of all agents at a specific time if all agents have the same information.]
$K^2_{\text{coercively\_causes}}se$	Agent s coercively causes event e.	s intentionally causes event e such that a transformation of a person against that person's will is necessarily part of the causal mechanism.

$O^1_{person}q$	q is a person.	
$O^2_{part\_of}\, a_1 a_2$	a_1 is part of a_2.	a_1 and a_2 could be matters, persons or events.
$O^2_{transformation}eq$	Event e consists of the physical transformation of q.	During event e some properties of q are added and some properties of q are destroyed.
$O^4_{intentional\_causation}\, e_1 e_2 e_3$	Event e_1 consists of the causal mechanism whereby agent s through event e_2 intentionally causes event e_3.	
$P^3_{purpose}se_1e_2$	Agent s has event e_2 as a purpose for allowing event e_1.	• s believes that event e_1 causes event e_2, • s allows event e_1, and • it is necessary that if s believes that event e_1 does not cause event e_2, then s do not allow event e_1 from happening.
$P^2_{final\_purpose}se$	s has event e as a final purpose	There is no such event z imagined by agent s that: • the imagined event z is not part of event e • s believes that event e causes the imagined event z, and • agent s has the imagined event z as a purpose for allowing event e.

Table 4.3 Sentences used to define production, work and consumption in this study

Sentence	Explanation	Detailed logical explanation in natural language
$\varphi_{1,1}$ [Matter transformation]	A matter is physically transformed.	Event $e_{matter\_transforms}$ consists of the transformation of q_{matter}.
$\varphi_{2,1}$ [Agent transformation]	The agent is physically transformed.	Event $e_{agent\_transforms}$ consists of the transformation of s_{agent}.
$\varphi_{2,2}$ [Intentional causation]	The activity consists in the agent intentionally causing the physical transformation of a matter.	Event $e_{intentional\_causation}$ consists of the causal mechanism whereby s_{agent}, through event $e_{agent\_transforms}$ intentionally causes event $e_{matter\_transforms}$.
$\varphi_{3,1}$ [Agent exteriority]	The object of transformation is exterior to the agent.	q_{matter} is not part of s_{agent}, and s_{agent} is not part of q_{matter}.
$\varphi_{3,2}$ [Purpose exteriority of activity]	The purpose of the activity lies outside of the activity [when combined with $\varphi_{2,2}$].	s_{agent} does not have event $e_{intentional\_causation}$ as a final purpose.
$\varphi_{3,3}$ [Purpose exteriority of agent self-transformation]	The purpose of the activity for the agent lies outside of the self-transformation of the agent	It is not the case that agent s_{agent} has event $e_{agent\_transforms}$ as a purpose for allowing event $e_{matter\_transforms}$.
$\varphi_{3,4}$ [Purpose exteriority of person subject matter]	If the object of transformation is a person that person views its transformation as a means to achieve something else.	If q_{matter} is a person, then q_{matter} has not event $e_{agent\_transforms}$ as a final purpose.
$\varphi_{3,5}$ [Social exteriority]	The agent does not cause the transformation of the object through social causation.	s_{agent} does not socially cause event $e_{matter\_transforms}$.
$\varphi_{3,6}$ [Humanity exteriority]	The object of transformation is not a person	q_{matter} is not a person.

Production, work and consumption 97

$\varphi_{4.1}$ [Non-social causation of final consumption]	It is possible that the transformation of the object will non-socially cause or overlaps with final consumption.	It is possible that there are/will be events $z_{intentional\_causation}$, $z_{agent\_transforms}$, and $z_{matter\_transforms}$, and object x_{matter} and person y_{agent}, such that: • event $z_{intentional\_causation}$ is the final consumption of x_{matter} by y_{agent} whereby event $z_{agent\_transforms}$ is the transformation of x_{matter} that is caused by event $z_{agent\_transforms}$, the transformation of y_{agent}, and either: • event $e_{matter\_transforms}$ non-socially causes event $z_{matter\_transforms}$, or • event $e_{agent\_transforms}$ is identical to event $z_{matter\_transforms}$, or • (event $e_{matter\_transforms}$ is identical to event $z_{matter\_transforms}$ and s_{agent} is not identical to y_{agent}), or • (event $e_{matter\_transforms}$ is identical to event $z_{matter\_transforms}$ and s_{agent} does not have event $e_{agent\_transforms}$ as a purpose for allowing event $e_{matter\_transforms}$).
$\varphi_{4.2}$ [Causation of final consumption]	It is possible that the transformation of the object will cause or overlaps with final consumption.	It is possible that there are/will be events $z_{intentional\_causation}$, $z_{agent\_transforms}$, and $z_{matter\_transforms}$, and object x_{matter} and person y_{agent}, such that: • event $z_{intentional\_causation}$ is the final consumption of x_{matter} by y_{agent} whereby event $z_{agent\_transforms}$ is the transformation of x_{matter} that is caused by event $z_{agent\_transforms}$, the transformation of y_{agent}, and either: • event $e_{matter\_transforms}$ causes event $z_{matter\_transforms}$, or • event $e_{agent\_transforms}$ is identical to event $z_{matter\_transforms}$, or • (event $e_{matter\_transforms}$ is identical to event $z_{matter\_transforms}$ and s_{agent} is not identical to y_{agent}), or • (event $e_{matter\_transforms}$ is identical to event $z_{matter\_transforms}$ and s_{agent} does not have event $e_{agent\_transforms}$ as a purpose for allowing event $e_{matter\_transforms}$).
$\varphi_{4.3}$ [Non-social causation of non-social production]	It is possible that the transformation of the object will cause or is part of non-social production.	It is possible that there are/will be events $z_{intentional\_causation}$, $z_{agent\_transforms}$, and $z_{matter\_transforms}$, and object x_{matter} and person y_{agent}, such that: • event $z_{intentional\_causation}$ is the non-social production, whereby event $z_{matter\_transforms}$ is the transformation of x_{matter} that is caused by event $z_{agent\_transforms}$, the transformation of y_{agent},

(Continued)

Table 4.3 (Continued)

Sentence	Explanation	Detailed logical explanation in natural language
$\varphi_{4.4}$ [Causation of comprehensive production]	It is possible that the transformation of the object will cause or is part of comprehensive production	• event $e_{intentional\_causation}$ is part of event $z_{intentional\_causation}$, and • event $e_{matter\_transforms}$ causes or is identical to event $z_{matter\_transforms}$, and • event $e_{agent\_transforms}$ is part of event $z_{agent\_transforms}$. It is possible that there are/will be events $z_{intentional\_causation}$, $z_{agent\_transforms}$, and $z_{matter\_transforms}$, and object x_{matter} and person y_{agent}, such that: • event $z_{intentional\_causation}$ is the comprehensive production, whereby event $z_{matter\_transforms}$ is the transformation of x_{matter} that is caused by event $z_{agent\_transforms}$, the transformation of y_{agent}, • event $e_{intentional\_causation}$ is part of event $z_{intentional\_causation}$, and • event $e_{matter\_transforms}$ causes or is identical to event $z_{matter\_transforms}$, and • event $e_{agent\_transforms}$ is part of event $z_{agent\_transforms}$.
$\varphi_{4.5}$ [Market saleability]	It is possible that the transformation of q_{matter} is part of or causes the transformation of a matter that is sold at the market.	

Table 4.4 Sentences used to define production, work and consumption in this study, expressed in logical and non-logical symbols (see Tables 4.1 and 4.2). Sentence $\varphi_{4,5}$ is explained in natural language in Table 4.3

Sentence	Logical expression
$\varphi_{1,1}$	$O^2_{\text{transformation}}e_{\text{matter\_transforms}}q_{\text{matter}}$
$\varphi_{2,1}$	$O^2_{\text{transformation}}e_{\text{agent\_transforms}}s_{\text{agent}}$
$\varphi_{2,2}$	$O^4_{\text{intentional\_causation}}e_{\text{intentional\_causation}}s_{\text{agent}}s_{\text{agent\_transforms}}e_{\text{matter\_transforms}}$
$\varphi_{3,1}$	$\neg O^2_{\text{part\_of}}q_{\text{matter}}s_{\text{agent}} \wedge \neg O^2_{\text{part\_of}}s_{\text{agent}}q_{\text{matter}}$
$\varphi_{3,2}$	$\neg P^2_{\text{final\_purpose}}s_{\text{agent}}e_{\text{intentional\_causation}}$
$\varphi_{3,3}$	$\neg P^3_{\text{purpose}}s_{\text{agent}}e_{\text{matter\_transforms}}e_{\text{agent\_transforms}}$
$\varphi_{3,4}$	$O^1_{\text{person}}q_{\text{matter}} \rightarrow \neg P^2_{\text{final\_purpose}}q_{\text{matter}}e_{\text{agent\_transforms}}$
$\varphi_{3,5}$	$\neg K^2_{\text{socially\_causes}}s_{\text{agent}}e_{\text{matter\_transforms}}$
$\varphi_{3,6}$	$\neg O^1_{\text{person}}q_{\text{matter}}$
$\varphi_{4,1}$	$\Diamond \exists z_{\text{intentional\_causation}}\, \exists z_{\text{agent\_transforms}}\, \exists z_{\text{matter\_transforms}}\, \exists y_{\text{agent}}\!: \exists x_{\text{matter}}$ $(A^5_{\text{final\_consumption}}z_{\text{intentional\_causation}}z_{\text{agent\_transforms}}z_{\text{matter\_transforms}}y_{\text{agent}}x_{\text{matter}} \wedge$ $((K^2_{\text{causes}}e_{\text{matter\_transforms}}z_{\text{matter\_transforms}} \wedge \neg K^2_{\text{socially\_causes}}e_{\text{matter\_transforms}}z_{\text{matter\_transforms}}) \vee (e_{\text{agent\_transforms}}=z_{\text{matter\_transforms}}) \vee$ $(e_{\text{matter\_transforms}}=z_{\text{matter\_transforms}} \wedge \neg(s_{\text{agent}}=y_{\text{agent}})) \vee (e_{\text{matter\_transforms}}=z_{\text{matter\_transforms}} \wedge \neg(s_{\text{agent}}=y_{\text{agent}})) \wedge$ $\neg(P^3_{\text{purpose}}s_{\text{agent}}e_{\text{matter\_transforms}}e_{\text{agent\_transforms}}))))$
$\varphi_{4,2}$	$\Diamond \exists z_{\text{intentional\_causation}}\, \exists z_{\text{agent\_transforms}}\, \exists z_{\text{matter\_transforms}}\, \exists y_{\text{agent}}\!: \exists x_{\text{matter}}$ $(A^4_{\text{final\_consumption}}z_{\text{intentional\_causation}}z_{\text{agent\_transforms}}z_{\text{matter\_transforms}}y_{\text{agent}}x_{\text{matter}} \wedge (K^2_{\text{causes}}e_{\text{matter\_transforms}}z_{\text{matter\_transforms}} \vee$ $(e_{\text{agent\_transforms}}=z_{\text{matter\_transforms}}) \vee (e_{\text{matter\_transforms}}=z_{\text{matter\_transforms}} \wedge \neg(s_{\text{agent}}=y_{\text{agent}})) \vee (e_{\text{matter\_transforms}}=z_{\text{matter\_transforms}} \wedge$ $\neg(P^3_{\text{purpose}}s_{\text{agent}}e_{\text{matter\_transforms}}e_{\text{agent\_transforms}})))$
$\varphi_{4,3}$	$\Diamond \exists z_{\text{intentional\_causation}}\, \exists z_{\text{agent\_transforms}}\, \exists z_{\text{matter\_transforms}}\, \exists y_{\text{agent}}\, \exists x_{\text{matter}}$ $(A^5_{\text{non-social\_production}}z_{\text{intentional\_causation}}z_{\text{agent\_transforms}}z_{\text{matter\_transforms}}y_{\text{agent}}x_{\text{matter}} \wedge$ $O^2_{\text{part\_of}}e_{\text{intentional\_causation}}z_{\text{intentional\_causation}} \wedge (K^2_{\text{causes}}e_{\text{matter\_transforms}}z_{\text{matter\_transforms}} \vee e_{\text{matter\_transforms}}=z_{\text{matter\_transforms}}) \wedge$ $O^2_{\text{part\_of}}e_{\text{agent\_transforms}}z_{\text{agent\_transforms}})$
$\varphi_{4,4}$	$\Diamond \exists z_{\text{intentional\_causation}}\, \exists z_{\text{agent\_transforms}}\, \exists z_{\text{matter\_transforms}}\, \exists y_{\text{agent}}\, \exists x_{\text{matter}}$ $(A^5_{\text{comprehensive\_production}}z_{\text{intentional\_causation}}z_{\text{agent\_transforms}}z_{\text{matter\_transforms}}y_{\text{agent}}x_{\text{matter}} \wedge O^2_{\text{part\_of}}e_{\text{intentional\_causation}}z_{\text{intentional\_causation}} \wedge$ $(K^2_{\text{causes}}e_{\text{matter\_transforms}}z_{\text{matter\_transforms}}=z_{\text{matter\_transforms}} \vee e_{\text{matter\_transforms}}=z_{\text{matter\_transforms}}) \wedge O^2_{\text{part\_of}}e_{\text{agent\_transforms}}z_{\text{agent\_transforms}})$

transformation of the matter, event $e_{\text{agent\_transforms}}$, and the physical transformation of the matter, event $e_{\text{matter\_transforms}}$.

The order of the objects in the definitions is important. For example, if $A^5{}_{\text{consumption}}e_{\text{intentional\_causation}}e_{\text{agent\_transforms}}e_{\text{matter\_transforms}}s_{\text{agent}}q_{\text{matter}}$ is a relation of consumption, and if q_{matter} is not a person, then $A^5{}_{\text{consumption}}e_{\text{intentional\_causation}}e_{\text{agent\_transforms}}e_{\text{matter\_transforms}}q_{\text{matter}}s_{\text{agent}}$ is false, i.e., there is no relation of consumption for that order of constants, given that consumption presumes an agent.

The sentences in Tables 4.3 and 4.4 can be divided into four groups, which conform to the four main conditions of production described at the beginning of the chapter:

1   $\varphi_{1,1}$ [Matter transformation] belongs to the first group given that it states conditions concerning the physical transformation of q_{matter}.
2   $\varphi_{2,1}$ [Agent transformation] and $\varphi_{2,2}$ [Intentional causation] belong to the second group by expressing conditions concerning the intentional causation by s_{agent} of the transformation of q_{matter}. $\varphi_{2,1}$ states that the agent is transformed, while $\varphi_{2,2}$ states that there is an activity consisting of the agent intentionally causing the physical transformation of a matter.
3   $\varphi_{3,1}$ to $\varphi_{3,6}$ belong to the third group and are different variants of exteriority conditions: $\varphi_{3,1}$ agency exteriority, $\varphi_{3,2}$ to $\varphi_{3,4}$ various purpose exteriorities, $\varphi_{3,5}$ social exteriority, and $\varphi_{3,6}$ humanity exteriority.
4   $\varphi_{4,1}$ to $\varphi_{4,4}$ belong to the fourth group and state various final utility conditions. For convenience, sentences $\varphi_{4,1}$ to $\varphi_{4,4}$ contain relations of final consumption or production, but it is possible to reformulate all sentences in Tables 4.3 and 4.4 by only using the sentences in Table 4.2 (there is no circularity involved). The sentence $\varphi_{4,5}$, market saleability, is also associated with this group.

The focus is on using as simple logic as possible. Therefore, temporal and higher-order logics are avoided. Although this book applies traditional logic, it is also recognised that there are limits to how exactly reality can be described by the presented definitions. In recent years, fuzzy logic has developed as an influential field that better mimics natural language compared to traditional Boolean logic that states that a sentence either has the value 1 (true) or false (0) (Selase et al., 2015). Fuzziness does not require that the logic is fuzzy, but rather that the assignment of whether a statement is true or false is vague, i.e., partially true or false at a continuum between 0 and 1. This, in turn, has to be distinguished from the probability of whether it is true or false. Concepts are social constructions but restrained by various conditions of the mind and the exterior world. This is fully compatible with critical realism, i.e., the view that given that we decide to use one or another definition, statements can under certain conditions accurately describe the exterior world, or fail to do so. Analytical rigour to explore a fuzzy world may be preferable compared to analysis based on conceptual fuzziness. As argued by Baran (1957, pp. 32–33) in relation to distinguishing between productive and unproductive labour (although without presenting the needed analytical rigour to establish such distinction):

> But that brandy and water mixed in a bottle cannot be separated, and that it may be impossible to establish accurately the proportions in which the two liquids are combined, does not alter the fact that the bottle contains both brandy and water and that the two beverages are present in the bottle in some definite quantities. What is more, to whatever extent the bottle may be filled, it can be safely asserted that in the absence of one or the other ingredient of the mix, it would be less full than in its presence. That we cannot at the present time neatly separate the wheat from the chaff, i.e., identify unequivocally the dimensions of the socially desirable output and of the economic surplus in our economy, is in itself an important aspect of the economic and social order of monopoly capitalism.

Some difficulties in classifying a phenomenon may be in itself interesting for some analytical purposes. Feminist economists and other researchers have pointed out that many women to a larger degree than men perform multitasking, where different work tasks are performed simultaneously, and leisure may be intertwined with work (Kalenkoski & Foster, 2016). However, that does not imply that analytically it is impossible to distinguish between leisure and work.

Both production and consumption involve processes, and sequences of events, which are temporarily intertwined, while the definitions presented in this book rest on a temporal order between events. For example, an artist producing a painting may, for simplicity, be considered to first transforms his or her body before transforming the matter that is to become the painting. In reality, the process of the transformation of the body of the artist and the transformation of the matter that is to become the painting is seemingly going on simultaneously. Analytically, we could still distinguish a temporal order, the cause precedes the effect, but would then have to describe the process as a series of acts of production, but for simplicity, it could be preferable to describe that process as one act of the self-transformation of the agent followed by the transformation of an exterior matter. Although this book does not apply fuzzy logic, the application of the definitions is to be regarded as fulfilling criteria of partial truth rather than absolute truth.

Consumption

A common feature of all definitions of consumption, production and work is that they are activities. They, therefore, include at least the sentences $\varphi_{1,1}$ [Matter transformation], $\varphi_{2,1}$ [Agent transformation] and $\varphi_{2,2}$ [Intentional causation], which describe how the transformation of the agent intentionally

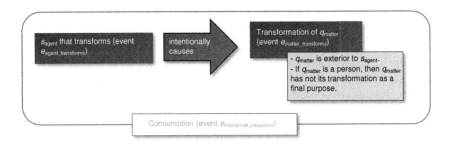

Figure 4.1 The definition of consumption applied in this book.

causes the transformation of the matter of transformation. Consumption is here defined as (see also Figure 4.1):

Consumption (event $e_{\text{intentional\_causation}}$) occurs if
$A^5_{\text{consumption}}e_{\text{intentional\_causation}}e_{\text{agent\_transforms}}e_{\text{matter\_transforms}}s_{\text{agent}}q_{\text{matter}}$,
which in turn occurs if and only if φ_1 [Matter transformation], and $\varphi_{2,1}$ [Agent transformation], and $\varphi_{2,2}$ [Intentional causation], and $\varphi_{3,1}$ [Agent exteriority] and $\varphi_{3,4}$ [Purpose exteriority of person subject matter].

In plain words, consumption (event $e_{\text{intentional\_causation}}$) occurs when a matter ($q_{\text{matter}}$) exterior to an agent ($s_{\text{agent}}$) is transformed (event $e_{\text{matter\_transforms}}$), intentionally caused by the agent's self-transformation (event $e_{\text{agent\_transforms}}$); and if the transformed matter (q_{matter}) is a person that person does not have its self-transformation (event $e_{\text{matter\_transforms}}$) as a final purpose. The relation of consumption between events $e_{\text{intentional\_causation}}$, $e_{\text{agent\_transforms}}$ and $e_{\text{matter\_transforms}}$, agent s_{agent} and matter q_{matter} is here labelled as $A^5_{\text{consumption}}e_{\text{intentional\_causation}}e_{\text{agent\_transforms}}e_{\text{matter\_transforms}}s_{\text{agent}}q_{\text{matter}}$.

$\varphi_{1,1}$ [Matter transformation] states that event $e_{\text{matter\_transforms}}$ consists of the physical transformation of matter q_{matter}. The transformation of the matter entails that some intrinsic properties are gained and some are lost. Sentence $\varphi_{1,1}$ [Matter transformation] requires that the transformed matter cannot be an object of the mind.

While production adds useful properties to a matter, consumption normally subtracts useful properties. Consumption is in this sense asymmetric to production, or what Marshall (1997, p. 62) calls "negative production". Usually, the lost properties entail that the matter of consumption loses its properties for future consumption, causing the ordered structure of q_{matter} to decrease. To some extent, this is self-evident in sentence $\varphi_{1,1}$ [Matter transformation] since transforming the matter q_{matter} involves destroying some of its intrinsic properties. The uses that presuppose the original properties are prevented, which constitutes an opportunity cost. Some matters are useless before being transformed, for example, waste that is disposed of, which makes it awkward to describe their transformation as a consumption. However, even in the case of waste, some people may, for example, be negatively affected by the waste being transported to their area of residence. For them, the waste is more "useful" at its original location.

Sentence $\varphi_{2,1}$ [Agent transformation] states that event $e_{agent\_transforms}$ is the physical transformation of s_{agent}. There are, therefore, two events constituting two different transformations, one transformation of s_{agent} (event $e_{agent\_transforms}$) and one transformation of q_{matter} (event $e_{matter\_transforms}$). Sentence $\varphi_{2,2}$ [Intentional causation] states what is the causal relationship between the two transformations. Both are part of the event $e_{intentional\_causation}$, which is the whole activity in question. Sentence $\varphi_{2,2}$ [Intentional causation] states that event $e_{intentional\_causation}$ consists of the mechanism whereby s_{agent} intentionally causes event $e_{matter\_transforms}$ through event $e_{agent\_transforms}$.

The time of production, work or consumption can be stretched longer than the involvement of the active agent s_{agent}. For example, bottled wine that is stored continues to change in a desirable way even after it has been bottled. Similarly, a house can continue to be consumed by the agent, even if the agent does not use the house for the time being.

Consumption should normally exclude the possibility of consumption of oneself, an exteriority condition. Therefore, sentence $\varphi_{3,1}$ [Agent exteriority] is added. $\varphi_{3,1}$ [Agent exteriority] states that the matter q_{matter} must be exterior to the agent s_{agent}.

One possibility is to state that the matter of transformation in consumption cannot be a person. For example, prostitution would then be excluded from the definition of consumption. However, services such as singing and medical treatment would then not be considered consumption activities, provided we could not somehow separate the physical effects of these services from the persons performing and consuming them. A quandary with the formulation of consumption used here is that it could be true for an activity involving hurting a person against the person's will. For example, cannibalism could be regarded as a final consumption of a person, even if that occurs against that person's will. By including the sentence $\varphi_{3,5}$ [Social exteriority], cannibalism could be excluded from final consumption in an alternative definition, but the choice here is not to add that sentence. Consumption is ultimately about destroying some of the useful properties of the matter.

Hobby-hunting does not involve the consumption of the hunter since the agent performs the activity for his or her own amusement. It expresses recreation, not the wearing out of the agent. Consumption of persons should involve changes of these persons that are not desirable for those persons. To exclude the possibility of two persons enjoying each other's company as consuming each other, sentence $\varphi_{3,4}$ [Purpose exteriority of person subject matter] is added, which is a purpose-exteriority condition. Sentence $\varphi_{3,4}$ states that if q_{matter} is a person, then q_{matter} has not event $e_{matter\_transforms}$ as a final purpose – the transformation of q_{matter} then involves some kind of disutility for q_{matter}. For example, we could not say that the student consumes the teacher if

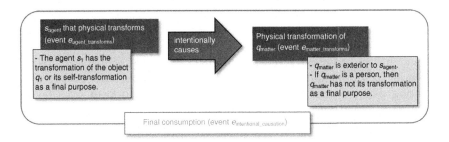

Figure 4.2 The definition of final consumption applied in this book.

the teacher performs the activity entirely for its own intrinsic pleasure. Ultimately consumption involves a potential disutility.

Final consumption

SNA 2008 (United Nations et al., 2009, p. 8) distinguishes between intermediate and final consumption as follows:

> Consumption is an activity in which institutional units use up goods or services, but there are two quite different kinds of consumption. Intermediate consumption consists of goods and services used up in the course of production within the accounting period. Final consumption consists of goods and services used by individual households or the community to satisfy their individual or collective needs or wants.

Defining what individual or collective needs are is difficult. In this book, final consumption is defined, as (see Figure 4.2):

> **Final consumption** (event $e_{\text{intentional\_causation}}$) occurs if
> $A^5{}_{\text{final\_consumption}}e_{\text{intentional\_causation}}e_{\text{agent\_transforms}}e_{\text{matter\_transforms}}s_{\text{agent}}q_{\text{matter}}$,
> which in turn is true if and only if φ_1 [Matter transformation], and $\varphi_{2,1}$ [Agent transformation], and $\varphi_{2,2}$ [Intentional causation], and $\varphi_{3,1}$ [Agent exteriority], and **either not $\varphi_{3,2}$ or not $\varphi_{3,3}$** [Purpose interiority of either activity or agent transformation], and $\varphi_{3,4}$ [Purpose exteriority of person subject matter].

In plain words, final consumption (event $e_{\text{intentional\_causation}}$) occurs when a matter ($q_{\text{matter}}$) exterior to an agent ($s_{\text{agent}}$) is transformed (event $e_{\text{matter\_transforms}}$), intentionally caused by the agent's (s_{agent}) self-transformation (event $e_{\text{agent\_transforms}}$); the agent ($s_{\text{agent}}$) has the transformation (event $e_{\text{matter\_transforms}}$) of the matter ($q_{\text{matter}}$) or its self-transformation (event $e_{\text{agent\_transforms}}$) as a final purpose; and if the transformed matter (q_{matter}) is a person that person does not have its self-transformation (event $e_{matter\_transforms}$) as a final purpose. The relation of final consumption between events $e_{intentional\_causation}$, $e_{agent\_transforms}$ and $e_{matter\_transforms}$, agent s_{agent} and matter q_{matter} is here labelled as

$$A^5_{final\_consumption}e_{intentional\_causation}e_{agent\_transforms}e_{matter\_transforms}s_{agent}q_{matter}.$$

Compared to the definition of consumption, the sentence "either not $\varphi_{3,2}$ or not $\varphi_{3,3}$" is added, which states that s_{agent} has either the transformation of q_{matter} as a final purpose ("not $\varphi_{3,2}$") or the purpose of the transformation of q_{matter} lies in the transformation of s_{agent} (sentence "not $\varphi_{3,3}$"). This is an opposite exteriority condition, i.e., an interiority condition.

Final consumption encompasses desirable effects as perceived by the consumer. These desirable effects might involve the consumer or the subject matter. Collective consumption does not necessitate any satisfaction of the needs of individuals.

Reproduction is here used as the description of purposeful transformation of humans, which can both involve self-reproduction, the transformation of oneself and the transformation of other human beings. While the ultimate purpose of production is final consumption, the ultimate purpose of final consumption is mostly, but not always, reproduction. We can identify various types of final consumption.

Final consumption is usually finally purposeful. An example is eating ice cream for its own enjoyment. Another example is feeding an infant, where the final consumption is finally purposeful, but exteriorly reproductive. Final consumption can be non-reproductively finally purposeful, for example, preserving nature for its own sake.

Final consumption does not necessarily encompass a final purpose. Consider teaching students to cook in a restaurant. It is possible that the student in the future will cook a meal in a restaurant. From the student's point of view, the activity of the teacher does not constitute final purpose as the purpose of the activity for the student lies outside the class. Students that attend the classes do not do that entirely for the intrinsic pleasures that can be derived from the teaching (i.e., sentence "not $\varphi_{3,2}$" is false). However, since the purpose of the transformation of the teacher for the student lies in the transformation of the student, s_{agent} (i.e., sentence "not $\varphi_{3,3}$" is true), we can say that the student finally consumes the teacher, q_{matter}.

In practice, as is well-known, it can be difficult to distinguish between intermediate and final consumption. For example, using a textbook to teach a person may be considered final consumption if the final purpose is to educate a person for its own sake, but also intermediate consumption if the textbook is about how to, for example, use a machine in production.

In national accounts, for a closed economy, it is generally assumed that gross output always equals final consumption, intermediate consumption and investment, which excludes the possibility of final consumption of non-produced matters. The definition of final consumption in this book opens for the possibility of final consumption of non-produced matters, for example, drinking water directly from a lake, breathing fresh air or enjoying

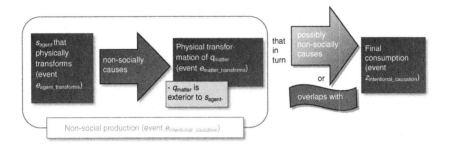

Figure 4.3 The definition of non-social production applied in this book.

nature, which can be related to the emphasis in ecological economics on the role of nature for human welfare. An alternative is to delimit final consumption to final consumption of produced matters, but final consumption of produced matters and non-produced matters could sometimes be indistinguishable. Drinking water from a non-produced container of water is not much different from drinking water from a produced container of water. Environmental degradation destroys types of final consumption that are not produced. Another dilemma is that a formulation of final consumption that presupposes produced matters is circular, given that the definition of production, as discussed below, in turn, depends on the definition of final consumption.

Non-social production

We should consider several definitions of production. All the definitions discussed in this book may fulfil different analytical purposes. In the end, it is of secondary importance how activities are labelled. What is crucial is to keep various definitions analytically separate and to offer clear delimitations.

The first articulation of production in this book is closest to what Marx describes as production in general, but also to the Classical and early institutional traditions. Deleting the sentence $\varphi_{3,4}$ [Purpose exteriority of person subject matter] and adding sentences $\varphi_{3,5}$ [Social exteriority] and $\varphi_{4,1}$ [Non-social causation of final consumption] to the formulation of consumption yields the following definition of non-social production (see also Figure 4.3):

> **Non-social production** (event $e_{\text{intentional\_causation}}$) occurs if
> $A^5{}_{\text{non-social\_production}}e_{\text{intentional\_causation}}e_{\text{agent\_transforms}}e_{\text{matter\_transforms}}s_{\text{agent}}q_{\text{matter}}$,
> which in turn is true if and only if $\varphi_{1,1}$ [Matter transformation], and $\varphi_{2,1}$ [Agent transformation], and $\varphi_{2,2}$ [Intentional causation], and $\varphi_{3,1}$ [Agent exteriority], and $\varphi_{3,5}$ [Social exteriority], and $\varphi_{4,1}$ [Non-social causation of final consumption]

In plain words, non-social production (event $e_{\text{intentional\_causation}}$) occurs when a matter ($q_{\text{matter}}$) exterior to an agent ($s_{\text{agent}}$) is transformed (event $e_{\text{matter\_transforms}}$) non-socially caused by the agent's (s_{agent}) self-transformation (event $e_{\text{agent\_transforms}}$); and it is possible that the transformation (event $e_{\text{matter\_transforms}}$) of the matter ($q_{\text{matter}}$) causes or overlaps with final consumption (event $z_{\text{intentional\_causation}}$). The relation of non-social production between events $e_{\text{intentional\_causation}}$, $e_{\text{agent\_transforms}}$ and $e_{\text{matter\_transforms}}$, agent s_{agent} and matter q_{matter} is here labelled as

$$A^5_{\text{non-social\_production}} e_{\text{intentional\_causation}} e_{\text{agent\_transforms}} e_{\text{matter\_transforms}} s_{\text{agent}} q_{\text{matter}}.$$

Sentence $\varphi_{2,2}$ [Intentional causation] necessitates intentional causation of the transformation of the matter q_{matter}. Intentional causation of a physical transformation presupposes that such transformation really occurs. If agents think one action will generate certain effects, but there is no possibility this will happen, such activity cannot be described as productive. The definitions in this book open for the possibility of failed production, which usually involves work. To give an example, for 3000 years, medical practitioners believed that bloodletting could cure illness (Greenstone, 2010). However, since such activity did not cure anything, except for a few select conditions, the activity was unproductive, while the present definition of SNA would put it, if paid, within the production boundary. The emphasis on actual transformations of matter having certain material effects by agents is consistent with materialism and objectivism, as a contrast to idealism and subjectivism. Production cannot be defined just in terms of subjective conceptions, as implicitly advocated by mainstream economics, but also by its objective effects.

It is sometimes possible that the agents of production do not know what is actually produced, for example, in a factory. That is, however, not a necessary condition for production activity, even if there is usually a person that intends the end-product. An unintentional action can be generated by an intentional action (Anscombe, 1957; Davidson, 1980). s_{agent} may, for example, intend to transform q_{matter}. This transformation may, in turn, cause the end-product without s_{agent} even intending the latter.

Including sentence $\varphi_{3,1}$ [Agent exteriority] entails that studying and work travel cannot be classified as production activity, in accordance with the third person criterion. If q_{matter} is the agent of the transformation, it is not exterior to the agent; the activity cannot then be delegated to a third person.

Theft and the services provided by a broker to raise the price of a property imply that the needs of one individual can be satisfied at the expense of other persons. No change is then made to the amount of final consumption possibilities available in society at large. Trade, financial services and advertising may add to the utility of products without decreasing utility for other persons through better allocation. However, the national accounting principle of no double counting involves quantification of production that is independent of the utility derived from the products. Otherwise, the level of aggregate production should be adjusted to equality as well as higher equality increases utility. While production must be quantifiable, changes in the choices persons make are difficult to quantify, especially if they are treated as objects of the mind.

Adding sentence $\varphi_{3,5}$ [Social exteriority] is a solution to such problems, which restricts the definition of production to non-social causation as discussed earlier in this chapter. Sentence $\varphi_{3,5}$ states that s_{agent} does not socially cause the transformation of q_{matter}. Sentence $\varphi_{3,5}$ requires that there could not be any coercive causation as well. Coercive activities, which change the choices people can make concerning their bodies, would not occur on Robinson Crusoe Island either. Robinson Crusoe could not have intentionally killed himself against his own will or waged a war against himself, at least not if he would be a rational person. The concept of security as a type of productive service and public good is contradictory as argued by a number of thinkers through history. For example, already Lao Tzu (1988, p. 57) noted:

> The more weapons you have, the less secure people will be.

Shaikh and Tonak (1994, p. 18) purport that there is a difference between output and outcomes. Activities such as policing, trade and finance are outcomes, social consumption that may be desirable, but not output. They do not fully explain the difference. For some reason, they (Shaikh & Tonak, 1994, p. 27) view fire departments as maintenance of social order similar to policing. The concept of social exteriority entails that the difference between productive and unproductive labour mainly concerns whether social causation is involved or not. For example, while fire departments protect against the destruction of a non-human force, an activity that could theoretically be performed at Robinson Crusoe Island, policing protects against human threats, which would not happen at Robinson Crusoe Island.

This does not entail that all activities that somehow hurt people against their will should be regarded as unproductive. For example, constructing a building may accidentally kill a person, but that is not part of the mechanism that causes the final consumption of the building. The building would be constructed even if the accident would not occur. In contrast, the attempt to murder a person would not have accomplished its aim if the person survived.

Counting trade, financial services and war activities as productive intermediate consumption is an alternative to avoiding double counting, but present national accounts treat those activities as final consumption services. Productive intermediate consumption still presupposes that such are technologically and materially necessary, which may be questioned concerning trade, financial services and war. They could be considered regrettables. Waging war may provide substantial material benefits to the winner, but that only redistributes what has previously been produced. Trade is socially necessary, given that a larger society cannot redistribute everything for free, but not technologically necessary.

Production involves a consciously directly transformation. However, consciousness only resides in the individual. The minds of two individuals are separate from each other. Those who cause transformations by delegating all conscious steps to other persons are not directly involved in a consciously directed process. If the capitalist employs the worker to produce, that does not make the capitalist the producer. However, providing information could be viewed as directly contributing to production. The information in itself could be regarded as existing in the form of a physical object. The writer productively contributes to the printing of a physical book. This is much an analytical distinction, which should not be conflated with how individual capitalists could act. Some entrepreneurial capitalists are part of the production process, but under modern capitalism, the entrepreneurial spirit is often separated from the ownership.

The same act could seemingly be either a productive or unproductive activity according to the definition applied here. Amputating a person's arm against that person's will involves coercive causation, even if the intent may be to save that person's life and could not occur on Robinson Crusoe Island. Amputating a person's arm if that person desires so for medical reasons is not a coercive act and could occur on Robinson Crusoe Island. There are, however, more difficult cases to judge. Amputating an infant's arm for medical reasons has obviously not been approved by the infant, but we could imagine that since it serves the infant's interest, and the infant cannot yet express its own intents, it does not constitute a coercive act. This is not clear-cut from the definition applied here, but the intent with these definitions is for them to serve as heuristic tools, not as rigid formulas.

The utilitarian tradition rests on the distinction between the person and the non-person, which is a value judgement. Infanticide has been practised in most cultures, whether active or passive. Darwin (1889, p. 592) contends that in "the Polynesian Islands women have been known to kill from four or five to even ten of their children, and Ellis could not find a single woman who had not killed at least one". Today infanticide would be defined as a coercive act in all countries, even with the approval of the parents. Why is the killing of animals different from killing new-born children? New-born children are obviously not more conscious than some of the most intelligent animals. The essential distinction between an infant and an animal is that the infant has the potential to develop into an intelligent being. However, what about abortion or persons that are permanently in a coma? There are no definite scientific answers to such questions as they concern value systems. Hence, even if this book attempts to provide a trans-historical formulation of production, value judgements cannot be avoided – but they should be transparent.

At present, the closest to a trans-historical definition of a human being would be all those that have been born to humans or are fully developed foetuses. Non-fully developed foetuses may be considered to belong to women's bodies before they are born, although biologically, this is not entirely correct, and the mother's immune system could act as if the foetus is an intruder and mount an immune response (Kramer & Bressan, 2015). On balance, an abortion could be regarded as a productive activity as long as it is not performed against the mother's will. Other definitions would, however, shift the production boundary of non-social production.

While forcing a slave to work may be considered non-production according to this definition, it does not automatically implicate that the work of the slave is non-production. If the slave intentionally transforms the matter, the slave does not force himself/herself against his/her own will to do that. Slaves are forced to labour. Also, wage labour can be perceived as being forced into production if the alternative is to starve, although a difference is that direct violence is not used against the wage worker, in contrast to the slave. Even when forced to labour, during the labour process, the slave and the wage-labourer become compliant since otherwise, they could not perform various tasks. They always have the "choice" to stop working, even under the threat of being punished or starved. In contrast, a person being beaten up, murdered or stolen from does not have such a choice. The work of the slave owner may be considered unproductive given that it presupposes the use of violence and force against slaves.

A productive activity should possibly cause future final consumption to fulfil the final utility condition, which is universally recognised by various economic thinkers. For example, Keynes (1973, p. 46) points out:

> All production is for the purpose of ultimately satisfying a consumer. Time usually elapses, however – and sometimes much time – between the incurring of costs by the producer (with the consumer in view) and the purchase of the product by the ultimate consumer. Meanwhile the entrepreneur… has to form the best expectations he can as to what the consumer will be prepared to pay when he is ready to supply them (directly or indirectly) after the elapse of that may be a lengthy period; and he has no choice but to be guided by these expectations, if he is to produce at all by processes which occupy time.

The final utility condition is difficult to formulate as we cannot beforehand state exactly how the production and consumption processes continue after the product has been created. As argued by Carl Menger (2007, p. 64–64):

> The goods-character of a thing is… dependent on its being capable of being placed in a causal connection with the satisfaction of human needs… a direct causal connection between a thing and the satisfaction of a need is by no means a necessary prerequisite of its goods-character. On the contrary, a large number of things derive their goods-character from the fact that they stand only in a more or less indirect causal relationship to the satisfaction of human needs…

> If, as the result of a change in tastes, the need for tobacco should disappear completely, the first consequence would be that all stocks of finished tobacco products on hand would be deprived of their goods-character. A

further consequence would be that the raw tobacco leaves, the machines, tools, and implements applicable exclusively to the processing of tobacco, the specialized labor services employed in the production of tobacco products, the available stocks of tobacco seeds, etc., would lose their goods-character.

Although production must be recognised by its objective consequences, its demarcation rests on the subjective perceptions of these consequences by the agents. Objective conditions and subjective perceptions are related. Production, work and consumption concern the reproduction of human life, in the long-term, the survival of the human species. Normally, people prefer subjectively what they objectively are in need of. Hungry persons tend to prefer food. However, a discrepancy is possible. Smokers prefer cigarettes subjectively, but objectively cigarettes deteriorate smokers' health. A value system based on subjective perceptions is therefore different from one based on objective conditions. For production, it is ultimately subjective purposes that must be served. Production that objectively are beneficial to human life, but which subjectively are discarded, will not be able to continue operating. Nevertheless, favourable objective conditions to human life cannot be disregarded when explaining agency. Governments can act to restrict smoking, voters vote for such action, and smokers make efforts to stop smoking.

When producing a good, the producer cannot predict what subjective utility a consumer will have from this good but can determine that the good is prospectively useful from the physical properties of the good. As noted by Carl Menger (2007, p. 69):

> A person with consumption goods directly at his disposal is certain of their quantity and quality. But a person who has only indirect command of them, through possession of the corresponding goods of higher order, cannot determine with the same certainty the quantity and quality of the goods of first order that will be at his disposal at the end of the production process.

The sentence $\varphi_{4,1}$ [Non-social causation of final consumption] states that the relation between production and possible final consumption can occur under four circumstances, either by possibly causing or overlapping with final consumption:

1   The transformation of the subject matter under non-social production may possibly non-socially cause final consumption, which requires that the two events are separate. An example is the recording of music that is later consumed. Another example is the manufacturing of a vehicle that is used to transport food, which in turn is finally consumed.

2   Production may entail that the agent of production is finally consumed. One example is a teacher that is finally consumed by students.
3   Production may involve the transformation of matter, a transformation that also constitutes final consumption, but where the agent of final consumption is different from the agent of production. An example is bus transport of passengers, whereby the driver is the agent of production and a passenger an agent of final consumption.
4   Production may involve the transformation of matter, a transformation that constitutes final consumption, but where the agent of production has not its own transformation as a purpose for the transformation of the matter. An example can be a person that helps saving an animal for the sake of the animal, which both constitutes production and final consumption.

In all four instances, the agency of production can be delegated to a third party, while this is not possible with final consumption for the sake of own self-transformation that does not generate anything useful for another person, for example, eating a meal for the purpose of satisfying the agent.

Although production usually is a type of consumption, production can also occur without any consumption during the production process (also note that the sentence $\varphi_{3,4}$ [Purpose exteriority of person subject matter] is not included). An example is a singer that performs for his or her own pleasure, but likewise produces music for a listener – there is no disutility to any of the participants.

The sentence $\varphi_{4,1}$ [Non-social causation of final consumption] entails that the production boundary is defined by the objective conditions up to the end of the production process. An alternative is to delete the modal operator "possible" in $\varphi_{4,1}$ and state that all production must result in final consumption. However, then an activity is categorised as production or non-production based on what happens after the activity. Production may not actually cause final consumption, for example, if the manufactured apple juice is never bought and therefore never finally consumed. However, principles of national accounting take this into account by registering wasted production as the depreciation of inventories, which is deducted from the net value added. There is, therefore, no need to place production that is wasted outside of the production boundary.

The definition of non-social production here excludes activities from the production boundary that cause final consumption in a manner that would not occur on a Robinson Crusoe island.

If Sara first picks an orange and later sells it to John, it implicates that Sara permits John to take the orange to finally consume it. The event "Sara sells an orange to John" causes the final consumption of the orange by John. Without the ownership change, John will not have access to orange. While the transformation of the owner of an orange from not allowing to take the orange to allowing to take the orange possibly causes the final consumption of the orange by a specific person, this transformation occurs through changing the intentional action of the owner of the orange. The intent of the owner was not to pass over the orange without anything in return. Such transformation would not occur in a Robinson Crusoe Island, or in a society of individuals that are completely altruistic towards each other. The picking of the orange by Sara causes final consumption through the mediation of trade, but picking the orange, which is non-social production, is a separate activity from the selling. Selling the orange is not a necessary part of the causation of its final consumption. Causation of final consumption of an orange through picking it from a tree could occur at a Robinson Crusoe island.

A more extreme example is the production of a weapon to kill a person. Murder requires both intentionality and actual causation. On the other hand, weapons can have other uses, and cars could be used in military operations, while neither the weapons nor the car company may be aware of these uses. Manufacturing of weapons and cars that are later used to hurt people per se does not involve social causation at the time of their production and could occur on a Robinson Crusoe island. However, causation of final consumption of an orange through the teaching of a thief how to steal it would not occur on a Robinson Crusoe island.

The intermediate consumption in trade, for example, of a credit card machine, or the use of weapons in war, are both types of waste. This should be taken into account in eventual satellite national accounts that distinguish between productive and unproductive labour. Shaikh and Tonak (1994) argue that intermediate consumption in unproductive activities should be deducted from national income. Such conduct can be implemented without classifying manufacturing weapons or construction of buildings used for banking as unproductive, which is further discussed in chapter 5.

Comprehensive production and social reproduction

Comprehensive production can be defined as:

> **Comprehensive production** (event $e_{intentional\_causation}$) occurs if $A^5_{comprehensive\_production} e_{intentional\_causation} e_{agent\_transforms} e_{matter\_transforms} s_{agent} q_{matter}$, which in turn is true if and only if $\varphi_{1,1}$ [Matter transformation], and $\varphi_{2,1}$ [Agent transformation], and $\varphi_{2,2}$ [Intentional causation], and $\varphi_{3,1}$ [Agent exteriority], and $\varphi_{4,2}$ [Causation of final consumption]

In plain words, comprehensive production (event $e_{intentional\_causation}$) occurs if a matter ($q_{matter}$) exterior to an agent ($s_{agent}$) is transformed (event $e_{matter\_transforms}$), intentionally caused by the agent's (s_1) self-transformation (event $e_{agent\_transforms}$); and it is possible that the transformation (event $e_{matter\_transforms}$) of the matter (q_{matter}) causes or overlaps with final consumption (event $z_{intentional\_causation}$). The relation of comprehensive production between events $e_{intentional\_causation}$, $e_{agent\_transforms}$ and $e_{matter\_transforms}$, agent s_{agent} and matter q_{matter} is here labelled as $A^5_{comprehensive\_production}e_{intentional\_causation}e_{agent\_transforms}e_{matter\_transforms}s_{agent}q_{matter}$.

Compared to the definition of non-social production, the sentence $\varphi_{3,5}$ [Social exteriority] is deleted and the sentence $\varphi_{4,1}$ [Non-social causation of final consumption] is changed to $\varphi_{4,2}$ [Causation of final consumption]. This articulation is closest to neoclassical theory and the third person criterion, given that the basic neoclassical model assumes no transaction costs and externalities and that transformation of oneself is excluded by sentence $\varphi_{3,1}$ [Agent exteriority].

Social reproduction can be defined as transformations involving social causation:

Social reproduction (event $e_{intentional\_causation}$) occurs if
$A^5_{social\_reproduction}e_{intentional\_causation}e_{agent\_transforms}e_{matter\_transforms}s_{agent}q_{matter}$, which in turn is true if and only if $\varphi_{1,1}$ [Matter transformation], and $\varphi_{2,1}$ [Agent transformation], and $\varphi_{2,2}$ [Intentional causation], and $\varphi_{3,1}$ [Agent exteriority], and **not** $\varphi_{3,5}$ [Social interiority]

Compared to comprehensive production, sentence "not $\varphi_{3,5}$" [Social interiority] is added and sentence $\varphi_{4,2}$ [Causation of final consumption] is deleted. Comprehensive production that is not non-social production is usually a type of social reproduction, although social reproduction not causing or overlapping with final consumption is not comprehensive production. These activities are conceptually related to Mill's description of distribution. Social reproduction causes a redistribution of power relations between individuals, including ownership rights.

Shaikh and Tonak (1994, p. 21) write that there are two main types of unproductive labour, distribution (mainly trade), which generates social access of produced objects to the users (which should be distinguished from transport that they classify as a productive activity), and social maintenance and reproduction, in which produced objects are used up to maintain social order. They show that distribution, social maintenance and reproduction, corresponding to social reproduction in this book, share some features with consumption:

[T]he classical distinction between production and nonproduction labor is essentially analytical. It is founded on the insight that certain types of labor share a common property with the activity of consumption – namely, that in their performance they use up a portion of existing wealth without directly resulting in the creation of new wealth. To say that these labors indirectly result in the creation of this wealth is only another way of saying that they are necessary. Consumption also indirectly results in production, as production indirectly results in consumption. But this hardly obviates the need for distinguishing between the two.

In this book, social reproduction is instead differentiated between coercive activities, which transform other persons against those persons' will, and non-coercive activities that intentionally transform agents to voluntary perform intentional actions. This distinction is partly recognised in modern national accounts – while murder and theft are not included in GDP, illegal sales of narcotics are. Even if social reproduction may involve the consumption of produced items, the main characteristic of social reproduction is the consumption (according to the definition presented earlier) of a non-produced entity, the transformed person. There is an essential difference between social reproduction and final consumption in that the former usually does not involve any self-reproduction. Final consumption should not be deducted from production in the same way as intermediate consumption of production. However, there is a point in treating the consumption of produced items in the process of social reproduction as intermediate consumption when applying the concept of non-social production, which would then yield a negative value added of the activity if the output of social reproduction is set to zero (in case of voluntary transactions) or negative (in case of coercive activities). Such conduct has some affinities with the welfare measures discussed in chapter 3. In contrast, when applying the concept of comprehensive production, social reproduction must be measured as both nominal and physical output, the practice of modern national accounts, which, as discussed in chapter 5, is challenging.

Considering that sentence $\varphi_{1,1}$ [Matter transformation] only refers to a transformation of a physical object, not a mental object, social reproduction comprises a physical transformation. Trade and financial services represent changes in ownership rights, which are mental objects, but the corresponding physical change comprises of transformations in the minds of persons. Social reproduction is here defined as transformations of humans, not as transformations of mental objects. Money only exist in the heads of people, but the heads of people are physical. Buying requires the buyer to transform the mind of the seller by releasing money to the latter, while selling requires the seller to transform the mind of the buyer by releasing a good or service to the buyer (O'Connor, 1975, p. 301). If the subject matter is the mind, sentence $\varphi_{1,1}$ [Matter transformation] is not violated. Although we can imagine trade taking place without any changes in the minds of persons, for example, if a computer buys something from another computer, at some level, at some time, it must involve agents intentionally causing such processes. However, in contrast to transport and storage, trade does not alter the intrinsic physical properties of the subject matter exterior to social relations.

Coercive activities – related to the political superstructure – could be seen as the redistribution of the control of a person's body to another person and transform the choices the person is able to make. Such activities could be described, in Marx's (1969, p. 175) words, as "destructive" and comprise of coercive social causation. Coercive labour must here be distinguished from coerced labour (van der Linden & García, 2016), such as slave labour, which is not the focus of this book. Coerced labour can perform either coercive or non-coercive work, and coercive work can consist of forcing coerced labour to work. That coercion can be described as social reproduction may seem peculiar. Nonetheless, as noted by Foucault (1991, p. 194), power is not only negative and destructive but also creative:

> We must cease once and for all to describe the effects of power in negative terms: it 'excludes', it 'represses', it 'censors', it 'abstracts', it 'masks', it 'conceals'. In fact power produces; it produces reality; it produces domains of objects and rituals of truth. The individual and the knowledge that may be gained of him belong to this production.

The following different types of coercive activities can be considered:

1   The annihilation by an agent s_1 of a person s_2 against the intent of the s_2, for example, homicide, genocide, waging war or killing somebody in defence. Homicide is the most drastic redistribution of power relations or change in the choices a person can make. However, euthanasia would not be a coercive activity if it occurs in accordance with the will of the person being killed.

2   Intentional action by an agent s_1 having the purpose to cause change of another agent s_2 against the will of agent s_2, by directly changing the intrinsic properties of agent s_2. Examples include rape, use of violence, torture and guarding inmates at a prison. Most coercive actions are not directed towards annihilation but comprise of the transformation of persons in accordance with the will of the perpetrator.

3   Intentional action by an agent s_1 having the purpose to cause change of another agent s_2 against the will of agent s_2, through changing matters exterior to s_2, which in turn change the capabilities for action by agent s_2. Examples of such action are: installing secure doors, stealing and expropriating. There is a difference between transforming the intrinsic and extrinsic properties of a matter, which is of relevance for social actions. Assume Sarah stops John from taking food from her farm by setting up a fence, which results in John starving to death, and transforms John against his own will. Starving to death is a change in the intrinsic properties of John. However, the purpose of stopping John to enter Sarah's farm is not to make John starve to death, only to transform John so he becomes incapacitated to take food, which is a change in the extrinsic properties of John. If John instead steals food from Sarah and Sarah starves to death, the action is of the same type. The intention is not to transform Sarah, but to transform the extrinsic properties of Sarah, i.e., her access to food. Guarding and stealing are therefore the same type of actions, irrespectively of whether we consider one to be legitimate and the other illegitimate.

4   Intentional action by an agent s_1 threatening to transform agent s_2 against the latter's wishes to force agent s_2 to perform an intentional action. Examples of such actions include policing and making somebody pay through threat.

Non-coercive social reproduction is an intentional action, event e_1, by an agent s_1 involving the causal mechanism to intentionally transform another agent s_2 to perform an intentional action, event s_2, in such a way that s_2 would not have preferred event e_2 if event e_1 would not occur, even when being past the information contained in event e_1. What constitutes voluntary and involuntary transactions can be vague. Trade involves a voluntary transaction. However, trade presupposes that ownership rights are guaranteed, mostly by a state that monopolises the violence in society. Are then not all transactions coercive? For example, threatening somebody to pay money is an action not much more coercive than trade. However, in this book, it is argued that there is a difference, because of the direct involvement of violence or threat of violence in coercive activities. Trade must be distinguished from activities supporting trade, such as guarding or punishing thieves. Of course, sometimes voluntary transactions can be intermixed with coercions, so here the distinction is primarily analytical.

The differentiation between social reproduction and self-production may be a grey zone. Consuming a Gucci bag may seemingly occur due to its direct positive effect on the person, but the wearer may own a bag only for the social status it lends. It is a type of conspicuous consumption, as described by Veblen (1899). The value of the Gucci bag is then not related to its functionality as a bag. It may be completely useless as a bag, or even constitute a disutility except for the social effects.

If a person hates smoking but practices it so as to develop a network of friends, then consuming a cigarette has no value for that person except for its social effects. People can have friends because they feel good about them – socialising is then not social reproduction in the sense used in this book – or as a means for something else, for example, as friends on Facebook to increase their social status. A growing share of what today is classified as final consumption in the national accounts maybe should not be classified as such. While online social networks are today much larger than earlier types of social network formations, they tend to make people less happy (Taylor & Strutton, 2016). Facebook users persistently compare themselves to other users, which increases narcissism and envy, reduces self-esteem and is linked to the conspicuous display of online consumption.

The definitions of this book entail that conspicuous consumption, if the purpose of the consumption is only to increase one social status, is not final consumption, but only consumption. Such acts of conspicuous consumption, as well as much of self-promotion activities using social media, is a kind of social reproduction, and may actually involve consumption and depreciation of the consumer, similar to work.

Time-frame-independent production and self-reproduction

One interpretation of the third-person criterion is that if the matter of production is the agent, then the activity could be considered unproductive. However, that is not self-evident since the criterion is ambiguous concerning what type of activity can be delegated. If an activity is defined as a change to a specific agent, it cannot be delegated. If we by an activity mean that a person causes a transformation to a matter in a longer time frame, then some self-reproductive activities could be delegated.

Several creation myths tell about a primordial god that self-creates, for example, Tonacateuctliff in Aztec mythology (Brundage, 1979, p. 32). Self-creation is a self-contradiction under existing physical laws, but self-reproduction, i.e., changing oneself once a person exists, can be seen as a relation between different selves in consecutive time periods, before and after the transformation. There is an identity over time between these selves. Self-transformation comprises two different events, first a self-transformation, which in turn causes another self-transformation. It represents a current self that transforms its future self with a time lag. Self-reproduction can involve several types of activities. The main difference is between self-reproduction whose purpose lies in itself and outside of the activity. Time use studies categorise the first as free time, or leisure, and the second as personal activities and studying (Gershuny, 2011).

For self-transformation whose purpose lies outside the activity, we may distinguish between those whose purpose is to cause future self-transformation and those whose purpose is to ultimately cause transformations of matters exterior to the agent. Brushing one's teeth or studying for future amusements belong to the first category, while studying for a profession and work travel belongs to the second category. For self-transformations whose purpose is to cause transformations of matters exterior to the agent, there are different time frames. For example, while walking from one side of the workplace to the other is normally considered work, travel to work is not. Studying for a profession exemplifies a more drawn-out process, but is not profoundly distinct from reading an instruction manual to operate a machine. It is not unreasonable that the production boundary, if possible, should be determined independently from the duration of the activity, i.e., independently of the time frame. As Becker (1980, p. 10) points out, as with market production and household production, human capital formation involves both goods and time spent on the investment. However, not all education is directed towards productive activity. The Italian abbot Genovesi noted in the 18th century that the productiveness of intellectual labour depends on the context, and in "primitive" stages, intellectual labour is hardly productive (Cosimo, 2019, p. 12).

Deleting sentence $\varphi_{3,1}$ [Agent exteriority] from the formulation of production opens the possibility that some self-reproductive activities could be regarded as productive. However, another exteriority condition is necessary. This can be accomplished by including the sentence "$\varphi_{3,1}$ or $\varphi_{3,2}$", which states that either the agent of transformation is separated from the matter of transformation (sentence $\varphi_{3,1}$ [Agent exteriority]) or the purpose of the activity for the agent lies outside the activity as such (sentence $\varphi_{3,2}$ [Purpose exteriority of activity]).

Two different variants of time frame independent production are considered, corresponding to the definitions of non-social and comprehensive production. In both variants sentence $\varphi_{3,1}$ [Agent exteriority] is replaced by "$\varphi_{3,1}$ or $\varphi_{3,2}$". Time-frame-independent non-social production, where sentence $\varphi_{4,1}$ [Non-social causation of final consumption] is replaced with $\varphi_{4,3}$ [Non-social causation of non-social production], can be defined as:

Time frame independent non-social production (event $e_{\text{intentional\_causation}}$) occurs if $A^5_{\text{time\_frame\_independent\_non-social\_production}} e_{\text{intentional\_causation}} e_{\text{agent\_transforms}}$ $e_{\text{matter\_transforms}} s_{\text{agent}} q_{\text{matter}}$, which in turn is true if and only if $\varphi_{1,1}$ [Matter transformation], and $\varphi_{2,1}$ [Agent transformation], and $\varphi_{2,2}$ [Intentional causation], and ($\varphi_{3,1}$ [Agent exteriority] or $\varphi_{3,2}$ [Purpose exteriority of activity]), and $\varphi_{3,5}$ [Social exteriority], and $\varphi_{4,3}$ [Non-social causation of non-social production].

The relation of time frame independent non-social production between events $e_{\text{intentional\_causation}}$, $e_{\text{agent\_transforms}}$ and $e_{\text{matter\_transforms}}$, agent s_{agent} and matter q_{matter} is here labelled as $A^5_{\text{time\_frame\_independent\_non-social\_production}}$ $e_{\text{intentional\_causation}} e_{\text{agent\_transforms}} e_{\text{matter\_transforms}} s_{\text{agent}} q_{\text{matter}}$.

A worker that eats during the lunch break performs a necessary activity to be able to work after the lunch break. There is certainly causality involved; eating causes the worker to be able to produce. Is that activity productive? One argument why not to consider eating during the lunch break as productive is that the purpose of that activity is for its own sake. The activitiy is, therefore, not part of the production process. Workers would not stop eating if they got unemployed. Only if the purpose of eating lies outside the activity as such, for example, if a sportsman consumes special nutrition to be able to perform at a contest to amuse the audience, can it be considered productive. Time frame independent production, therefore, requires that a process must at some stage cause the transformation of matters exterior to the agent.

The other definition of production allows for human capital formation without conditions of social exteriority. Time frame independent comprehensive production is defined as:

Time frame independent comprehensive production (event $e_{\text{intentional\_causation}}$) occurs if $A^5_{\text{time\_frame\_independent\_comprehensive\_production}}$ $e_{\text{intentional\_causation}} e_{\text{agent\_transforms}} e_{\text{matter\_transforms}} s_{\text{agent}} q_{\text{matter}}$, which in turn is true if and only if $\varphi_{1,1}$ [Matter transformation], and $\varphi_{2,1}$ [Agent transformation], and $\varphi_{2,2}$ [Intentional causation], and ($\varphi_{3,1}$ [Agent exteriority] or $\varphi_{3,2}$ [Purpose exteriority of activity]), and $\varphi_{4,4}$ [Causation of comprehensive production]

The relation of time frame independent comprehensive production between events $e_{\text{intentional\_causation}}$, $e_{\text{agent\_transforms}}$ and $e_{\text{matter\_transforms}}$, agent s_{agent} and matter q_{matter} is here labelled as $A^5_{\text{time\_frame\_independent\_comprehensive\_production}}$ $e_{\text{intentional\_causation}}e_{\text{agent\_transforms}}e_{\text{matter\_transforms}}s_{\text{agent}}q_{\text{matter}}$.

For example, while military training would be included in the production boundary when applying the definition of time frame independent comprehensive production, it would not be included when applying the definition of time frame independent non-social production.

Humanity exterior production

The Marxist conception of productive activity is often confused with Adam Smith's view that only goods production is productive. A definition close to Adam Smith's, is to further restrict the production boundary by including sentence $\varphi_{3,6}$ [Humanity exteriority], which only considers activities as productive if they involve a transformation of non–persons:

> **Humanity exterior production** (event $e_{\text{intentional\_causation}}$) occurs if $A^5_{\text{humanity\_exterior\_production}}e_{\text{intentional\_causation}}e_{\text{agent\_transforms}}e_{\text{matter\_transforms}}$ $s_{\text{agent}}q_{\text{matter}}$, which in turn is true if and only if $\varphi_{1,1}$ [Matter transformation], and $\varphi_{2,1}$ [Agent transformation], and $\varphi_{2,2}$ [Intentional causation], and $\varphi_{3,6}$ [Humanity exteriority], and $\varphi_{4,1}$ [Non–social causation of final consumption].

The relation of humanity exterior production between events $e_{\text{intentional\_causation}}$, $e_{\text{agent\_transforms}}$ and $e_{\text{matter\_transforms}}$, agent s_{agent} and matter is here labelled as $A^5_{\text{humanity\_exterior\_production}}e_{\text{intentional\_causation}}e_{\text{agent\_transforms}}$ $e_{\text{matter\_transforms}}s_{\text{agent}}q_{\text{matter}}$.

The articulation of humanity exterior production contains the most restrictive exteriority condition as all transformations directed towards other persons are classified as unproductive. According to this notion, many services, such as child care and medical treatment, are categorised as unproductive. However, services such as cooking, cleaning, storage, goods transport and washing are categorised as productive since they are directed towards transforming non-persons. Therefore, this definition deviates from Adam Smith's original intention.

Market comprehensive production

None of the definitions of production discussed above is close to the SNA definition in view of the fact that no sentence states that production must be, or potentially be, sold at the market. The closest to the Keynesian and SNA conception of GDP is to replace sentence $\varphi_{4,2}$ with sentence $\varphi_{4,5}$, stating that it is possible that the transformation of q_{matter} generates a matter that can be sold at the market:

> **Market comprehensive production** (event $e_{\mathrm{intentional\_causation}}$) occurs if $A^{5}_{\mathrm{market\_comprehensive\_production}}e_{\mathrm{intentional\_causation}}e_{\mathrm{agent\_transforms}}e_{\mathrm{matter\_transforms}}$-$s_{\mathrm{agent}}q_{\mathrm{matter}}$, which in turn is true if and only if $\varphi_{1,1}$ [Matter transformation], and $\varphi_{2,1}$ [Agent transformation], and $\varphi_{2,2}$ [Intentional causation], and $\varphi_{3,1}$ [Agent exteriority], and $\varphi_{4,5}$ [Market saleability].

The label for the relation of market comprehensive production is $A^{5}_{\mathrm{market\_comprehensive\_production}}e_{\mathrm{intentional\_causation}}e_{\mathrm{agent\_transforms}}e_{\mathrm{matter\_transforms}}$ $s_{\mathrm{agent}}q_{\mathrm{matter}}$. Introducing such expression violates the trans-historical criterion, but the notion of market production could serve important analytical purposes, for example, to investigate the relation between money supply and inflation. It should then be rid of inconsistencies such as the inclusion of non-market goods production. However, there are conceptual problems with the market principle tradition. For example, the construction of a house may be entirely for self-use, but after the owner dies, decades later, the house could be sold.

A further alternative is to replace non-social causation of final consumption in the definition of non-social production with a sentence stating that the activity generates a surplus or profit in accordance with the surplus tradition, which is not further explored in this book.

Work and leisure

The third person criterion describes work rather than production. The discussion in the preceding chapters shows that operational definitions such as the third person criterion are in need of reformulation. Preferably, such

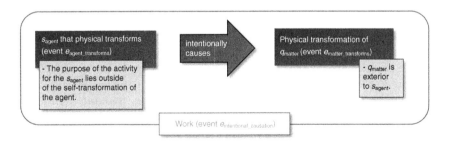

Figure 4.4 The definition of work applied in this book.

definition should be reduced to propositional and predicate logic, and/or only describe an actual world. A reformulation of the third person criterion should at least state that an agent intentionally causes the transformation of a matter and that the matter of the activity must be exterior to the agent of transformation. A definition of work does not require a final utility condition nor a social exteriority condition.

Since work involves a kind of disutility for the agent, there should be a purpose exteriority condition, which is not a necessary characteristic of production. However, sentence $\varphi_{3,2}$ [Purpose exteriority of activity], stating that the agent has not the transformation of the matter as a final purpose, may be problematic in a definition of work. For example, a parent may work to satisfy a child's need and have the latter as a final purpose. The purpose exteriority condition could instead be stated through sentence $\varphi_{3,3}$ [Purpose exteriority of agent self-transformation], i.e., that agent s_{agent} has not its own transformation as a purpose for causing the transformation of matter q_{matter}. The critical aspect of work is that it is not self-reproductive and that the transformation of the agent implicates a disutility for the agent (a kind of consumption of the agent). Thus, one definition of work is (see Figure 4.4):

> **Work** (event $e_{\text{intentional\_causation}}$) occurs if $A^5_{\text{work}}e_{\text{intentional\_causation}}$ $e_{\text{agent\_transforms}}e_{\text{matter\_transforms}}s_{\text{agent}}q_{\text{matter}}$, which in turn is true if and only if $\varphi_{1,1}$ [Matter transformation], and $\varphi_{2,1}$ [Agent transformation], and $\varphi_{2,2}$ [Intentional causation], and $\varphi_{3,1}$ [Agent exteriority], and $\varphi_{3,3}$ [Purpose exteriority of agent self-transformation].

The relation between events $e_{\text{intentional\_causation}}$, $e_{\text{agent\_transforms}}$ and $e_{\text{matter\_transforms}}$, agent s_{agent} and matter q_{matter} constituting work is here labelled as $A^5_{\text{work}}e_{\text{intentional\_causation}}e_{\text{agent\_transforms}}e_{\text{matter\_transforms}}s_{\text{agent}}q_{\text{matter}}$.

Himmelweit (1995) points to three features of work in the feminist literature, that (1) work is a purposeful activity, (2) it takes time and energy and (3) is separable from the person who performs it (she adds the condition of a division of labour, but a lone person isolated on an island can perform work). In the above articulation, these three features relate to intentional causation (sentence $\varphi_{2,2}$), purpose exteriority of agent self-transformation (sentence $\varphi_{3,3}$) and agent exteriority (sentence $\varphi_{3,1}$), respectively. Separability is a precondition for the third person criterion. If an activity is self-reproductive, then it cannot be delegated.

Why do people work if it generates a disutility? The reasons are different. It could be to satisfy some later needs, for example, cooking a meal to consume it directly afterwards. In the latter case, work and final consumption constitute the same process. Part of the process can, however, be delegated to a third party. Another type of work is directed towards satisfying other persons' needs. Such work can be conducted for altruistic reasons, for example, to cook a meal for one's children, as part of a voluntary transaction, for example, as wage labour, or due to coercion, for example, as slave labour.

Given that production and work are defined differently, we can distinguish between productive and unproductive work. If we here only consider non-social production, productive and unproductive work can be defined as followed:

Productive work (event $e_{\text{intentional\_causation}}$) occurs if
$A^5{}_{\text{productive\_work}}e_{\text{intentional\_causation}}e_{\text{agent\_transforms}}e_{\text{matter\_transforms}}s_{\text{agent}}q_{\text{matter}}$,
which in turn is true if and only if $\varphi_{1,1}$ [Matter transformation], and $\varphi_{2,1}$ [Agent transformation], and $\varphi_{2,2}$ [Intentional causation], and $\varphi_{3,1}$ [Agent exteriority], and $\varphi_{3,3}$ [Purpose exteriority of agent self-transformation], and $\varphi_{3,5}$ [Social exteriority] and $\varphi_{4,1}$ [Non-social causation of final consumption].

Unproductive work (event $e_{\text{intentional\_causation}}$) occurs if
$A^5{}_{\text{unproductive\_work}}e_{\text{intentional\_causation}}e_{\text{agent\_transforms}}e_{\text{matter\_transforms}}s_{\text{agent}}q_{\text{matter}}$,
which in turn is true if and only if $\varphi_{1,1}$ [Matter transformation], and $\varphi_{2,1}$ [Agent transformation], and $\varphi_{2,2}$ [Intentional causation], and $\varphi_{3,1}$ [Agent exteriority], and $\varphi_{3,3}$ [Purpose exteriority of agent self-transformation], and (either not $\varphi_{3,5}$ [Social exteriority] or not $\varphi_{4,1}$ [Non-social causation of final consumption]).

Under the definition of comprehensive production, it is also possible for work to be unproductive if "not $\varphi_{4,1}$" is true. Even Marshall, who had a very broad perception of production, opened to that possibility.

A widening of the definition of work is to follow Marshall, i.e., to define work as an activity with a view to some good other than the pleasure derived directly from the activity. This could be interpreted as a disutility condition, stating that the agent of transformation must consider the activity as inferior to a possible other activity the agent could perform in its place if the outcome of the activity would be the same. Another way to formulate this condition is to state that the subject matter of the transformation cannot be the current self only, i.e., if the subject matter is the agent, the time period at which the matter attains certain properties must occur after the activity has ended (i.e., it must then be the future self). An activity whose purpose is to transform the current self cannot even logically be delegated to a third person, given that such activity in itself presupposes that the current self takes part in the activity. Activities whose purpose is the transformation of the future self can at least theoretically be delegated to a third person.

Work is sometimes contrasted with leisure. Nevertheless, not all non-work activities are leisure. Today, a residual definition of leisure is used, as activities that are not paid or unpaid work, learning activities or personal activities

(Roberts, 1999). Using the conceptual framework developed in this chapter, leisure could instead be defined as follows:

> **Leisure** (event $e_{\text{intentional\_causation}}$) occurs if $A^5{}_{\text{leisure}}e_{\text{intentional\_causation}}$ $e_{\text{agent\_transforms}}e_{\text{matter\_transforms}}s_{\text{agent}}q_{\text{matter}}$, which in turn is true if and only if $\varphi_{1,1}$ [Matter transformation], and $\varphi_{2,1}$ [Agent transformation], and $\varphi_{2,2}$ [Intentional causation], and **not**$\varphi_{3,3}$ [Purpose interiority of agent self-transformation].

Leisure is an activity where the purpose lies in the self-transformation of the agent. The distinction between personal time and free time or leisure is noteworthy. Personal time involves the reproduction of the body for the future maintenance of the body. These activities are usually not performed if they are not necessary. For example, if technological innovation would make people sleep 2 hours per day instead of 8 hours, without any side-effect of choosing the first option, many would probably prefer to increase their time towards other activities. There is also a difference between conscious personal activities – such as eating, bathing, brushing one's teeth, etc., – and unconscious personal time – sleep.

An alternative is to consider leisure as self-reproduction of the current self, in contrast to self-reproduction of future selves. Leisure can, of course, involve the transformation of other matters, but they serve as the instruments of the transformation of the current self. Self-transformations, where the purpose lies outside the activity, for example, learning oneself to perform an activity in the future or brushing one's teeth, is not leisure; the activity is then directed towards transforming the future self.

One confusion with the third person criterion is that some activities that could be regarded productive could not be delegated to a third party as the person performing the activity enjoy it in itself. Leisure and production are not contraries. However, leisure and work are contraries given that $\varphi_{3,3}$ [Purpose exteriority of agent self-transformation] is true for relations of work, but false for relations of leisure. Leisure production, which occurs without the effort of any work, can be defined as:

> **Leisure production** (event $e_{\text{intentional\_causation}}$) occurs if $A^5{}_{\text{leisure\_production}}$ $e_{\text{intentional\_causation}}e_{\text{agent\_transforms}}e_{\text{matter\_transforms}}s_{\text{agent}}q_{\text{matter}}$, which in turn is true if and only if $\varphi_{1,1}$ [Matter transformation], and $\varphi_{2,1}$ [Agent transformation], and $\varphi_{2,2}$ [Intentional causation], and $\varphi_{3,1}$ [Agent exteriority], and not $\varphi_{3,3}$ [Purpose interiority of agent self-transformation], and $\varphi_{3,5}$ [Social exteriority] and $\varphi_{4,1}$ [Non-social causation of final consumption]

Activities such as painting for one's own pleasure, playing with children for one's own sake, free-time research, hobby-hunting and hobby-knitting can generate products that can benefit others than the agents of transformation, without the involvement of any work. Some of these products are included in official national accounts, even if the activities are not registered as working time. Hobby-hunting and hobby-knitting would be performed even if the result would not be used later. They cannot be delegated to a third person given that they are leisure activities and would lose their purpose if they were delegated. Still, the meat from a hunt and the textile from knitting can be used by others and could be sold to finance the hobby as an extra bonus. Some research has a similar character. Many professional scholars continue to write articles and books even after retirement without receiving any extra payment for the activity. Some of women's productive activities are performed under such conditions, and using the third person criterion may risk underestimating women's contribution. The distinction between work and leisure has become fuzzier, with people contributing to Wikipedia in their free time or using their leisure activities to support their work (Coyle, 2014, p. 145).

The driving forces of leisure production are different from productive work as the latter would normally not occur without any or too low compensation. Estimating the imputed value of leisure production by the costs may therefore be misleading.

Comparison of definitions

Table 4.5 summarises the definitions of consumption, production and work in this book and other related concepts. The table reveals the large similarity between these concepts. The sentences are combined through conjunctions.

An activity is the most general type. It encompasses a transformation of an agent that intentionally causes the transformation of a subject matter. Production, work and consumption are all activities, but so is leisure, self-reproduction and social reproduction. Sleep is not an activity given that it is unconscious, but it is a type of personal time.

This chapter presents various categories of exteriority conditions. Exteriority entails that the activity is directed towards phenomena exterior to the agent, the community of agents, their social relations or the purpose of the activity.

The condition of agent exteriority is imperative for the definition of production, work and consumption. In contrast, self-reproduction is an activity where the agent is the subject matter. However, if the production boundary is expanded to include activities taking place in a longer time horizon, then human capital formation can be viewed as productive.

Purpose exteriority is a characteristic of work, while leisure by definition cannot have an exterior purpose. Albeit production usually involves work, production is not required to have an exterior purpose. Leisure production can

Table 4.5 Labels of relations and sentences used in the definitions of various activities

Label of relation	$\varphi_{1,1}$ Matter transformation	$\varphi_{2,1}$ Agent self-transformation	$\varphi_{2,2}$ Intentional causation	$\varphi_{3,1}$ Agent exteriority	$\varphi_{3,2}$ Purpose exteriority of activity	$\varphi_{3,3}$ Purpose exteriority of agent self-transformation	$\varphi_{3,4}$ Purpose exteriority of person subject matter	$\varphi_{3,5}$ Social exteriority	$\varphi_{3,6}$ Humanity exteriority	$\varphi_{4,1}$ Non-social causation of final consumption	$\varphi_{4,2}$ Causation of final consumption	$\varphi_{4,3}$ Causation of non-social production	$\varphi_{4,4}$ Causation of comprehensive production	$\varphi_{4,5}$ Market saleability
$A^5_{activity}$	$\varphi_{1,1}$ and	$\varphi_{2,1}$ and	$\varphi_{2,2}$											
$A^5_{consumption}$	$\varphi_{1,1}$ and	$\varphi_{2,1}$ and	$\varphi_{2,2}$ and	$\varphi_{3,1}$ and	(not $\varphi_{3,2}$	or not $\varphi_{3,3}$), and	$\varphi_{3,4}$							
$A^5_{final\_consumption}$	$\varphi_{1,1}$ and	$\varphi_{2,1}$ and	$\varphi_{2,2}$ and	$\varphi_{3,1}$ and	(not $\varphi_{3,2}$	or not $\varphi_{3,3}$), and	$\varphi_{3,4}$							
$A^5_{non-social\_production}$	$\varphi_{1,1}$ and	$\varphi_{2,1}$ and	$\varphi_{2,2}$ and	$\varphi_{3,1}$ and				$\varphi_{3,5}$ and		$\varphi_{4,1}$				
$A^5_{comprehensive\_production}$	$\varphi_{1,1}$ and	$\varphi_{2,1}$ and	$\varphi_{2,2}$ and	$\varphi_{3,1}$ and				$\varphi_{3,5}$ and			$\varphi_{4,2}$			
$A^5_{time\_frame\_independent\_non-social\_production}$	$\varphi_{1,1}$ and	$\varphi_{2,1}$ and	$\varphi_{2,2}$ and	($\varphi_{3,1}$ or	$\varphi_{3,2}$) and							$\varphi_{4,3}$		
$A^5_{time\_frame\_independent\_comprehensive\_production}$	$\varphi_{1,1}$ and	$\varphi_{2,1}$ and	$\varphi_{2,2}$ and	($\varphi_{3,1}$ or	$\varphi_{3,2}$) and								$\varphi_{4,4}$	
$A^5_{humanity\_exterior\_production}$	$\varphi_{1,1}$ and	$\varphi_{2,1}$ and	$\varphi_{2,2}$ and	$\varphi_{3,1}$ and					$\varphi_{3,6}$ and	$\varphi_{4,1}$				
$A^5_{market\_comprehensive\_production}$	$\varphi_{1,1}$ and	$\varphi_{2,1}$ and	$\varphi_{2,2}$ and	$\varphi_{3,1}$ and										$\varphi_{4,5}$
A^5_{work}	$\varphi_{1,1}$ and	$\varphi_{2,1}$ and	$\varphi_{2,2}$ and	$\varphi_{3,1}$ and		$\varphi_{3,3}$								
$A^5_{productive\_work}$	$\varphi_{1,1}$ and	$\varphi_{2,1}$ and	$\varphi_{2,2}$ and	$\varphi_{3,1}$ and		$\varphi_{3,3}$ and		$\varphi_{3,5}$ and		$\varphi_{4,1}$				
$A^5_{unproductive\_work}$	$\varphi_{1,1}$ and	$\varphi_{2,1}$ and	$\varphi_{2,2}$ and	$\varphi_{3,1}$ and		$\varphi_{3,3}$ and		(not $\varphi_{3,5}$ or not $\varphi_{3,5}$		not $\varphi_{4,1}$)				
$A^5_{social\_reproduction}$	$\varphi_{1,1}$ and	$\varphi_{2,1}$ and	$\varphi_{2,2}$	$\varphi_{3,1}$ and										
$A^5_{leisure}$	$\varphi_{1,1}$ and	$\varphi_{2,1}$ and	$\varphi_{2,2}$			not $\varphi_{3,3}$								
$A^5_{leisure\_production}$	$\varphi_{1,1}$ and	$\varphi_{2,1}$ and	$\varphi_{2,2}$ and	$\varphi_{3,1}$ and		not $\varphi_{3,3}$ and		$\varphi_{3,5}$ and		$\varphi_{4,1}$				

occur if the agent transforms a matter that possibly causes final consumption, while the activity is performed for its own sake.

Social exteriority is used in this book to elaborate on the Classical distinction between productive and unproductive work. Without a notion of social and non-social causation, the distinction between productive and unproductive work remains vague. Rejecting such distinction implicates that, for example, war activities and income streams held from copyrights are considered productive. Social reproduction comprises of the transformation of social relations and is excluded from the notion of non-social production. Comprehensive production includes socially reproductive activities that possibly cause or overlap with final consumption. The condition of humanity exteriority is compatible with social exteriority. Humanity exterior production excludes all transformations of humans from the production boundary, which resembles the physicalist conception of productive labour, for example, of the Material Product System applied in the Soviet Union.

The possible causation of final consumption is a condition for all definitions of production presented in this chapter, including time frame independent production, given that the latter is part of a production process when the time frame is expanded. Work does not have to possibly cause final consumption, while leisure might.

Both non-social and comprehensive production include non-market activities that are excluded from the production boundary by modern national accounts. The articulation of market comprehensive production is closest to, but not identical with, the SNA notion of the production boundary.

As Marx (1993, pp. 90–91) points out while being opposites, production involves consumption of at least three matters: (1) the labourer, (2) the means of production that become worn out, and (3) the raw materials. Work is a consumption of the worker. Similarly, final consumption normally encompasses the production of the human body and mind, i.e., the reproduction of individuals (as distinguished from social reproduction). Production has the purpose of final consumption and would not be production without such purpose. The intent of production is ultimately the reproduction of human life. As ecological economists recognise, this is an effect of the second law of thermodynamic. In a world without decay, order would be eternally preserved, but there would also be no life.

Which types of reproductions should be included in the production boundary? While the concept of non-social production includes some activities directed towards reproducing individuals, social reproduction is excluded. Some socially reproductive activities are, however, included in the concept of comprehensive production. The time-frame-independent production includes some self-reproductive activities, although not leisure. Reproduction can likewise be either subjectively positive or negative, in that some reproductions are preferred by the person transformed, and others are not. Coercive activities involve the transformation of individuals against their will, i.e., coercive social causation. Work is a type of reproduction that is not desired but is performed to accomplish other purposes of the activity. Reproduction could be objectively either positive or negative as well. For example, smoking is subjectively positive reproduction, given that the activity is preferred to not performing it, but objectively negative reproduction.

5 Possible applications of the framework

Introduction

This chapter sketches various possible applications of the framework presented in chapter 4 and how it potentially can contribute to theories of long-term economic growth and history. The intent is not to depict any full-fledged analysis, new models or empirical examples, which would each require substantial investigations of its own.

First chapter investigates how production, work and consumption can be quantified using the definitions developed in chapter 4. Quantities of different types of products can, however, not be aggregated. A discussion is followed on value theory, and how such value theory can move beyond the market prices. The following two sections discuss the mainstream neoclassic growth models and assumptions concerning exploitation, capital, and the productivity of capital that are counterposed to the concept of social causation introduced in chapter 4. The Marxist theory of exploitation is related to the Classical differentiation between productive and unproductive labour. The final section is more speculative. It discusses how the trans-historical framework could be used to analyse stages in the development of intelligent life. The demarcation between coercive activities, non-coercive social reproduction and non-social production is akin to the Marxist distinction between political superstructure, relations of production and productive forces. The section likewise deliberates whether non-humans can produce, which relates to animal rights, and the consequences of artificial intelligence on work.

Quantifying production, work and consumption

Quantities in national accounts are measures of the physical processes during production and seemingly should be established objectively. Despite this, physical quantity in national accounting is a difficult concept. Measurement is strongly related to the definition of what is measured. Performance measurement of universities, a trend in New Public Management, has caused researchers to take shortcuts to focus on what is measured. At the same time, the quality of education is lowered to reach targets for the number of students

DOI: 10.4324/9781003057017-5

who graduated (Kallio et al., 2017). New Public Management has similarities with the Soviet system, whereby the government rewarded managers for quantity with disregard for quality (Coyle, 2014, p. 59). That entailed, for example, that if coal was to be delivered in quantity, it was provided in a lower quality to execute or exceed plan targets (Winiecki, 2011, p. 5).

Production, work and consumption comprise of transformations of agents and matters. Table 5.1 displays measures of various aspects of these transformations.

At the most general level, the production process could be measured by the general physical properties of the subject matter and its transformations (category 1). An example is the Kardashev scale measuring energy use of civilisations (Kardashev, 1964). Type I civilisations harness the energy of the whole planet, type II civilisations of a star system and type III of a galaxy. Similar scales could also be used to measure information storage, population and the mass of constructions (Gray, 2020).

As discussed in chapter 4, Jevons distinguishes between different concepts of utility, crucially between prospective and actual utility. Prospective utility is related to the functionality of a good or service (category 2). Actual utility and disutility are about effects on the consuming agent or how the agent perceives these effects (category 3). Production, work and consumption generate effects outside of the intentional causal mechanism, for example, natural degradation. From an ecological-economic point of view, the utility and disutility can be related to increases and decreases in the ordered structure of various matters.

Functionality, as defined in this book, is determined by the physical properties of a transformation or matter that objectively may cause a specific utility. Still, it should not be reduced to just these physical properties or the particular utility. Production possibly causes final consumption due to the transformed matter having certain physical properties that make it useful. Nevertheless, as discussed in chapter 4, final consumption is not inevitable, and its utility may depend on who consumes it. An orange has certain physical properties that make it suitable as food for humans, but it may never be consumed. As Shaikh and Tonak (1994, p. 23) write:

> In a factory, a set of workers produces a car. This car has objective material properties – shape, color, engine displacement, etc. – which make it an object of our consumption. These properties are the car's useful objective characteristics and serve as the material basis for the subjective satisfaction we may derive from the car, but they are clearly distinct from this satisfaction itself.
>
> Now consider the case of so-called services. A barber uses scissors to transform the shape of someone's hair, thus producing a material effect which is the object of the customer's personal consumption, an effect whose useful objective properties are evident in the mirror, to the touch, and even in a photograph. Similarly, a singer who projects a song into the

Table 5.1 Various measures of the production and consumption process

Broad category	Fine category	Gains in ordered structure, functionality or utility		Losses in ordered structure, functionality or utility	
		Examples	*Measures*	*Examples*	*Measures*
1. General physical properties	1. Physical properties of matters in the production and consumption processes	Produced bus, meat, heart medicine	Mass of output, energy use, Kardashev Scale	Metals used in bus production	Mass of matters used, ecological footprint, CO_2 emissions
2. Gains and losses in functionality	2a. Gained or lost physical properties of matters that have functionality of lasting duration.	Produced bus, meat, heart medicine	Quantity of output of goods measured by functionality.	Killed animal, used up tools, depreciation of machinery	Quantity of intermediate consumption, environmental degradation
	2b. Gained or lost physical properties of physical effects that have functionality of non-lasting duration.	Number of passengers using the bus, warm meal, heart transplant.	Quantity of services measured by functionality	Work to produce bus	Working time

(Continued)

Table 5.1 (Continued)

Broad category	Fine category	Gains in ordered structure, functionality or utility		Losses in ordered structure, functionality or utility	
		Examples	*Measures*	*Examples*	*Measures*
3. Actual utility and disutility	3a. Objective utility/disutility or capability. The prospective physical properties of the "inside" effects on agents.	Objective effects on passengers. The effect of the meal or heart transplant on human body.	HDP, average life span, MEW, ISEW, GPI.	Objective negative effects of work on workers, cigarette smoking	Negative health effects of work
	3b. The subjective utility/disutility. The subjective perception of the agent on the physical inside effects of the consuming object.	The perceived benefit to consumer of using a bus, eating the meal or receiving heart transplant.	Individual utility, happiness index.	Perceived negative impact of work, individual time preferences	Indices of work satisfaction, time preferences
	3c. The inter-subjective comparisons of subjectively perceived utility/disutility.	The social valuation of bus transport, the meal or heart transplant.	Value, price, GDP	Price on capital, land and labour	Cost side of GDP

air produces an object of consumption so material that it can be captured on a record and reproduced electronically. In both cases, the useful objective material properties of this song are very different from the satisfaction one may or may not derive from them.

Functionality can be differentiated between storable and non-storable effects (categories 2a and 2b in Table 5.1), which exist in the form of a good, and production that involves immediate consumption, i.e., a service. Adam Smith only considers the production of storable utilities as productive. Still, as explained by Shaikh and Tonak there is no essential difference between the physical properties of a good and the physical effects of a service that has objective functionality. A good should only be quantified in accordance with the inner physical properties. An apple should be set equal to another apple if its qualitative properties are the same, i.e., irrespectively of whether the first is consumed by a starving child and the second by an overweight rich person. Quantifying services for their inner physical properties is much more difficult, but the argument is the same as for the apple. It is the "outside" effects that are to be quantified, not the "inside" effects on a consumer. For example, a heart transplant should be quantified as equal to another heart transplant if performed under the same conditions, irrespective of the long-term effect on the patient or subjective perceptions.

  National accounts regard the physical quantity of 10 apples as worth 10 times more than one apple, even if an individual consumer views the consumption of 10 apples in say one day, not at par with the consumption of 10 apples consumed over a long period. One reason is that 10 apples are divisible so the 10 apples can be consumed by 10 different consumers instead of just one consumer. As long as we treat the sale of 10 apples as the sale of the same commodity as the sale of one apple, 10 apples are valued 10 times more than one apple. In reality, a consumer can buy apples in bulk, so 10 apples cost say five times more than one apple. These could be treated as two different physical entities since they have different objective functionalities. In the *Consumer Price Index Manual*, it is recommended to adjust for quality of size (ILO et al., 2004, pp. 113–114):

> In the pharmaceutical context, for example, prices of bottles of pills of different sizes differ. A bottle of 100 pills, each having 50 milligrams of a drug, is not the same as a bottle of 50 pills of 100 milligrams, even though both bottles contain 5,000 milligrams of the same drug. If there is a change, say, to a larger size container, and a unit price decrease of 2 per cent accompanies this change, then it should not be regarded as a price fall of 2 per cent if consumers gain less utility from the larger and more inconvenient containers. [...]

> The rationale behind the quality adjustment process is to ask: does the difference in unit price in each case reflect different levels of utility? If so,

adjustments should be made to the unit prices to bring them into line. If not, adjustments should be made to the unit prices for that proportion attributable to differences in utility gained from, say, more convenient packaging or the availability of smaller lots.

The argument in the *Consumer Price Index Manual* that convenient packaging yields higher utility per unit is problematic given that different individuals may have different utilities from exactly the same properties of a matter, which should be disregarded by a CPI. The CPI does not adjust for more equal distribution of consumption, despite that such increases the total utility of the same bunch of items. A more stringent argument is that more convenient packaging adds additional objective functionality than less convenient packaging.

Given that the quantities of different qualities cannot be aggregated into another physical property, the actual transformation of the subject matter of production or consumption should be measured by a vector of quantities of the new acquired or lost properties that are desirable. Gained properties are equivalent to the quantity measures of output. From an ecological-economic point of view, it usually increases the ordered structure of the transformed matter. The transformation of the matter and the surrounding environment can also be quantified by the vector of the loss of desirable properties. It is equivalent to the input measures of output, which is a vector, and usually decreases the ordered structure of the surrounding environment. The transformation under production both increases and decreases various aspects of the ordered structure of the subject matter. For example, the living animal transformed into meat has some of its ordered structure destroyed and some enhanced.

A challenging topic concerning the conceptual framework developed in chapter 4 concerns quantification of social reproduction. While human reproduction in principle is quantifiable, coercive activities and voluntary transactions are not. For example, what is the physical output of war? Usually, preventing war is considered more successful than waging war, but preventing war simply means that nothing is changed. Does social reproduction belong to the law of physics or the law of the mind? In the case of trade and financial services, the objects transformed are ownership rights, but the latter are ultimately imagined entities, following the laws of the mind. In contrast, information is not imagined in the same way and has a physical existence, following the laws of physics. Ownership rights can be changed retroactively, but that is because they are not physical entities. While the quantity of information cannot be infinite as there is a physical limit to its storage, there are no such limitations for ownership rights, precisely because they are imagined. For example, it is possible to earn an amount of imagined money that approaches infinity without having any material correspondence. Infinite quantities occur because the language is mixed up with the metalanguage, as discussed in chapter 3. We must distinguish between the changes to the physical object and how these changes are perceived and, in turn, distinguish between these perceptions and the perceptions of these perceptions, and so on.

As discussed in chapter 3, hedonic regression quantifies qualitative change by explaining the product's price by its physical characteristics. However, if these characteristics are not direct measures of functionality, they may result in erroneous estimates of economic growth and inflation. Another problem is that some of the characteristics of a product may not concern their functional qualities but social networks, status and externalities. A bag with exactly the same qualities as a Gucci bag, but produced by an unknown company, would have a much lower price than an actual Gucci bag. This goes beyond information asymmetries. In a study of a large market-driven virtual world, Hoefman et al. (2018) conclude:

> Our analysis reveals that consumers appraise the social quality of a product in the same general way as its functional quality: incremental increases in the social quality of a product lead to exponential increases in the price consumers are willing to pay for the good embodying those qualities... Economy theory suggests that firm investments in branding in part signal the firm's willingness to engage in a long term relationship with its clients and therefore in equilibrium reduces the information asymmetry about the product's quality on the part of the consumers, rendering them more willing to pay a price mark-up. This argument has lead observers to predict that the ongoing digital revolution, by reducing information asymmetries between firms and consumers, would erode the value of brands and shrink price mark-ups. We show that social value considerations make consumers value labels even if they have incentives to behave rationally and their information is complete. This may inform further theoretical advances on the deeper drivers of social value and suggests that top brands' price mark-ups may well survive the digital revolution, because their value hinges not only on the presence of information asymmetries, but also on social value.

Adding social status to goods and services may be considered social reproduction rather than a productive activity, as discussed in the previous chapter. However, generating network effects is not social reproduction given that it could occur on Robinson Crusoe Island, but such effects are different from the physical properties of a specific good or service. Network effects change the functionality of the same product despite that its intrinsic physical qualities do not change. The functionality of the same matter with the same physical characteristics may depend on the physical context, which in turn must be analytically distinguished from social status and context.

Imagine that a new model of a computer is valued 100 per cent more than an old model and a new model comes every second year and is twice as fast as the preceding model. Then, applying a hedonic price index, a computer today is worth one million computers that are 40 years old because it is one million times faster. However, because a customer values a new computer twice as much as the previous version, that does not mean the same customer today would value a computer that is 38 years old twice as much as a computer that is 40 years old, even if the same customer 38 years ago would actually do that. The price differences are not additive over time. The customer today is situated in a different context than 38 years ago. Neither the 38-year-old nor the 40-year-old computers are on the market today. These contexts cannot simply be accumulated.

Even if today's computer would be one million times faster than a 40-year-old computer, today's computer could not be used by one million persons as a calculator at the same time. The difference with a computer that is one million times faster than another computer is that the faster computer cannot be divisible into one million slower computers. Theoretically, we could imagine that one million customers provide tasks for the fast computer to calculate. Then, such a computer would quantitatively be on par with one million slower computers. Under such circumstances, it would be reasonable to quantify the fast computer as equivalent to one million slower computers. However, in reality, fast computers are not divisible into slow computers in this way. Quantification must be based on functionality coming from the potential utility that a matter can have. Consider that the value of a new computer reflects a difference in physical properties so that each doubling of a computer calculating power enables the user to perform yet another function and the doubling of computer power occurs every second year. Imagine now that the slowest computer, the first one that was produced 40 years ago, could only perform one function, for example, like a calculator. The fastest computer could therefore perform 21 functions. The 40-year-old computer is not on the market today, and the only equivalent is a calculator. From such a perspective, and if all functions are of equal importance, it would be more reasonable to quantify the fastest computer as equivalent to 21 computers from 40 years ago than one million old computers.

The large differences in the price of old and new computers do not only reflect their functionality but likewise, that older computers will be used for a shorter time than a new computer given the changing technology level. Computers are valued in relation to other computers. A new computer is valued much more given that old versions become obsolete. If the decisive price difference between a new versus an old computer is the network effects, then the price difference between two old computers is not comparable to the price difference between a new and old computer as two older computers both lack such network effects.

The transformation of the agent of production can be measured by the negative effects on the agent, usually measured in working time. However, leisure production does not involve any loss of desirable properties. Some work may be beneficial for workers and contribute to a more ordered life besides the increased income from work. We should distinguish between the time agents are involved in the production and the objective and subjective negative effects of work.

Actual utility can be objective, subjective or inter-subjective (category 3).

In the utilitarian tradition, objective utility (category 3a in Table 5.1) has been formulated by various thinkers. A related notion is capability that Amartya Sen (1989) contrasts with the utility approach. A commodity may have a functionality that has different effects on the capability of different persons. Capability could be measured, for example, by how many years the patient will live after receiving a heart transplant, which should be distinguished from the functionality of a heart transplant. The final consumption that has taken place after the end of the production process can be quantified by the array of the newly acquired properties by the consuming agent. This usually increases the order of the agent of consumption, i.e., objective utility (category 3a). It is linked to various measures of welfare, for example, the impact of life expectancy, a component in the Humans Development Index. On the other hand, work can also cause loss of desirable properties of the agent and affect health negatively.

One possibility is to define production in terms of being productive of objective utilities. This would make it possible to define, for example, prostitution and the manufacturing of cigarettes and narcotics as unproductive. Such reconceptualisation is very difficult to implement and uses some kind of inter-subjective valuation. However, it would be possible to operationalise the notion if some measure of objective utility could be found, for example, on how various products and services affect the human body. The simplest measure is the average human life span, but a further challenge would be to judge how an individual product affects such life span.

Revealed preferences in mainstream economics belong to the category of the subjectively perceived benefit for a person (category 3b). Two patients that will receive an equal number of years added to their life after a heart transplant may value those years differently – a happiness index measures such subjective utility.

The final meaning of utility is the inter-subjective comparisons of subjectively perceived welfare (category 3c). A focal example is the market price. The price of a heart transplant does not reflect the subjectively perceived utility. A poorer patient may simply lack the money to pay a high price for a heart transplant if medical services are entirely provided at the market.

Value theory

The question of where to draw the production boundary is related to value theory. The market principle entails that only market activities are included in the production boundary. Feminist economics want to include unpaid domestic services in the production boundary, but, likewise, tend to use the market principle on the non-market sector. Human capital formation is placed outside of the production boundary, given that it does not contribute to value added in the current period, although it may in the long-term. The Marxist distinction between productive and unproductive labour is based on what constitutes surplus value, which in turn is related to the labour value theory. Ecological economics questions whether only human activity generates value.

Value theory or axiology is about what things are good and bad and how good and bad they are (Schroeder, 2021). It is by assigning a value to various items of production that those can be summed up. The condition of intentional causation in production, work and consumption, as presented in chapter 4, implicitly entails that various agents put a value on the processes and their end result. Distinguishing between productive and unproductive activities is to make such a rudimentary value judgement. Deciding between what is saleable and what is not is also a value judgement. Air and common ants have no prices; gold and apples are priced.

Since a value system is a guide for intentional action, it is a subjective or social construct. Some social constructs are better for specific analytical purposes, which may be possible to judge objectively, but then we need a meta-value system for making such an assessment. We may say that valuing human lives is vital for the survival of humankind – this can be evaluated scientifically. We may come to the conclusion that it may be good for society if people are killed under some circumstances, exemplified by the death penalty or the right to control one's own life. While instrumental value can be established using a scientific method, there are no objective criteria for intrinsic value. However, value systems have not been formed ad hoc entirely. Various value systems could be explained as evolutionary, even if not reduced to biology (Kitcher, 1994). What is best for the survival of the species has tended to evolve into something valuable, while what is detrimental to something negative.

Mainstream economics has long abandoned the objectivist theories of value. All value is reduced to the market price, which in turn is nothing more than the revealed preferences at the market. The abandonment of the distinction between exchange and use value could be described as monism. Monism is a view that there is only one intrinsic value, but is open to more than one instrumental value (Schroeder, 2021). In contrast, this book professes pluralist value theory. All actions cannot be priced. There are alternative value systems to the market. The value system at the market may differ from valuation made at the level of society, for example, the value of saving one human life. Finding shadow prices for unpaid domestic services or natural degradation is often quite difficult. Many activities that are impossible to price, such as parental care, belong to those that are considered of the highest value for people. Finding appropriate market prices is made increasingly difficult for activities included in GDP (Hoekstra, 2019, pp. 59, 65). There is no actual market for government services, and such are often measured by the costs incurred by providing these services, which entails that net profit is assumed to be zero. ICT makes it even more difficult to observe an actual price. For example, the price of an airplane ticket can vary from hour to hour.

In national accounts, a distinction is made between transfers and productive contributions, entailing that the value added is not entirely determined by the price formation at the market. GDP is measured in nominal prices, which is an inter-subjective valuation at the market, but economists want to eliminate the effect of price levels so that GDP is measured in constant prices or as volume values. GDP in volume value is sometimes interpreted as the physical output. Yet, only in the special case of an economy producing one commodity is physical output and volume measure equivalent. Despite this, the special case of a one-commodity economy is the main model in growth theory. The advantage of such a model is that it is easier to grasp and control what is happening. The quandary is that the production and capital consist of a number of goods and services, and they can only be aggregated by using prices, which, in turn, is circular given that nominal values have to be deflated and weighting depends on the deflation technique.

Chapter 4 shows that production comprises of physical transformations, some intended and some unintended such as environmental degradations. The physical properties of these transformations must not be conflated with how they are valued by various agents.

Modern capitalism erodes alternative value systems under a process of commodification. Even friendship has an implicit price tag. However, even under capitalism, not everything can be bought and sold. For example, modern capitalism forbids slavery and murder. The price is a value system for the individual market agent, not for society as a whole. Society may regard purchases of cars driven by gasoline as undesirable, despite that consumers may demand such products. The standard mainstream solution is to introduce externalities and shadow pricing – then the sum of utilities at the individual level equals utility at a social level. However, even the same individual may have different sets of preferences that are incompatible. How people reveal their short-term preferences may not be the long-term preferences they hold. As discussed in chapter 3, in climate research, mainstream economists introduce the concept of time preferences, entailing that the distant future becomes almost worthless. That is not how the distant future is perceived in the general debate and here, there exist an alternative underlying value framework related to the long-term survival of the species. In fact, a biological species that behave in a way that endangers its long-term survival may become extinct. Another moral principle is to act so that future generations are not worse off than the present, in accordance with Kant's categorical imperative, to solve a classical conundrum of Prisoner's dilemma where externalities cannot be privatised. Such moral rule for action may not correspond to the market logic.

As discussed in chapter 4, the ultimate purpose of production is consumption, which in turn involves the reproduction of human life. Reproduction of humans is more difficult to price than physical outputs of various goods.

Modern national accounts value production, work and consumption in prices. The market principle practised by national accounts excludes non-market services, but what if we are dealing with an economy that does not know of any prices, for instance, a self-subsistence economy? Surely, it should be possible to form volume indices over economic growth for such an economy as well? One solution is to use the relative prices of a modern economy, but such relative prices could be completely different from the technical relations of the economy under study.

Time use studies provide the most comprehensive account of human activities. Time use surveys are not conducted annually, and at best there is a survey once a decade (Edvinsson & Nordlund Edvinsson, 2017). Combined with data on work from national accounts, it can also provide data on how time has been divided between the various categories developed in chapter 4 of this book. How to apply the division of time use is not clear-cut. For example, cloth-making for own consumption could be classified as paid work given that all goods production is an SNA activity, unpaid work if considered that there are no monetary transfers involved or as free time if categorised as a hobby.

Working time or time use (in the case of leisure production) provides an alternative valuation than price and could, therefore, uncover the relations that exist prior to the price.

One motivation for the use of labour values is to analyse how society organises its productive time. The labour theory of value provides a principal foundation to estimate the level of productivity in various societies. Reproductive production, as well as self-reproduction, may be classified according to the positive effect they have on the human body. The human body can be stimulated in various ways, according to various needs. Physiological needs – air, water, food, sleep, clothing, sex and shelter – are the most basic. Maslow (Maslow, 1943) distinguishes between the hierarchy of needs – once more basic needs are satisfied, other needs tend to consciousness. The distinction between productive and unproductive work provides an essential conceptualisation of which work actually results in a product and which only redistributes existing production. However, some labour is more efficient than other labour. Methodological individualism can lend support to the use of labour values as an alternative to prices. It is the individual agent involved in the production and non-socially causing the transformation of a subject matter that contributes to production, not an abstract institutional unit or passive owner that controls resources through ownership.

Anthropologists studying societies, for example, hunters and gatherers, that do not know of money or prices, often use information over hours worked per week in different activities to describe the economic structure of these societies (Cashdan, 1989; Bossen, 1989). If prices are proportional to labour values, such a volume index gives exactly the same result as the volume index based on relative prices. When prices and labour values diverge, the labour value volume index gives a higher weight to activities that have a low (market) value added per worked hour, such as, for instance, government services and household services. Obviously, differences in labour productivity should be considered, but without data on prices, such comparisons can only be made for the same product. The productivity of child care cannot be compared to the productivity of car production if no other information is given than quantities produced and labour time. Paradoxically, the value added of 1-hour child care is usually much lower than the value added of 1 hour of producing a car, in spite of society valuing children more than cars.

Table 5.2 exemplifies two economies using three different methods to weigh quantities produced: prices, labour values and calories. Imagine an economy, Village A, consisting of 10 women and 10 men, with a strict, gender-segregated division of labour. The women produce 20 kilograms of bread per day of work, while the men produce 10 kilograms of cheese per day. A day of work consists of 8 hours. This means that the productivity for Village A is 0.25 kilograms of bread per working hour and 0.125 kilograms of cheese per working hour. Due to gender discrimination and due to the strict gender-segregated division of labour women's work is valued less than men's. In our example, the bread price is set at one pound per kilogram and for cheese at 4 pounds per kilogram, even if the labour value, i.e., hours to produce an output, is 4 hours per kilogram of bread and 8 hours per kilogram of cheese. This means that women's work is valued at half of men's. Assume further that both bread and cheese contain 3000 kcal per kilogram. This means that one pound buys four times more calories of bread compared to cheese, while 1 hour in production of bread yields twice as many calories for final consumption.

Now imagine another economy, Village B, not in any trading relation with Village A, with no gendered division of labour and slightly higher productivity of cheese than Village A, but not of bread. 10 women and 10 men produce 35 kg of grain in 140 hours and 4 kg of cheese in 20 hours. To estimate the production volume for economy Village A compared to Village B, we can use the usual method based on constant prices. In the prices of Village A, one-day production of Village B is valued at 60 pounds, 15 per cent below the production in Village A, despite Village B being more productive than Village A. However, in the prices of Village B, which reflect no discrimination of labourers producing bread instead of cheese, a day's production of Village B is worth 23 per cent more than a day's production of Village A. This is the classical index problem, discussed in chapter 3, where prices not only reflect technical conditions, but other circumstances as well, including social power, status, fashion trends, or in this example, gender discrimination. Under perfect market conditions, if men and women were to produce the same amount of bread and cheese per hour, there would be no price difference between an hour of the output of bread and cheese, respectively. In reality, gender discrimination or religious customs may cause women to be prevented from performing men's work and vice versa. In history, women workers have generally been paid much less than men (Humphries & Weisdorf, 2015). There has been a clear gender division of labour.

Comparing the two economies in labour values instead of prices generates another interpretation. In the labour values of Village A, production at Village

Table 5.2 Illustration of how to compute a volume index to compare two economies using prices, labour values and calories, respectively

Economy	Production per day	Labour productivity	Labour values	Price	Volume value				Kcal produced per labourer and an 8-hour day
					One days production in prices of Village A	One days production in prices of Village B	One days production in labour values of Village A	One days production in labour values of Village B	
Village A	• 20 kg bread (80 hours) • 10 kg cheese (80 hours)	• 0.25 kg bread per hour • 0.125 kg cheese per hour	• 4 hours per kg bread • 8 hours per kg of cheese	• 1 pound per kg bread • 4 pounds per kg cheese	60 pounds	65 dollars	160 hours	130 hours	4500
Village B	• 35 kg bread (140 hours) • 4 kg cheese (20 hours)	• 0.25 kg bread per hour • 0.2 kg cheese per hour	• 4 hours per kg bread • 5 hours per kg cheese	• 2 dollar per kg bread • 2.5 dollars per kg cheese	51 pounds	80 dollars	172 hours	160 hours	5850
Per cent difference villages B to A					−15 per cent	+23.1 per cent	+7.5 per cent	+23.1 per cent	+30 per cent

B is 7.5 per cent higher than Village A. The relative labour values of Village B are the same as the relative prices, given there is no discrimination, which implicates that the difference in the volume level of production is the same in the labour values and prices of Village B. There is, however, a difference in the comparison of the two economies in labour values, showing that the index problem pertains to labour values as well, given the relative labour values differ between economies. However, the advantage of labour values is that they only reflect objective technical conditions. While the comparison in prices of Village A reflects how much inhabitants of this economy can buy of the production of Village B at its own relative prices, labour values reflect how much labourers of this economy would have to work to produce the output of Village B under its own level of labour productivity.

An advantage of labour values is that information on prices is not necessary. For example, Village A and Village B may be self-sufficient economies and may not even know about prices, money and trade. In that case, only a volume index based on labour productivity should be calculated, given that the use of prices for a third economy may be misleading.

The last comparison of the two economies is based on calories, which shows that Village A produces much less calories than Village B by focusing half of its hours worked on cheese production instead of on bread production. If Village A would entirely switch to bread production, it would, under its own technical conditions, produce more calories than Village B. Here there is no index problem since the relative calorie content is the same. The predicament is that it is difficult to find a physical measure that can be applied to all types of commodities and services.

Using embodied hours worked instead of price weights have some interesting properties for volume measures. One difference is that volume values using prices as weights are affected by time preferences, while volume value estimated from embodied hours worked are not. Having a volume measure that is basically independent of time preferences is a clear advantage. Time preferences and consumer preferences are not an attribute of the production process as such. National accounts strive to measure the volume of production irrespectively of utilities. Still, if time preferences and consumer preferences are to have an impact on the volume values, utility has an impact. A problem with labour values is, of course, that a more productive worker can produce more in 1 hour than a less productive worker, but for the same commodity or service, an average can be taken.

National accounting using working time as weights could be used to detect some anomalies that occur in national accounting using prices as weights. In the case of Irish statistics in 2015, it is evident that what was a huge increase in value added was not reflected in an increase of similar magnitude in working time. Similarly, the huge sector of real estate is not reflected in the amount of labour input. Most part of the value added of real estate is capital income from owning buildings, but the value added of the construction of these buildings has already been accounted for in earlier data on GDP. The value added of the "housing services" of owner-occupied buildings is not assigned any working time at all in present national accounts, implicitly entailing that their labour productivity is infinite. Another advantage with labour values, as with embodied CO_2 emissions or other embodied physical characteristics, is that the value added then never can be negative as embodied labour of an activity must always be larger than the current labour input. This is, however, not the case if unproductive labour is assigned zero labour value.

If human capital formation is included in the production boundary, then learning is included in the concept of GDP, corresponding to the time-frame-independent production as defined in the previous chapter. The concept of work should then be expanded in the model to include studying and learning. Learning does not increase production under all circumstances, and it usually contributes to economic growth only in the long term. Learning and studying represent a diachronic division of work. As with unpaid domestic services, a difficulty is how to price the time of pupils and students. A shadow price could be set quite differently. Using labour values simplifies the problem.

Another shortcoming of historical national accounts is the inclusion of social reproduction. Neither labour values nor prices take into account the difference between social reproduction and production. In today's national accounts, the bombing of a building entails a positive value, as is the construction after the war to rebuild it.

The quantitative difference between non-social and comprehensive production can be illustrated by an example. Assume trade causes labour productivity outside of trade to increase four-fold due to specialisation, while the share of trade in total working time increases from nil to half. With the same value added per productive hour and with total hours worked kept constant, the value added of comprehensive production then records a four-fold increase, while that of non-social production only a doubling. Although trade causes an increase in utility, that increase in utility could be seen as already accounted for by the doubling of non-social production. It is doubtful whether it should be counted twice.

The difference between coercive and non-coercive social reproduction is that while the gross output of voluntary transactions generally could be set to zero, coercive activities signify destruction. Some of the welfare measures discussed in chapter 3 estimate some of this destruction. The value added of voluntary transactions would still be negative if intermediate consumption is deducted from the zero gross output. If intermediate consumption and destruction of social reproduction are to be deducted, then a concept of non-social net domestic product (NSNDP) could be calculated as follows (from the production side and in price terms):

NSNDP = output of non-social production − intermediate consumption of non-social production −
− capital depreciation of non-social production −

– intermediate consumption of social reproduction – capital depreciation of social reproduction –
– destruction from coercive activities

The relation to the SNA definition of GDP would then be:

NSNDP = SNA GDP + output of non-social production excluded by SNA –
– output of social reproduction included by SNA +
– intermediate consumption of non-social production excluded by SNA +
+ intermediate consumption of social reproduction included by SNA –
– capital depreciation of non-social production – capital depreciation of social reproduction –
– intermediate consumption of social reproduction – destruction from coercive activities

An alternative is not to deduct the intermediation consumption and capital depreciation of social reproduction and destruction from coercive activities. Such measure of the domestic production then also includes what is wasted by social reproduction. However, waste is normally deducted in national accounts, for example, if part of the inventory stock is destroyed.

Time invariant production can be calculated by adding the output of productive self-reproduction and deducting intermediate consumption and capital depreciation for those activities.

Interestingly, environmental national accounts similarly involve additional deductions to the value added. Environmental NDP deducts natural depletion and degradation. The following aggregate measure could be estimated:

Environmentally Adjusted Non-Social Net Domestic Product = Non-Social Net Domestic Product – natural depletion and degradation.

As discussed in chapter 3, how to measure natural degradation has been extensively researched and problematised. The problem is that deducting natural degradation caused by human production from output necessitates a measure, and such must be related to human activity. Natural degradation occurs not because of intentional action, and no social causation is involved. Valuing environmental degradation, therefore, is different from the principles of national accounting. People place value on the environment, but such value is not easily priced or assigned a labour value. In fact, as pointed out by ecological economics, physically production increases total disorder in the world, even if order can be increased in one area (the product). This is opposite from how production is valued, where the physical output is considered to be larger than the capital depreciation and intermediate consumption.

As discussed in chapter 3, the disappearance of wolves as species may be set at either a positive or a negative price (Lindmark, 2019). If all wolves disappear, they cannot be recreated, but if that is a loss, and how much the loss is valued depends on how humans value such incidence. The price of the existence of a species could almost be anything. Even if labour values provide a more objective basis to estimate how many hours of work are required to restore nature to its original state, what is a satisfactory original state is a matter of subjective opinion. Both killing and protecting wolves require labour input.

Taking the environment into account raises the question about the role of negative utility involved in the production process. If there are very large negative impacts that should be deducted from GDP, then could we not finally derive a negative GDP? According to the outline of this book, measuring production must be made from the point of view of humans that perform intentional actions (towards the end of the chapter, a possible expansion of the definition of the agent of transformations is discussed). Production occurs because it benefits humans. Some activities that are considered productive in the *System of National Accounts* cause more overall destruction than benefits, but such activities could not predominate – otherwise, humans would not survive for long. Given, for example, that the negative utility of coal power may be larger than its positive utility, it may be questioned whether coal power is a productive activity at all. On the other hand, if we define coal power as unproductive, that means it should be excluded from production, but how can we then analyse the impact of production on the environment?

The framework in this book considers activities productive as long as they potentially non-socially cause final consumption, i.e., as long as the output is positive, they are productive, even if the net value added could be negative after deducting intermediate consumption and capital depreciation. According to this framework, we must distinguish between one production process that causes a specific output and the future production processes that may or may not be necessary to replace the wear and tear caused by the first production process. The production processes must be distinguished from their valuation.

A company arranging a festival may buy cleaning services to restore the town area to its original state. A company arranging a festival without buying such cleaning services would earn a higher profit, but would we consider it to have a higher value added? The cleaning services can be considered intermediate consumption, which is deducted from the output to derive value added. Those services are not causally necessary to provide the festival service, so cleaning services are a separate production process. If the town environment is considered an asset or capital that people have invested efforts to maintain at a certain level, then deterioration of this environment is a depreciation in the same way as the machine is worn during the production process and must be replaced after some time. While the gross value added only deducts intermediate consumption from the output, the net value added also deducts depreciation. Including depreciation of the environment seems reasonable, which presupposes that the concept of capital is widened compared to present practices, but since there is a great degree of subjectivity involved in valuing the natural capital, environmental national accounts introduce a great uncertainty of the validity of the estimates.

Social causation versus the productivity of capital

In most mainstream models of economic growth, there is no exploitation. All factors of production are assumed to be paid for their marginal productivity. The differences between the income of women and men, rich and poor and ethnic majorities and minorities in such theoretical framework also depend on the marginal productivities of their contributions. Applying the definition of non-social production, inequalities rather occur due to social power and social relations.

Interpreting a multi-commodity economy as a one-commodity economy implies that value is reduced to physical property. An objectivist theory of value is sneaked back in through the backdoor. Being more straightforward, representatives of the neo-Austrian school see capital entirely from a subjectivist perspective, avoiding mixing it up with physical properties. For example, von Mises (1949, p. 260) writes:

> From the notion of capital-goods one must clearly distinguish the concept of capital. The concept of capital is the fundamental concept of economic calculation, the foremost mental tool of the conduct of affairs in the market economy. Its correlative is the concept of income.

A dilemma of stating that time preferences and opportunity costs are contributing to the value of a commodity is that these costs are actually not accruing and are only fictitious imaginations of an alternative world. The sacrifices of the capitalists lie in their heads, but that is precisely the point made by Austrian economists.

In reality, the marginal productivity of capital equals the marginal disutility of waiting for the owner only as an equilibrium condition under perfect competition. Monopoly models show that payment to capital does not equal marginal productivity but marginal revenue. Ownership of capital is similarly a type of monopolisation, a social relation rather than a technical one. In the framework of this book, the capitalist earns an income from the ownership of capital defended by socially reproductive activities, ultimately the power of the state. Of course, a building may be necessary for production, but the objective properties of a building are different from its social characteristics, most importantly, who owns it. The income stream of a labourer rests on the power wielded by labour and the prohibition of slavery by the modern state. In today's society, income streams also come from other sources, for example, copyrights, branding and social standing. The state earns income from its power to tax its citizens, not very different from how the capitalist earns its income, but taxation as such is not considered payment for a productive contribution in growth models.

One argument against the labour theory of value from neo-Ricardian economists is that Marx' argument that only labour contributes to value added is circular. As contended by Joan Robinson (1966, pp. 17–18):

> Marx uses his analytical apparatus to emphasise the view that only labour is productive. In itself, this is nothing but a verbal point. Land and capital produce no *value*, for *value* is the product of labour time. But fertile land and efficient machines enhance the productivity of labour in terms of real output... Whether we choose to say that capital is productive, or that capital is necessary to make labour productive, is not a matter of much importance.

> What is important is to say that *owning* capital is not productive activity. The academic economists, by treating capital as productive, use to insinuate the suggestion that capitalists deserve well by society and are fully justified in drawing income from their property.

The point made by Robinson that owning capital is not a productive activity is, however, indirectly supporting the view that it is the labour that sets material capital in motion. Production is a human activity. Capitalists and landowners contribute to production, but this is acted through ownership, i.e., by restricting others to access capital and land. Labour is the contribution a person makes to production through the control of the movement of his or her body and not through forcing or convincing other persons to perform. It is true that land contributes, for example, to agricultural output, but so is the sun. If the sun is blocked, for example, due to a volcano eruption, crops are directly affected. Why is not the sun classified as a kind of capital that contributes to production? The answer is that while the land is owned by persons that can charge rent, the sun is not owned, so the contribution of land is through ownership, which as Robinson admits is not a productive contribution. The "contribution" of nature to production is free of charge. Like the sun, land in itself does not charge anything for its "services". It is the person owning the land and excluding non-owners from using it without permission that charges the rent.

The reduction of social relations to technical conditions rests on an atomistic method that separates the contribution of capital from technological level and labour, instead of considering the production process as an organic whole. As explained by Felipe Jesus (2006):

> Suppose one bakes a cake. One combines flour, yeast, water, sugar, etc. Then after the cake is baked, one makes the following claim: 30 per cent of the size (or of the taste) is due to flour; another 5 per cent is due to

the water....and a residual 10 per cent is due to the baker's cooking skills. This may seem silly. However, this is what growth accounting does. One thing is to ask: what would happen to the cake (economy) if one added a given amount of extra flour (capital)? Or one may speculate about what it would have happened to the cake (economy) if it had been baked (managed) by a more competent baker [...] But this is different from apportioning the overall result to the individual components. Growth cannot be split the way it is done in growth accounting exercises because it does not make sense [...] Growth is the result of the interaction of a myriad of factors.

If the capital stock per labour increases, the technological level should change, but not so according to the simple Solow model. To separate the contribution of produced capital and labour is problematic given that capital represents past labour. Of course, an increase in the capital stock, under conditions of constant labour input, contributes to higher production, but this is through contributing to the productivity of the present labour. As Paul Sweezy (1942, p. 129) explains, the reduction of the analysis to price calculations

> mystifies the underlying social relations of capitalist production. Since profit is calculated as a return on total capital, the idea inevitably arises that capital as such is in some way 'productive'. Things appear to be endowed with an independent power of their own... it is easy to recognise this as a flagrant form of commodity fetishism.

In this book, it is argued that the labour value theory and the distinction between productive and socially reproductive labour are related. The common denominator is social causation, which is placed outside of the production boundary in the formulation of non-social production. The labour value theory states that the net value added of production comes from labour and not from capital. The conceptual outline of this book supports the Marxist notion of exploitation of workers in the capitalist system, given that it is only labour that non-socially causes the productive transformation. The exercising of ownership rights, if involving work, could be seen as a socially reproductive activity. The definition of comprehensive production, as presented in chapter 4, entails that social causation can contribute to production, but then by productivity is meant something else than a purely technical relation.

It is only intelligent beings that produce in a purposeful way. Capital as a physical entity is causally related to production, but as dead labour, where the intentional non-social causation runs through the contribution of past labour and through the purposeful activity of present labour. A criticism of the neoclassical distribution theory should not be mixed up with an ethical criticism of capitalism as an unequal system. Private ownership of the means of production may be the most efficient social system, but this then stems from social necessity, not a technical necessity.

Neoclassical theory of the marginal productivity of capital and labour has predictive power of how income is distributed, but this only occurs due to the specific social settings of an assumed perfect market economy and technical conditions where the marginal productivity of labour and capital is decreasing, or settings that approach such ideal. If the marginal productivity of labour is higher than the wage, the capitalist employs more workers until the wage equals the marginal productivity of labour. If a capitalist would pay the worker a wage below the productivity of labour, the labourer would simply seek to be employed by another capitalist. However, in other social settings, this may not hold.

Even under capitalism, risk in employing workers due to laws that protect against being fired, monopoly power, learning effects and redistribution through the financial markets entail that the marginal productivity of capital may not equal the compensation to capital.

If the labourers were the owner of capital, the whole value added would belong to labour. This is the main argument put forward by socialists for the existence of exploitation under capitalism. A counter-argument is that if the labourer is an owner, he or she is also a capitalist. However, ownership may not be in the form of capital if the labourer would not be able to sell his or her ownership rights. A company can theoretically change ownership from external owners to employees without entailing any change in the productive contributions and activities of the employees.

If labourers were turned into slaves or serfs, the remuneration to the worker could be lowered to below the present wage, given that the labourer would then not be free to change jobs. In a perfect free market economy allowing slavery, the slave owner hiring out slaves to capitalists would earn an income equal to the marginal productivity of labour, while the consumption of the slave would be equivalent to deprecation. The slave owner would have an interest in the slave being able to reproduce his or her labour-power, but no consumption above that level. A slave owner that owns physical capital will earn a profit both from the physical and slave capital, while a capitalist employing free labour but having a firm that produces the same value added would only earn profit from the physical capital and therefore receive a lower capital share. For example, assume that the necessary consumption of a labourer to reproduce is 70 per cent of the marginal productivity, the profit rate is 10 per cent, and the (physical) capital share is 40 per cent. A slave would then consume 30 per cent less than a free labourer, the rest being earned as profit for the slave owner, and due to slavery, the slave would not be able to change jobs. The ratio of slave capital to value added under slavery would be 1.8, while the ratio of physical capital to value added would be 4. An owner of both physical capital and slaves would have a larger share in the value added, 58 per cent, and would also own 45 per cent more capital than a capitalist operating after slavery had been abolished under the same technical conditions of production. Both the amount of capital and the capital share is here determined by the social context, i.e., whether slavery is allowed or not.

The argument that free labour is not exploited under capitalism, while slaves and serfs are exploited, ultimately rests on the argument that while private property of physical non-human capital is justified, slavery and serfdom are not. It is an argument made within the context of an idealised version of modern bourgeois law (Ellerman, 2021) rather than being based on the natural science of technical restraints or mathematics. The exact mathematical formulations of the labour value theory are here not decisive in showing the unproductive nature of capital ownership – this is largely a conceptual question, where the formal framework is to be judged by its consistency and usefulness for scientific analysis. Agents performing leisure production that does not involve any work can also be exploited by capitalists, for example, when online portals encourage users to become travel agents (Fioramonti, 2017, p. 67).

Moses Abramovitz (1956, p. 11) calls the total factor productivity, a weighted average of labour and capital productivity "some sort of measure of our ignorance about the causes of economic growth". It is well known that total factor productivity is not the same as technical change, even if the impression is given sometimes that it is so. However, what actually is technical change is very difficult to establish in these models.

The difficulty is how to interpret capital productivity. Output per capital ("capital productivity") is, of course, not irrelevant, for instance, as a measure of how much milk a cow "produces" every day, but capital needs to be seen as a product of labour itself (Lipietz, 1986). In a multi-sector model, where the prices of capital goods decrease in comparison to the general price level, capital per labour could grow much faster than output per labour at constant prices (Marquetti, 2003).

A fictive example can illustrate this. Assume that a labourer only uses a machine as capital and increases her output by 50 per cent by having a machine that has 200 per cent higher computing power. If the constant price is proportional to computing power, this will implicate that the capital productivity falls dramatically by 50 per cent. Even if the labour productivity increases by 50 per cent, assuming capital and labour are paid equal shares, the total factor productivity falls by 13 per cent (assuming a Cobb–Douglas function). However, if the relative labour time to produce a unit of computing power decreases dramatically, the nominal capital-output ratio could stay the same or even decline. Then the output per total labour input, the sum of the labour time using the capital goods and the labour content of the depreciation of the machines, increase substantially. Looking at how society has organised its labour it has become more efficient, despite data showing falling total factor productivity. This anomaly would not occur in a one-commodity economy. It arises because the price of production versus capital can change substantially, especially in the era of ever more efficient computers used as capital. Thomas Rymes (1971, pp. 89–90) puts it as follows:

> [T]he traditional treatment neglects the fact that commodity inputs are capable of being produced with ever increasing efficiency. In the world of technical change, the fact that commodities… are not primary inputs like labour and natural agents, becomes clear. The neglect of this fundamental point invalidates neoclassical analysis.

In one-commodity models, if the same output is produced with the same amount of labour and capital, then technology stays the same. However, the same amount of capital can be valued differently relative to the output over time and in different countries. A high price of capital relative to output results in less efficient production. While modern growth theory attempts to abstract from nominal prices by using only constant prices, constant prices embody social and nominal relations, i.e., that of the base year, which may be quite irrelevant for the compared year.

The concept of capital productivity is also problematic when viewing the effects on the production of capital as defined in the Solow model, which involves at least three main types of capital – machinery, buildings and stocks. These are causally differently related to output. Machinery most obviously has a causal relation to the output. Buildings are where the production takes place and usually do not directly impact on the output. Stocks of finished products are accumulated after the production process has ended, so this type of capital cannot have a causal relation to production, given that causation cannot run backwards. As pointed out by Hoekstra (2019, p. 175) in his book *Replacing GDP by 2030*:

> The founding father of modern economics, Adam Smith, starts his most famous book, *The Wealth of Nations*, looking at the production line of a pin factory and describing the various steps of the pin-producing process. Economists of that era were also interested in technology and the organisation of production. They would analyse the inner workings of factories. However, as economists started to adopt the "production function", the focus moved away from the engineering aspects of production but turned to mathematical representation of various inputs. In these types of models it is implicitly assumed that the production process is a black box with regular mathematical features.

There is a difference between capital that can be reproduced and non-reproducible natural resources such as land and mining resources. For example, if a square kilometre of land can feed 10 times more people, that represents genuine technological progress, even if labour productivity would stay the same or decline somewhat. In the pre-industrial era, the main form of technological progress was the increase in land productivity. Today, some countries can increase their GDP per capita substantially because of control of scarce natural resources, for example, oil. According to Mankiv et al. (1992), "one should not expect standard growth models to account for measured GDP in these [oil-rich] countries". Control of such resources is not based on the previous production of these resources and often involves a large amount of investment in socially reproductive activities. Oil income is a notable explanation of international wars, although the effect varies with the characteristics of the petrostate (Colgan, 2013). Colonialism has largely been motivated by the resting control of valuable natural resources, with catastrophic consequences for the indigenous people. Between 1493 and 1700, the American colonies of Spain transferred to Europe 51,100 tons of silver, roughly equivalent to 50 million annual workers' wages in Sweden in 1700 (Söderberg, 2010). America's indigenous population was substantially reduced, in Mexico by as much as 97 per cent between 1500 and 1620, which in turn motivated the slave trade to repopulate the workforce (Habib, 2017).

One of the arguments of this book is that production involves intentional causation. The concept of labour productivity denotes a causal link between labour and output. The concept of land productivity also signifies a causal link between land and output, although it is not intentional. Land only becomes productive because of the intentional causation of labour.

Despite their advancement in the understanding of growth dynamics, new growth models aggravate the problem of atomistic separation of the contribution of different production factors, especially as these models tend to separate the intrinsic capabilities belonging to labour from labour itself. Even if the learning-by-doing model recognises that if capital stock per labour increases, the technological level should also change, it takes for granted that the effect of increased capital per labour as capital could be separated from its effect on increasing knowledge. Kenneth Arrow (1962, p. 159) attempts to rescue the distribution theory by making the highly unrealistic claim that learning effects are not compensated by the market and that the private marginal productivity of capital is, therefore, less than the social marginal productivity. As the new growth models show, separating the contribution of capital from technical progress can be difficult. If more types of capital are included, for instance, human and knowledge capital, the total factor productivity dwindles.

One consequence of the exclusion of socially reproductive activities from the production boundary is the need to reformulate growth theories. In the Solow model, only one commodity is produced, and all work is devoted to its production. All capital is produced capital. However, we can imagine that part of the work is unproductive. Social reproduction and its specific institutional forms have an impact on production, but it is primarily not technical.

The production function is a technical relation between inputs to production – mainly labour, accumulated capital and output. A company may evict indigenous people to cultivate a crop and may have to employ a large number of guards against the resistance of the evicted people. The labour input of guards is not determined technically but socially. An agreement with the indigenous people, for example, by giving them shares in the company, may suddenly remove the need for the labour input of guards. In the Schumpeterian sense, this would involve a social innovation. However, the innovation is here entirely social, not involving changing the technical relations of a production function. The concept of productivity is meaningless both in relation to transactions and social power.

Including institutions and distinguishing between unproductive and productive work in the analysis make it difficult to apply deterministic models of the traditional growth models. Socially reproductive activities can enable more effective technological solutions, for example, laws that abolish feudal restrictions but likewise cause destruction. Acemoglu et al. (2002; 2005) purport that the effect of colonialism as an institution on economic growth has been different depending on the context. While in Latin America dense population of indigenous people contributed to their exploitation, in northern America, this was not feasible. Free trade may increase the productivity of two countries by enabling them to specialise, without that requiring that trade as such should be included in the production function. The trade between the new and old world developed the Atlantic slave trade, which raised the wealth of European merchants at the expense of others. The role of free trade in de-industrialising India's textile industry in the 19th century has been a debated topic (Roy, 2002; Clingingsmitha & Williamson, 2008). Doucouliagos and Ulubaşoğlu (2008) conclude that democracy does not have a direct effect on economic growth (using conventional measures of GDP), but there is a positive indirect effect through higher human capital formation and economic freedom, and lower inflation and political instability.

What is capital?

A major question in growth models is what to be included in capital (Lewina & Cachanosky, 2018) and what it actually is. As Joan Robinson (1962, p. 117) underlines:

> The 'capital' in the traditional production function is neither fish, flesh nor good red herring. It mixes up the physical and the value relations and cannot tell us anything about either.

The shortcoming with equating capital with time and considering it productive is that it mixes up capital as (1) an object with specific physical properties, (2) a social relation involving power (ownership defended by a state), and (3) the subjective perception of the owner of capital. Capital is a special social form but is also a sub-category of a more general type that exists in all human societies, that of physical or social assets. In the Solow model, capital and labour are categorised as two different production factors, but capital itself is accumulated labour if reproducible. Natural assets are not reproducible in the same way, and they are not a product of technology.

A large part of the value of capital consists of social power rather than embodied production. Some capital involves control over physical resources such as buildings, land, machinery and inventories, while other types of capital are directly socially reproductive, i.e., directly involve social power over human beings, consisting of monopoly power, goodwill, social influence, copyrights, etc. Historically, a large part of capital has existed in the form of slavery. Although endogenous growth models expand the concept of capital to knowledge, they usually disregard some forms of capital that do not directly contribute to production but still earn an income stream. As argued by Bourdieu (1986):

> Capital is accumulated labor (in its materialized form or its 'incorporated,' embodied form) which, when appropriated on a private, i.e., exclusive, basis by agents or groups of agents, enables them to appropriate social energy in the form of reified or living labor. [...]

> Depending on the field in which it functions, and at the cost of the more or less expensive transformations which are the precondition for its efficacy in the field in question, capital can present itself in three fundamental guises: as economic capital, which is immediately and directly convertible into money and may be institutionalized in the forms of property rights; as cultural capital, which is convertible, on certain conditions, into economic capital and may be institutionalized in the forms of educational qualifications; and as social capital, made up of social obligations ('connections'), which is convertible, in certain conditions, into economic capital and may be institutionalized in the forms of a title of nobility.

The largest part of capital today consists of transactional or intangible capital, such as the ownership of brands or copyrights, which generate income streams directly from social power rather than control of physical resources. Some of the monopoly profits are retained through investments, such as adverts, lobbyism, etc. Most of the value of Facebook is neither material assets nor information but is related to its social standing. Some physical capital may be used in socially reproductive activities, for example, vehicles used to transport military troops, while some socially reproductive capital involves the control of resources that technologically contributes to production, for example, ownership of copyrights or of slaves.

The book or share value of companies is obviously not the same as the capital defined in the Solow model. Endogenous growth models potentially take into account the wider notion of capital. International national accounts now classify research and development as an investment (United Nations et al., 2009, p. 206). Much of what new growth theories include cannot easily be capitalised by private companies. Under capitalism, what is sold on the labour market is not the labourers, but the use of the labourers for a temporary period of time. Human capital is not capital but a capability of labour. As noted by Piketty (2014, p. 46), human capital "cannot be owned by another person or traded on a market (not permanently at any rate)". It is a rival, excludable and owned item, but it is not owned as capital, because the owner cannot freely sell his or her body to another person. The concept of human capital implicitly mixes up physical properties and social forms. Turning labour into capital entails slavery, which is an alternative social form to free labour. The expenses a company have in educating its employees do not imply it can stop the employees from leaving the company, although labour contracts can be written restricting the form of knowledge that an employee can consider as his or her own and use in future employment (May, 2002). Competition presupposes free flows of information, which inhibits the transformation of specific knowledge into capital. As argued by Foray (2004, p. 91):

> A firm finds it far more difficult to control its knowledge than its machines, for numerous opportunities for leaks and spillovers arise.

If copyrights are classified as physical capital, income from ownership of copyrights is categorised as a productive payment to capital, which may be difficult to distinguish from a transfer. What companies can do is to try to block the access for others to the knowledge they are using, through patents, secrecy, etc., i.e., making it excludable and transforming knowledge into a commodity, but this is rather a monopolistic behaviour (May, 2002, pp. 323–326). Such monopolistic capitalisation of knowledge is limited and insecure precisely because of the non-rival, social nature of knowledge. According to Dominique Foray (2004, pp. 136–137), although there are many advantages of patents, the mechanism is not used frequently. Firms often prefer to keep their findings secret.

A remarkable feature of, for example, holding a chemical patent is that when this patent expires, the de facto destruction of the intangible capital causes increases in the production of the generic drug driven by other companies. The more capital held as copyrights would be destroyed, the more would production increase. The more human knowledge that would be capitalised on, the lower would be the production. Capitalisation of knowledge requires the exclusion of people from accessing it. This type of capital behaves opposite to the neoclassical assumptions of the production function, where the marginal productivity of capital is never assumed to be negative. This demonstrates why capital as a social form must be distinguished from the role of physical assets in the production process. This does not indisputably undermine the argument for copyrights, as a necessary incentive for companies to invest in knowledge production. However, such circumstances stem from social necessity, how humans act in relation to each other in a market system, not a technical necessity that could neatly fit into a production function.

A major contribution of endogenous growth models, for example, unified growth theory, is the emphasis on the size of the population for the technological level. This is related to Adam Smith's thesis that technological progress primarily comes from an increased division of labour, which is why, for example, international trade leads to a more efficient global economy. The advantage of the labour theory of value is that (produced) capital is not considered as something separate from labour, but as dead labour. "Dead labour" is the labour performed earlier in time, while "living labour" is the labour performed in the present (Marx, 1965, p. 233), a relation in production between labour in different periods. The relation between the capital stock and output can be seen as a diachronic division of labour. A large capital-output ratio could be seen as an advanced division of labour in time. If, for instance, one unit of a commodity is produced by work performed in 1 hour and the depreciation of capital represents 1-hour work in the capital producing sector, then the value added represents 1 hour of labour, and the total value of the commodity embodies 2 hours of labour.

Increased investments in human capital formation can be seen as a diachronic division of productive activity as well if the production boundary is widened in line with the definition of time-frame-independent production. Abstract knowledge accumulation, both learning effects and specialised research, a product of labour in endogenous growth models, is in itself similar to human capital formation, in that society as a whole is learning over generations. Abstract knowledge accumulation may be considered a much more advanced division of labour than capital formation, human capital formation as well as synchronic division of labour. The total stock of knowledge as measured in worked hours outpaces other types of assets in relation to production.

Social stages in the development of intelligent life

Production and work carried out by intelligent beings share similarities with activities among animals (Blattner et al., 2020). Recently, Eigenraam and Obst (2018) consider an expansion of the production boundary by classifying ecosystem units as producing units, which violates the assumption that production is a process involving an institutional unit or agency. From an ecological perspective, coerciveness involves the increase of free energy of one individual by forcefully decreasing it for another individual. If the social exteriority condition is expanded so that any animal is classified as a "person", then killing animals for food is an unproductive activity. If the concept of "person" is expanded to all life, then agriculture and all food-gathering of animals would be considered unproductive, while productive activity would be mostly restricted to the transformation of non-life, mainly the metabolism of plants. Violence against humans has some similarities with the exploitation of nature.

The concept of production is used in ecology that studies interactions between organisms and their environment. Given that economics studies human agents, there are some noticeable affinities. In biology, primary production is defined as the synthesis of organic compounds from atmospheric or aqueous carbon dioxide. The Gross Primary Production is the creation of new biomass.

Consumers reduce the existing stock of the biomass. What is important is the Net Primary Production, i.e., the Gross Primary Production less the biomass used by the organism that produces the biomass (Amthor & Baldocchi, 2001). Productivity in ecology differentiates between primary and secondary productivity. Secondary production is the generation of heterotrophic biomass, involving the transfer of organic matter between trophic levels. This differentiation is linked to ecological economics, which emphasises the importance of deducting natural degradation from measures of GDP. Theoretically, Net Primary Production, but not Gross Primary Production, could be negative (Roxburgh et al., 2005), which is similar to the possibility of value added, but not gross output, to be negative in the system of national accounts. The categorisation into primary and secondary production in ecology has some affinity with the distinction between non-social production and social reproduction presented in this book. While secondary production in ecology only transfers organic matter but does not generate new organic compounds containing additional energy, social reproduction typically redistributes existing production between individuals.

In *Poverty and Philosophy*, Marx (1956, p. 122) famously emphasises the level of technology as the driving force of history and society:

> Social relations are closely bound up with productive forces. In acquiring new productive forces men change their mode of production; and in changing their mode of production, in changing the way of earning their living, they change all their social relations. The hand-mill gives you society with the feudal lord; the steam-mill, society with the industrial capitalist.

Marx describes a dynamic between social reproduction and production. Purposeful beings enter into social relations and change one another in order to satisfy their needs. The driving force for the increased complexity of social relations and the institutions that set the rules for socially reproductive activities is the change in the mode of transforming exterior nature, although causality runs both ways. Why are some productive factors related to some types of socially reproductive activities, and what types? Certain institutions are only possible for larger populations. Such larger populations can only arise at a certain stage of production. For example, states could not have been formed before the neolithic revolution. Socially reproductive activities are shaped by institutions, the formal and informal rules of society, while the Marxist concepts of political superstructure govern coercive social reproduction. Financial services exist because there is a state that guarantees ownership rights and allows interest rates. War would not appear under a global institution that would prevent violent conflicts. Trade with slaves disappears or is pushed underground when slavery is abolished. Some socially reproductive activities, such as theft and murder, occur in spite of institutions that condemn and punish such acts. As Darwin (1889, p. 117) notes, "No tribe could hold together if murder, robbery, treachery, etc., were common" – they take place outside of the predominant institutions. Institutions are both enabled and enabling. The upholding of institutions, such as policing or protection of democratic rights, and institutional change, such as political reforms, revolutions and the rise of new religions, are in themselves socially reproductive activities.

Coercive reproduction is the last resort for humans to impose power over other humans – and the ultimate imposition of such power is lethal violence, whether enacted legally or illegally. Coercive social reproduction is more costly than non-coercive social reproduction. Lethal violence is more costly than non-lethal coercive social reproduction. Many institutions develop to regulate relations between humans through voluntary transactions, for example, trade, finance and religion, or to minimise lethal consequences. All major religions condemn the killing of other human beings.

Table 5.3 describes the condition of 11 different activities under various stages of society: hunter-gatherers, pre-urban agrarian society, urban agrarian society and industrialism. In addition, two types of animal ecologies are used for comparison, expanding the concept of production: ants and termites, and great apes. Finally, the stage of post-singularity is presented, when artificial intelligence possibly becomes more intelligent than humans, with the assumption that both AI and humans (or the intelligent species that has developed AI) continue to coexist. The 11 studied activities can be grouped into four main categories:

1   Non-reproductive production, which in turn, can be differentiated between transformations of non-biological material, transformations of dead biological material (including transformation from living to dead material, i.e., killing life) and reproducing living biological organisms.
2   Reproductive production, which in turn can be differentiated between reproduction of current and new individuals, the latter being raising children.
3   Social reproduction, which can be further differentiated between voluntary transactions, non-lethal coercion and lethal acts against individuals of the same species or members deemed to have personhood.
4   Self-reproduction, which in turn can be differentiated between time-frame-independent productive self-reproduction, mainly learning and work travel, and unproductive self-reproduction, which in turn can be differentiated between personal activities and leisure.

The dynamic relation between work and leisure is noteworthy. A simple model can illustrate it. Consider that the result of work (food) can be measured in calories, but that work results in additional calorie consumption of the body. Work generates both a utility and a disutility. Calories are the objective utility. The effect on the body is the loss of calories compared to a state where no work would be performed. If the purpose is the maximisation of net calories

Table 5.3 Condition of 11 different activities under various stages of society

		Ants and termites	Great Apes	Hunter and gatherers	Pre-urban agricultural societies	Agrarian urban societies	Industrialism	Post-singularity society
Non-reproductive production	**Production transforming non-biological material**	Constructing nests of non-biological material	Occasional tool making	Stone tool, crafting	Unspecialised stone and metal crafting, rural construction	Specialised crafts, mining, rural and urban construction	Factory manufacturing	AI: Probably main focus. Humans: Likely non-existent
	Production transforming from or to dead biological material	Foraging, constructing nests of biological material	Hunting, foraging	Hunting, foraging, food preparation, cloth-making, etc.	Manufacture of agrarian products, cooking, etc.	Manufacture of agrarian products, specialised crafts	Manufacture of agrarian products and associated services	Manufacturing to support biological humans
	Production reproducing life outside of the species	Cultivate fungi, keeping other species in captivity	Non-existent	Virtually non-existent	Agrarian activities predominate work	Agrarian activities predominate work	Shrinking agrarian activities	Preservation of biological life.

Productive reproduction							
Production reproducing current (adult) individuals	Uncommon for adult individuals	Uncommon for adult individuals	Within band	Within households and villages	Within households or villages	Within household, at the market and public sector.	AI: Probably less common Humans: Unknown
Production reproducing new individuals	Collectively by the colony	Mainly by mothers	Shared by parents and relatives	Shared by parents and relatives	Shared by parents and relatives	Child rearing shared by parents, relatives, the market and the state	AI: Takes short time Humans: Likely important
Social reproduction							
Voluntary transactions	Non-existent	Non-existent	Religious activity, sharing, gifts	Occasional trade, gift economy, slave trade	Trade, money, financial services, labour market (of minor importance)	Mainly capitalist organisation (Soviet type system as alternative), elections	Likely at low level
Non-lethal coercion	Defence, slavery, domination	Occasional violence, domination, rape	Occasional violence, dominance and rape	Patriarchy, chiefdoms, slavery, rape	State, patriarchy, slavery, serfdom	Modern state, patriarchy	Likely at low level within AI civilisation, but debated whether AI benevolent to others.

(Continued)

Table 5.3 (Continued)

		Ants and termites	*Great Apes*	*Hunter and gatherers*	*Pre-urban agricultural societies*	*Agrarian urban societies*	*Industrialism*	*Post-singularity society*
	Lethal violence	Lethal violence mainly against individuals outside colony. Warfare common.	Occasional killings at group level. High level of interpersonal lethal violence	Prevalence of warfare debated. High level of lethal violence between persons.	High level of warfare and homicides	High level of warfare, but decreasing lethal violence in some late agrarian societies.	Decreasing level of lethal violence, but variation in violence is large.	Probably non-existent within AI civilisation, but debated whether AI benevolent to others.
Self-reproduction	**Human capital formation, work travel, etc.**	Information sharing through tandem running, travelling	Some learning from adults, travelling	Learning skills from adults, spread of cultures, travelling long distances	Learning skills from adults, spread of cultures	Learning skills within household, learning institutions	Schools and universities, work travel	AI: Learning takes very short time. Humans: Learning has no productive purpose
	Personal activities	Eating, sleeping	Eating, sleeping.	Eating, sleeping	Eating, sleeping	Eating, sleeping	Increased importance	Important activity
	Leisure	Resting	Resting, sex	Resting, sex	Resting, sex	Leisure is decreased	Increased importance	AI: Depends on definition Humans: Main activity

(under the assumption of decreasing marginal calorie addition and increasing marginal calorie consumption of work), the individual will continue to work until the marginal increase in calories is equal to the marginal decrease in calories. We can imagine an animal in which effort adds to calories, but also increase calorie consumption.

For animals, production, final consumption and self-reproduction are usually the same processes, but many animals produce for later use, for example, storing food. Some animals are involved in the intentional transformation of exterior nature, for example, through tool use, including the manufacturing of tools. The extent of cultural transmission of tool use among chimpanzees is an ongoing scientific debate (Tennie et al., 2020). Some insects have partly reached an agricultural stage and complex social division of labour. As already Darwin (1889, p. 147) notes:

> Ants certainly communicate information to each other, and several unite for the same work, or for games of play. They recognise their fellow-ants after months of absence, and feel sympathy for each other. They build great edifices, keep them clean, close the doors in the evening, and post sentries. They make roads as well as tunnels under rivers, and temporary bridges over them, by cringing together. They collect food for the community, and when an object, too large for entrance, is brought to the nest, they enlarge the door, and afterwards build it up again. They store up seeds, of which they prevent the germination, and which, if damp, are brought up to the surface to dry. They keep aphides and other insects as milch-cows. They go out to battle in regular bands, and freely sacrifice their lives for the common weal. They emigrate according to a preconcerted plan. They capture slaves. They move the eggs of their aphides, as well as their own eggs and cocoons, into warm parts of the nest, in order that they may be quickly hatched; and endless similar facts could be given.

The level of intentionality among ants and termites to change nature is an ongoing research field. Their level of cooperation is classified by biologists as the highest form of sociality, i.e., eusociality. Eusociality is usually defined as encompassing the following characteristics: cooperative brood care, overlapping generation within a colony of adult individuals, and a division of labour between reproductive and non-reproductive adult individuals (Crespi & Yanega, 1995; Wilson, 1971). Evolutionary, the non-reproductive individual of eusocial species could be seen as the extended phenotype of the gene. A related concept is that of a superorganism, a buzzword of the 1920s, entailing that individuals act in concert in order to generate phenomena governed by the collective (Kelly, 1994, p. 98). These concepts raise the question of the difference between individuals and society. As Darwin (1889, p. 292) notes:

> For instance, Pierre Huber, whose accuracy no one doubts, separated some ants, and when, after an interval of four months, they met others

which had formerly belonged to the same community, they recognised and caressed one another with their antennae. Had they been strangers they would have fought together. Again, when two communities engage in a battle, the ants on the same side sometimes attack each other in the general confusion, but they soon perceive their mistake, and the one ant soothes the other.

Under the stage of hunters and gatherers, human production is not very different from the Great apes, in that the main focus is on transforming living organisms into food (Lucassen, 2021, p. 16), without being involved in the process of reproducing these living organisms as in agriculture. A distinction from the Great ape stage is the much more prevalent use of complex tools and the use of fire among humans, which creates an environment for further social development (Ko, 2016). Bands among foragers are characterised by cooperation, which can involve organised violence. Chimpanzees are known to conduct organised violence as well, which can be exemplified by the following incidence (Zinner & Wheeler, 2013):

A gang of eight males from the Kasakela community travelled purposefully towards the boundary of their territory, crossed the border and pushed silently further, monitoring carefully the neighbourhood. From time to time they stopped and listened. Then they spotted an adult male of the neighbouring Kahama community. They faced him up and attacked him brutally. After twenty minutes they desisted from their victim and moved back into their own territory. The victim died after some days due to his severe injuries. Similar events followed and after five years, the Kahama community was wiped out and its territory was taken over by the Kasakela community.

To what extent the Neolithic revolution caused an increased level of violence or not is a matter of a long debate (Allen, 2016). While Hobbes argued that civilisation saved humanity from a state of war of all against all, Rousseau suggested that civilisation brought more oppression, conflict and violence. Today, anthropologists generally agree that the level of lethal violence was high among foragers or hunters and gatherers. There is a difference between those arguing for a long chronology of war, entailing that warfare was prevalent throughout all of human history, and those maintaining a short chronology of war, and only accepting that warfare has been common in agricultural and complex hunters–gatherers societies. Partly, the question is semantic of how warfare is defined. For example, if war can only be conducted between polities, then warfare would be impossible among foragers if their societies are defined as non-polities. Empirical evidence tends to point in different directions, but it seems that violence and warfare are not always present. The level of violence can change quickly for the same societies.

With the advent of agriculture, humans became directly involved in re-producing non-human life, first through plant and animal management, and subsequently through cultivation and domestication (Lucassen, 2021, pp. 51–52). Production involving reproducing non-human life is in need of land. In economic history, Malthusian restrictions on pre-industrial society have been discussed for a long period (Edvinsson, 2015). Although Malthus was proved wrong by the industrial revolution and the demographic transition, his model has some relevance to the dynamics of agricultural society. In a Malthusian society of overpopulation, control of land and the people living on this land is crucial. Scarce resources constitute a noticeable explanation of conflicts.

Social class is a type of institution, or a consequence of institutions, and concerns what type of relation there is between people entering into production. Social class involves both coercive and non-coercive social reproduction. Class in pre-capitalist formations usually involved coercion. A slave owner causes production by forcing a slave to work. A feudal lord does not direct production but forces the labourer to pay a feudal rent in kind, money or work. The term tributary mode of production has been used to describe class society during the agrarian stage (Haldon, 1993). The state was mainly dominated by coercion, i.e., a military apparatus. The society could be termed a coercive mode of production, which was combined with the household mode of production.

During the late agrarian and industrial stages, there has instead been a strong tendency for the growth of voluntary transactions. In Europe, there has been a decline in the rate of homicide since the Middle Ages, which can be associated with the rise of state power that monopolises violence (Eisner, 2013). Advanced capitalist countries largely rest on institutions of voluntary transactions. A capitalist intentionally causes production by entering a voluntary agreement with a worker, and this agreement presupposes a state that guarantees ownership rights and monopolises violence. In a modern state, its subjects are forced to pay tax, but a difference to feudalism is that the modern state is not composed of an owning class and employment in the state cannot be transferred to heirs.

Not all industrial societies minimise coercive social reproduction. There are large variations between today's countries in homicide rates. Dictatorships beget an increased amount of coercion. The Soviet system imposed a dictatorship with some similarities to a tributary system, but there was no owning social class, and workers were able to choose education and employment. Even in the Soviet Union, there was a market, and money was used to pay wages and buy consumption goods and services. Genocide and forced labour have been implemented by some industrial capitalist societies, for example, Nazi Germany, but voluntary transactional were predominant for the majority of the population. The Nazi government did not desire to expropriate private ownership of the means of production and even took steps to denationalise, although the market mechanism was heavily regulated (Nathan, 1944).

One question is whether leisure production can replace productive labour in a future society, i.e., whether work may disappear (Braunschweig & Ghallab, 2021; Fioramonti, 2017, p. 117). There are some tendencies that point in that direction. At present, there is an ongoing discussion of what happens when work is overtaken by artificial intelligence. Much work is conducted as voluntary work where work in itself yields satisfaction. Many young people prefer less paid employment that yields satisfaction over higher paid employment of lesser satisfaction. Employers today need to think about motivating their staff. But is it really work when the worker performs tasks for pleasure and not for earning a wage? The possible disappearance of work poses dangers. It is not certain that a society of leisure production is an equal society. The dynamism of capitalism has largely rested on organising work and making it more effective through capital accumulation and the implementation of new technology. As already noted by Aristotle (*Politics*, 1.1253b, translated by H. Rackham):

> [If] shuttles wove and quills played harps of themselves, master-craftsmen would have no need of assistants and masters no need of slaves.

If workers no more are needed, who will support them? There are proposals of a citizen's salary, but why should those who control resources be interested supporting people that no longer are needed? Democracy may be in danger as democracy was largely based on the power that the working class and middle social layers could rest, while recipients of a citizen's wage no longer have such power.

Some researchers, for example, Nick Bostrom (2003), mostly outside of the mainstream AI community, predict that the point of singularity, when artificial intelligence develops beyond human intelligence causing an explosion in the development of ever improving AI, may lie quite near in the future. One argument against the perspective of imminent singularity is that computing speed does not alone bring about human-like intelligence. A fast-thinking dog does not necessarily play chess. Another argument is that there are diminishing returns to computer speed (Walsh, 2017). Work requiring actual human interaction, for example, care, may never be replaceable by machines.

Given that we do not know anything about possible extra-terrestrials intelligence, the only empirical information is the development of life and intelligent life on Earth. On Earth, animal life displays different levels of sociality. An extra-terrestrial intelligence possessing similar biological properties as humanity, concerning the level of sociality, reproduction patterns and feeding strategies, living under similar contexts may have developed analogous to humans, from hunters and gatherers, via a Neolithic and urban revolution giving rise to a state and a class structure and finally industrial capitalism and the rise of artificial intelligence. However, what about extra-terrestrial intelligence with different traits than human beings, for example, a eusocial or solitarity-but-social intelligence? Would there be a transition from agrarian to industrial society if an intelligent biological species would not decrease its fertility as a consequence of rising incomes, causing the Malthusian trap to never be escaped? Such counterfactual speculations are not out of place. It is common in the cliometric tradition, for example, Fogel's (1964) investigation of what would have happened if no railways had been developed in the United States.

Eusocial societies or superorganisms, if ever evolved to an intelligent state, have similarities with the hypothetical society of individuals with the same preferences for actions described in chapter 4 for the definition of social action. The Argentinian ant can form a super- or megacolony whose individuals are not mutually aggressive, spanning several continents (Vogel et al., 2010). If an extra-terrestrial species would consist only or predominantly of one super- or mega-colony and individuals of such colonies would display non-violence against each other, it would mean that coercive activities would be kept to a minimum and probably voluntary transactions as well. The history of such species may be much less violent between members of the same community than in human history, although violence between mega-colonies could still be prevalent.

Could a eusocial intelligent species develop capitalist relations? One possibility for eusocial capitalism would be if such species would act similarly to human households, and the colony would consist of a smaller number of individuals, but that would preclude larger colonies. An industrial revolution in non-capitalist forms is more likely. The Soviet system reached an industrial stage under non-capitalist relations, even though it was based on copying technology from the West (Allen, 2003). Whether an industrial stage could be reached before developing human type individual intelligence or by biological evolution is an interesting question. A eusocial intelligence may have developed a high division of labour as a biological characteristic, for example, in agriculture. Such evolution may therefore have taken more time than for humans, and it may hinder faster economic growth, which, nevertheless, could be an advantage for long-term survival.

Voluntary transactional activities may be a more successful pathway towards cooperation between social groups than altruism based on eusociality. In human society, the level of altruism of households or small bands has not been extended to society or humanity at large. From an evolutionary point of view, there is difficult to see a pathway for the biological development of universal altruism, i.e., high-level altruism practised to all individuals of any species. As known from human societies, dictatorships often see change as a potential threat to their own power. China in the 15th century chose to isolate itself. The failure of the Soviet system indicates why it is problematic to impose a collective will on the human species. The development of a harsh dictatorship after the Russian revolution, originally motivated by mass action for the rule of the people and the abolishment of class hierarchies, indicates egalitarian collectivism risk running being evolved into a new type of caste system. Economic growth at the technological frontier has tended to be fostered in countries with a high level of individualism, the Netherlands in the 17th century, UK in the 18th and 19th centuries and the USA in the 20th century. A eusocial society may develop an industrial society if it learns how to change its culture. Ants can make adaptive group-level decisions, for example, by combining social information, such as trail pheromones, with private information that mostly consists of their own memories (Czaczkes et al., 2015). A high level of altruism in a eusocial civilisation may be compatible with openness to new ideas, but such a society probably needs some kind of fostering of individualism to allow for innovation.

A post-biological evolution may open up a pathway to universal altruism, given that such development would not be restrained by biology. A major question is instead whether an advanced alien civilisation or artificial intelligence surpassing human abilities after singularity is reached would be benevolent to humanity. One fear is that a machine culture would see people as unnecessary and therefore dispose of humanity altogether or just keep some alive in reservations as study objects. In 2014, Stephen Hawking told BBC (Cellan-Jones, 2014):

> The development of full artificial intelligence could spell the end of the human race... It would take off on its own, and re-design itself at an ever increasing rate... Humans, who are limited by slow biological evolution, couldn't compete, and would be superseded.

If the social exteriority condition involves all intelligent beings, then an alien civilisation that exterminates other intelligent beings is conducting an unproductive activity, which is extremely destructive. Whether evolution favours sociality and non-violence is a debated issue. Human civilisations have evolved from coercive to non-coercive social reproduction, an institutional change that has benefited all humanity. The concern for non-human life has a long historical tradition. Jainism influenced Indian philosophy, including Hinduism and Buddhism, by its view of non-violence and a vegetarian diet, while in the earlier Vedic period, there was no ban, for example, on eating meat from a cow (Gittinger, 2017). Plants are more plentiful than animals, given that consuming others is less resource effective. An advanced alien civilisation may be inclined towards being beneficial to others, i.e., minimising coercive activities. If alien civilisations generally would show disrespect for other alien civilisations that would lead to conflicts. Some of the civilisations that are prone to be annihilated by a more advanced civilisation, may suddenly develop technologically, for example, after reaching singularity. Such conflicts, if not resolved quickly, would not be beneficial for the long-term survival of intelligent life, but the outcomes of such repeated prisoner-dilemma-type games are uncertain.

The anarchist writer Kropotkin (1919) emphasises that biological evolution benefits social cooperation before struggle between individuals. He points out that the most successful species on Earth are social animals. Kropotkin's key concept is mutual help. People are, by nature, social and collaborative. They are able to identify their interests with those of their fellow human beings. This sociality is what constitutes the morality of societies. Kropotkin believes that the struggle for existence in nature is of great importance, but as a struggle against unfavourable conditions rather than between individuals of the same species. According to Kropotkin (1924, p. 51), species that do not develop sociality risk being outcompeted.

Kropotkin could be described as an early proponent of group selection. If the exact mechanism of group selection is difficult to locate, experiments since the 1970s have shown that it is more prevalent than traditional evolutionary models have assumed (Wade, 1977). In socio-biology, kinship-based selection to some extent replaces the individual/organism with genes (Wilson, 1975; Dawkins, 1976) and is therefore not entirely a group selection. Models of group selection where individuals are not related have been formulated in recent years (Wilson, 2005). According to Multilevel Selection Theory, natural selection can take place at different levels: the gene, the cell, the organism and the group (Okasha, 2006; Wilson & Wilson, 2008). This theory moves beyond methodological individualism (to explain group selection through selection at the individual level). It is in line with Kropotkin's original view that evolution acts on several different levels.

Some biologists, on the other hand, point out that increased sociality entails that some types of violence increase, for example, punishment of individuals that do not subordinate to the group and attack of individuals outside of the group (Clutton-Brock & Parker, 1996; Heinze, 2004). Queens among wasps and naked mole rats, which are both eusocial species, often display aggression against lazy or inactive workers. Eggs laid by worker ants are destroyed. Civilisations at a much higher technological level than today will have the possibility to consciously move beyond previous biological constraints. Still, history shows that more advanced human civilisations have exploited or sometimes annihilated less advanced civilisations, as happened after the transatlantic contact of the 15th and 16th centuries. Carlos Santana (2021) purports that an advanced extra-terrestrial eusocial civilisation may have evolved through cooperation within the colony, but possess a lower ability or willingness to cooperate outside the hive. Even if benevolent, AI civilisation could be paternalistic and therefore force its will on others.

Yet, history exposes that extrapolating past trends may not always be the best guide for future conditions in a radically different context, at a much higher level of technological development. Some of the gloomy predictions by Classical economists on overpopulation, stagnation and declining living standards discussed in chapter 3 have not emerged. Path dependence could be a major factor as well.

Conclusions

This chapter discusses some possible applications of the formalisation mainly developed in chapter 4, which attempts to define production, work and consumption trans-historically. An impasse of present national accounts is the dependence on a market view of production. Neoclassical models tend to reduce economic, technological and social relations to the perceptions of a market economy, based on the ideal type of a utility maximising individual. Developing a transhistorical analysis should move beyond these limitations.

Inclusion of non-market activities, for example, unpaid domestic services or learning, in the production boundary is made problematic because these activities are not priced, and shadow prices may be constructed in different ways, yielding quite different estimates. A radical move would be to construct national accounts that are not dependent on prices at all, but instead use labour values as weights, or some other objective phenomenon such as natural degradation. It would describe how the economy organises its labour or use natural resources to produce for final consumption.

Modern national accounts define a productive activity such that increases the value added, i.e., the value of the output less the value of intermediate consumption. This difference is ostensibly measured using the market prices. Most of the production outside the market is not included. Even in modern national accounts, value is not the same as the market price. One reason is that there are always deviations from the law of one price. Various methods have been developed to estimate the "true price" of subsidised goods and services. Economic growth cannot be estimated without calculating volume values, i.e., where the goods and services in one year are valued at the prices of other years to eliminate the effect of inflation, which can be chained, but this deviates from the notion of one market price. There is no common market of the society this year with the same society as the preceding year, and no goods can be sold and transferred back in time.

The labour theory of value and the distinction between productive and unproductive work, two important contributions of Marxist economics, have not been sufficiently anchored in historical materialism. This can, in turn, be explained by the fact that Marxists, including Marx himself, have theorised productive labour as specific to a capitalist economy, rather than to human societies in general. The focus on the special case of capitalism has confused some of the crucial features of the labour value theory and the distinction between productive and unproductive labour. As explanations of the mechanisms of capitalism, the two Marxist contributions are redundant, precisely what is shown by neoclassical economists. The two contributions are essential if we want to situate and compare the capitalist economy in the broader setting of the evolution of human society. For example, the labour theory is redundant to explain price formation at the market, but most non-capitalist societies in history did not price their products. To analyse past non-market sectors, mainstream economists suggest we should use shadow prices, but that means that we are valuing past GDP mostly by prices that actually never existed. The working time to produce various goods is the actual, non-fictitious weight that could be used to make such a comparison, but Marxists at the same time only use the labour theory of value to analyse capitalist society and consider non-capitalist production, including unpaid domestic services, as unproductive.

Marxist labour value theory states that the value comes from work. Capital is therefore not productive, only labour is. Women are not less productive than men. Rather there occurs a transfer of embodied labour value from women to men. Employing natural degradation as weights instead of prices or labour values (for example, CO_2 emissions), although a much more difficult endeavour, has the potential to expose how the West has exploited the rest of the world by using up the natural resources at the disposal for future generations.

Various Marxist theories distinguish what is socially and technologically necessary beyond the price tags attached. Labour productivity is usually used as a measure of technological development. However, technology is about changing a material world, not a fictitious world, for example, an imagined reality of ownership rights and monetary relations. The socially constructed fictitious world is free of technological constraints, given that it does not exist physically. While Marxists are often accused of being ideological, it may be the other way around. This book suggests that official national accounts reflect a capitalist perspective on social relations, describing capitalism as technologically rather than socially necessary. Such a perspective should not be mixed up with a political stance, i.e., that a socialist system is superior to a capitalist either ethically or in terms of efficiency. This book does not take an evaluative stance. A capitalist system may still be superior because it is more efficient, more ethical, or both. We should bear in mind that the Marxist contribution to productive and unproductive labour and the labour value theory actually is a development of Classical economics. While Adam Smith, Ricardo and Mill advocated free trade, they still regarded trade as unproductive.

A common criticism from heterodox economists of mainstream growth models is their neoclassical assumptions (Jesus & McCombie, 2020), entailing that social relations are reduced to the technical conditions of the production function. Various extensions of the Solow model attempt to explain why the convergence predicted by the Solow model has not occurred, but are usually based either on a similar reductionism of social relation to technical ones or the incorporation of other factors as external to the model similar to Solow's treatment of total factor productivity. All agents are assumed to have perfect information and act rationally. The concept of zero transaction costs is indirectly retained by assuming that all market activities are productive, even if some models incorporate institutions as exogenous factors (Breton, 2004).

The formal outline presented in this book implicates that a genuine model of economic growth should not treat socially reproductive activities as a productive activity with a specific technical relationship between inputs and outputs. In any growth model, labour should be divided between productive and socially reproductive labour (if not considered labour that is neither productive nor socially reproductive). The concept of capital is also in need of further reformulations in such models.

Theories of the evolution of human society are based on concepts such as institutions, production and social relations. In this book, it is proposed that the differentiation between unproductive and productive activities is crucial to understand the long-term dynamics of society. The concept of what constitutes agency and individuality and whether production is a distinctly human activity may in itself be further investigated. If the demarcations of what an agent is are widened, the concepts of this book could be applied to non-human life. All life, and even a possible machine culture, transforms exterior nature to reproduce. This process is similar to how humans produce, work and consume. The purpose of production, work and consumption normally involves the increase of free energy in one sphere by decreasing the free energy in other spheres. Consumption destroys properties and therefore tends to decrease the ordered structure of the transformed matter, but the final consumption usually increases the ordered structure of the agent of consumption. Production tends to increase the ordered structure of the matter of transformation, but it comprises consumption, which tends to decrease the ordered structure. Work tends to decrease the ordered structure of the agent. The natural environment is the existential precondition for all life and its transforming processes.

6   The contribution of this book

The purpose of this book

This book professes the need to formally redefine the basic economic concepts of production, work and consumption with the aim to be relevant to all human societies and not just to today's economic policy. How the production boundary is expressed by the *System of National Accounts* (SNA) is inconsistent from a scientific perspective. For example, while some non-market and illegal services are classified as productive, others are not. Services and goods are treated differently. The so-called third-person criterion, advocated by many feminist economists, is in some aspects trans-historical and consistent but misses other key attributes of production, such as intentionality, satisfaction of human needs and the differentiation between productive and unproductive work. Although the third-person criterion is wider than the market principle to define the production boundary, one interpretation, as in the criticism of the criterion by Wood (1997), is that the possible world is a market economy, which non-market economies are ultimately reduced to.

Important issues concern how to deal with coercion, double counting, self-reference of transaction costs, human capital formation and non-market activities. The answers are different in various theoretical traditions – for example, Classical, Neoclassical, Institutional, Marxist, Feminist and Keynesian Economics.

The intent of this book is not to side with heterodox economics against the mainstream conception of GDP and economic growth. Various theories and measures serve their purposes. The intent of this book is rather to discuss the limits of various frameworks for some analytical purposes, how competing conceptualisations may be related and synthesised, and why a theory of human evolution, or intelligent life in general, may require a trans-historical formalisation. Modern national accounts and economics have developed a high level of sophistication, which reflect general insights into human conditions, and may therefore be used as a starting point for further investigations.

What humans can produce depends on a number of factors: their technological skills, the number of persons involved in the production process, how

DOI: 10.4324/9781003057017-6

they cooperate and the available natural resources. People throughout history have consciously changed themselves, other human beings and the non-human nature for various purposes. A theory of human history should examine these interactions and attempt – if possible – to define, measure and predict them.

Despite the large differences between various definitions of production, there is a core of common assumptions and intuitive understandings across paradigmatic and historical borders. Measuring production and productivity is eventually about measuring the capacity of humans in changing their exterior physical environment in order to satisfy human needs. Differences occur in what that exactly means. Only a more formalised approach can clarify these differences. The various definitions proposed in chapter 4 could fulfil different analytical purposes. In this respect, this book attempts at synthesising seemingly incompatible paradigms.

Production, work and consumption

In chapter 4, production, work and consumption are defined as relations between three events, an agent and a subject matter and reduced to non-economic sentences. First-order logic is used, complemented with modal operators for some of the sentences. It is proposed that production, work and consumption all fulfil three conditions: (1) they comprise of a physical transformation of a subject matter, entailing that some properties of the latter are destroyed, and some are added, (2) the transformation is intentionally caused by an agent and (3) the subject matter must be exterior to the agent. A feature of the third-person criterion is that delegation of a task cannot involve the delegation of oneself. Therefore, all types of self-reproduction, purposeful transformation of oneself, are excluded from the definition of production and work. The purpose of final consumption must lie in the activity itself or in the transformation of the agent. A production activity must potentially be able to cause the satisfaction of human needs, or final consumption, by adding new useful properties to the matter, which is not a condition for work nor required by the third-person criterion. For work, the purpose of transforming the matter must not lie in the transformation of the agent. Products can be generated that will not be consumed, for example, goods that are wasted. Productivity is measured by the changes in the physical world and not the subjective or inter-subjective utility derived from such a change.

In this study, various definitions of production are presented:

1   Under the articulation of non-social production, all socially reproductive activities are put outside the production boundary, which comes close to the distinction made by Classical and Marxist economists between productive and unproductive work. This book uses a criterion

applied by the institutional economist Cheung to identify transaction costs as costs that would not occur in a Robinson Crusoe economy. The mental construct of a Robinson Crusoe economy is in no way evaluative – such an economy would not even be desirable. It is merely used as a theoretical tool to analytically identify which work is technologically necessary and which is, as Marx (1969: 289) puts it, "necessary only because of the faulty social relations". Social reproduction involves either the forceful transformation of a person or the transformation of a person's intentional actions under the condition of conflicting interests. The income from capital stems from capital as a social form, i.e., from social power, not from capital as a physical entity. The activity of a capitalist is, therefore, social reproduction, not a productive contribution, which also relates to the Marxist theory of labour value and exploitation.

2   The formulation of comprehensive production is close to the third-person criterion, but the possible causation of future final consumption is included as a condition for productive activity. This definition relates to the assumptions of no transaction costs in some neoclassical modes. Trade causes final consumption through the transformation of ownership rights to a matter, which, in turn, involves the transformation of the agent's minds' (old and new owners). Social reproduction that likely causes or overlaps with final consumption fulfils the criterion of comprehensive production, but not non-social production. Social reproduction can be coercive or non-coercive.

3   Under the definitions of time frame independent production, human capital formation and work travel are included in the production boundary.

4   Humanity exterior production only includes the transformation of non-persons. It is close to Adam Smith's notion of productive labour as well as the Soviet Material Product System.

5   Market production comes close to Keynesian theory and the present notion of SNA, with the difference that it excludes non-market goods production. It requires a type of household exteriority where the household is considered an agent.

From a historical materialist position, it is important to distinguish between material conditions and ideas of these conditions. We must also separate language from meta-language to avoid circularity and self-reference. Although it is true, as suggested by Marshall, that trade rearranges matter, the mental objects associated with ownership rights have no independent material existence per se – they are imagined in the same ways as a character of a fantasy novel that is unrestricted by the laws of physics. Counting the change in ownership of a product, a change in the mental object associated with the physical product, as an addition to total aggregate production involves double counting and confuses language with meta-language. By reducing mental objects to physical objects, i.e., social relations to technical conditions, the neoclassical tradition mixes up the physical relation between humans and their exterior world with how this relation is imagined. For example, while we as material beings are able to decide that an infinite number of transactions of equal value was made during a limited period, in an infinite regress, this infinite amount is entirely imagined and meaningless as a material equivalent that can be quantified in national accounts (the sum of a geometric series of declining values is, however, not infinite). Philosophically, realists and idealists form incompatible paradigms. However, a naïve realist position, de facto the conduct of neoclassical models, is that there is no difference between how we perceive reality and reality itself. A naïve realist position, in its extension, opens up for idealism since it equates ideas with reality.

Can formalisation of definitions be driven too far?

One question is whether overly formalised and too exact definitions can be counterproductive for science. Should not science occupy itself mainly with the empirical world? Does a different formulation of GDP add any new knowledge about the economy? Should not social sciences use the natural language of society? The history of science shows that formalised definitions matter under some circumstances. What we can investigate is limited by our concepts. Determining which definition is most suitable for a specific analytical purpose is likewise a scientific question if testable according to specific criteria.

Although it may be argued that the concepts of production, work and consumption are far too complex to be expressed using formal logic, the purpose of this book is not to present a fixed way of how to articulate these notions. It must be stressed that the definitions presented in this book likely contain flaws and should be further problematised and re-elaborated. They are, at best, sketchy suggestions to promote interdisciplinary dialogues on this subject. More precision often generates more problems and questions. More complicated logic could be applied, for example, fuzzy logic that recognises partial truths (Selase et al., 2015), although more complexity could diminish relational oversight. The formalisation of causation is in need of further revisions, not least how to specify causation of final consumption or to identify intentional and social causation. During the writing of this book over several years, the various definitions had been reformulated numerous times and, if given more time, would most likely have been reformulated further. This hermeneutic circle has not been fully visualised in this book.

Even natural science may not always rest on a clear conceptual framework. Ancient Greeks counted the moon as a planet. Until recently, there was no clear definition of a planet. When Eris was discovered, it turned out to be as large as Pluto, which was defined as a planet. It caused a debate on what constitutes a planet. There was much resistance against declassifying Pluto as a dwarf planet. Nevertheless, having a clear notion of a planet is essential as it reflects our understanding of the mechanism and evolution of the solar system. As argued by Steven Soter (2006):

> Attempts to define "planet" in terms of upper and lower mass limits have not been satisfactory. An upper mass limit corresponding to the onset of deuterium fusion is complicated by the existence of some brown dwarfs in close orbits around stars... A lower mass limit to distinguish planets from smaller nonplanets is also problematic... Nature does, however, provide a suitable criterion for planetary status based on a wide gap in a physically significant parameter, namely, the measure of the extent to which a body dominates the other masses in its orbital zone... Brown... proposed a definition of "planet" based on the natural division of objects into solitary bodies and members of populations... A modification of Brown's definition can link it explicitly to the dynamics of planet formation: a planet is a body that has swept up or scattered most of the mass from its orbital zone in the accretion disk around a central star or substar.

Similarly, the articulation of the production boundary impacts the analysis of the long-term economic growth and evolution of human society. For example, models of growth depend on what should be included in production and capital. A theory of history depends on whether material or ideal conditions are seen as the principal driving force. An alternative production boundary may treat all wars as unproductive. A production measure including human capital formation grows faster during expansions of the education system. The notion of market production could serve crucial analytical purposes, for example, to investigate the relation between money supply and inflation, but should be rid of inconsistencies such as the inclusion of non-market goods production. In the Marxist tradition, there would be no fantastic growth in Irish GDP in 2015, simply because income from copyrights is not based on performed work, but on ownership, i.e., social power. Whereas the definition of a planet should be appropriate for the analysis of the dynamics of planet formation in all solar systems, a definition of production, work and consumption should be relevant for the analysis of the dynamics of society and economy during the entire human history, or even intelligent life in general.

The need for clear definitions for some scientific purposes must be made in recognition of, but not eclipsed by, the fuzziness of the world. Even in physics, a celestial body may have not completely swept up most of the mass from its orbital zone without necessarily implying that the new definition of a planet is deficient. "Most of the mass" is somewhat vague, but for the purpose of the definition of a planet, the current degree of vagueness may be desirable at the same time as the higher precision accomplished by the new articulation is motivated from the point of view of studying planet formations. The definition of a planet may undergo further changes in the future, but it will most likely not return to the state before reclassifying Pluto as a dwarf planet. Modern national accounts are far from fuzzy in that there are very specific instructions on what to include in the production boundary, without that implicating a very coherent definition.

Bibliography

Abramovitz, M., 1956. Resource and Output Trends in the United States since 1870. *American Economic Review*, Volume 46, pp. 5–23.

Acemoglu, D., Johnson, S. & Robinson, J. A., 2002. Reversal of Fortune: Geography and Institutions in the Making of the Modern World Income Distribution. *Quarterly Journal of Economics*, Volume 118, pp. 1231–1294.

Acemoglu, D., Johnson, S. & Robinson, J. A., 2005. The Rise of Europe: Atlantic Trade, Institutional Change and Economic Growth. *American Economic Review*, Volume 95, pp. 546–579.

Allen, M., 2016. Hunter-gatherer conflict: The last bastion of the pacified past?. In: M. Allen & T. Jones, eds. *Violence and warfare among hunter-gatherers*. London; New York: Routledge, pp. 15–46.

Allen, R., 2003. *Farm to Factory; A Reinterpretation of the Soviet Industrial Revolution*. Princeton: Princeton University Press.

Alvey, J., 2003. *Adam Smith's View on History: Consistent or Paradoxical?* s.l.: Massey University. https://core.ac.uk/download/pdf/7082591.pdf

Amthor, J. & Baldocchi, D., 2001. Terrestrial higher plant respiration and net primary production. In: *Terrestrial global productivity*. San Diego: Academic Press, pp. 33–59.

Anscombe, G. E. M., 1957. *Intention*. Oxford: Basil Blackwell.

Aquinas, T., 1981. *Summa Theologica*. English Dominican Fathers ed. s.l.: New York.

Aristotle, 1976. *Ethics*. London: Penguin.

Aristotle, n.d. *Economics*. [Online] Available at: http://perseus.uchicago.edu/perseus-cgi/citequery3.pl?dbname=GreekFeb2011&query=Arist.%20Oec.&getid=1

Aristotle, n.d. *Politics*. [Online] Available at: http://www.gutenberg.org/files/6762/6762-h/6762-h.htm

Arrow, K., 1962. The Economic Implications of Learning by Doing. *Review of Economic Studies*, Volume XXIX, pp. 155–173.

Árvay, J., 1994. The material product system (MPS): A retrospective. In: *The accounts of nations*. Amsterdam, Oxford, Washington DC, and Tokyo: IOS Press.

Backhouse, R., 2000. Austrian Economics and the Mainstream: View from the Boundary. *Quarterly Journal of Austrian Economics*, Volume 3(2), pp. 31–43.

Baran, P., 1957. *The Political Economy of Growth*. New York: Monthly Review Press.

Beall, J., Glanzberg, M. & Ripley, D., 2020. *"Liar Paradox", The Stanford Encyclopedia of Philosophy (Fall 2020 Edition)*, E. N. Zalta (ed.). [Online] Available at: https://plato.stanford.edu/archives/fall2020/entries/liar-paradox/ [Accessed 25 December 2021].

Becker, G., 1980. *A Treatise on the Family.* Cambridge, Massachusetts, and London: Harvard University Press.

Becker, G., 1994. *Human Capital: A Theoretical and Empirical Analysis with Special Reference to Education.* Third Edition ed. Chicago: The University of Chicago Press.

Bhattacharya, T. & Vogel, L., 2017. *Social Reproduction Theory: Remapping Class, Recentering Oppression.* London: Pluto Press.

Blattner, C. E., Coulter, K. & Kymlicka, W., 2020. *Animal Labour, A New Frontier of Interspecies Justice?.* Oxford: Oxford University Press.

Bolander, T., 2017. "Self-Reference", *The Stanford Encyclopedia of Philosophy (Fall 2017 Edition),* E. N. Zalta (ed.). [Online] Available at: https://plato.stanford.edu/archives/fall2017/entries/self-reference/ [Accessed 25 12 2021].

Bolt, J. & van Zanden, J. L., 2014. The Maddison Project: Collaborative Research on Historical National Accounts. *The Economic History Review,* Volume 67(3), pp. 627–651.

Bossen, L., 1989. Women and economic institutions. In: S. Plattner, ed. *Economic anthropology.* Stanford: Stanford University Press.

Bostrom, N., 2003. When Machines Outsmart Humans. *Futures,* Volume 35, pp. 759–764.

Bourdieu, P., 1986. The forms of capital. In: J. Richardson, ed. *Handbook of theory and research for the sociology of education.* New York: Greenwood, pp. 241–258.

Braunschweig, B. & Ghallab, M. eds., 2021. *Reflections on Artificial Intelligence for Humanity.* Switzerland: Springer.

Breton, T., 2004. Can Institutions or Education Explain World Poverty?. *Journal of Socio-Economics,* Volume 33, pp. 45–69.

Brewer, A., 1988. Cantillon and the Land Theory of Value. *History of Political Economy,* Volume 20(1), pp. 1–14.

Broadberry, S. et al., 2015. *British Economic Growth, 1270–1870.* Cambridge: Cambridge University Press.

Brundage, B. C., 1979. *The Fifth Sun: Aztec Gods, Aztec World.* Texas: University of Texas Press.

Brynjolfsson, E., Hu, Y. & Smith, M., 2003. Consumer Surplus in the Digital Economy: Estimating the Value of Increased Product Variety at Online Booksellers. *Management Science,* Volume 49(11), pp. 1445–1615.

Cámara, S., 2006. A Value-Oriented Distinction Between Productive and Unproductive Labour. *Capital & Class,* Volume 30, pp. 37–63.

Cameron, R., 2018. "Infinite Regress Arguments", *The Stanford Encyclopedia of Philosophy (Fall 2018 Edition),* E. N. Zalta (ed.). [Online] Available at: https://plato.stanford.edu/archives/fall2018/entries/infinite-regress/ [Accessed 25 December 2021].

Cantillon, R., 2010. *Essay on Economic Theory.* Auburn, Alabama: Mises Institute.

Carchedi, G., 1991. *Frontiers of Political Economy.* London, New York: Verso.

Cashdan, E., 1989. Hunters and gatherers: Economic behaviour in bands. In: S. Plattner, ed. *Economic anthropology.* Stanford: Stanford University Press.

Cellan-Jones, R., 2014. *Stephen Hawking Warns Artificial Intelligence Could End Mankind.* [Online] Available at: https://www.bbc.com/news/technology-30290540 [Accessed 09 11 2021].

Central Statistics Office [Ireland], 2016. *National Income and Expenditure Annual Results.* [Online] Available at: https://www.cso.ie/en/releasesandpublications/er/nie/nationalincomeandexpenditureannualresults2015/ [Accessed 10 10 2021].

Cheung, S. N. S., 2005. *Economic Explanation.* Hong Kong: Arcadia Press.

Clark, J. B., 1891. Distribution as Determined by a Law of Rent. *Quarterly Journal of Economics*, Volume 5(3), pp. 289–318.

Clingingsmitha, D. & Williamson, J., 2008. Deindustrialization in 18th and 19th century India: Mughal decline, climate shocks and British industrial ascent. *Explorations in Economic History*, Volume 45(3), pp. 209–234.

Clutton-Brock, T. H. & Parker, G. A., 1996. Punishment in Animal Societies. *Nature*, Volume 273, pp. 209–216.

Coase, R., 1960. The Problem of Social Cost. *Journal of Law & Economics*, Volume 3(October), pp. 1–44.

Coase, R., 1992. The Institutional Structure of Production. *The American Economic Review, Sep., 1992, Vol. 82, No. 4 (Sep., 1992)*, Volume 82(4), pp. 713–719.

Cohen, A. & Harcourt, G. C., 2003. Whatever Happened to the Cambridge Capital Theory Controversies?. *Journal of Economic Perspectives*, Volume 17(1), pp. 199–214.

Colander, D., 2000. The Death of Neoclassical Economics. *Journal of the History of Economic Thought*, Volume 22(2), pp. 127–143.

Colgan, J., 2013. *Petro-Aggression*. Cambridge: Cambridge University Press.

Confucius, 2015. *The Analects of Confucius: A Teaching Translation*. s.l.: s.n. https://scholarworks.iu.edu/dspace/bitstream/handle/2022/23420/Analects_of_Confucius_%28Eno-2015%29-updated.pdf?

Cosimo, P., 2019. *Unproductive Labour in the Political Economy: The History of an Idea*. London and New York: Routledge.

Coyle, D., 2014. *GDP: A brief But Affectionate History*. Princeton: Princeton University Press.

Crespi, B. & Yanega, D., 1995. The Definition of Eusociality. *Behavioral Ecology*, Volume 6(1), pp. 109–115.

Cronin, B., 2001. Productive and Unproductive Capital: A mapping of the New Zealand system of national accounts to classical economic categories, 1972–95. *Review of Political Economy*, Volume 13(3), pp. 309–327.

Czaczkes, T., Czaczkes, B., Iglhaut, C. & Heinze, J., 2015. Composite Collective Decision-Making. *Proceedings of the Royal Society B*, Volume 282, p. 20142723.

Darwin, 1889. *The Descent of Man and Selection in Relation to Sex*. New York: D. Appleton and Company.

Davidson, D., 1980. *Essays on Actions and Events*. Oxford: Oxford University Press.

Dawkins, R., 1976. *The Selfish Gene*. Oxford: Oxford University Press.

Domar, E., 1946. Capital Expansion, Rate of Growth, and Employment. *Econometrica*, Volume 14(2), pp. 137–147.

Domar, E., 1946. Capital Expansion, Rate of Growth, and Employment. *Econometrica*, Volume 14, pp. 137–147.

Dore, M., 1996. The Problem of Valuation in Neoclassical Environmental Economics. *Environmental Ethics*, Volume 18(1), pp. 65–70.

Doucouliagos, H. & Ulubaşoğlu, M. A., 2008. Democracy and Economic Growth: A Meta-Analysis. *American Journal of Political Science*, Volume 52(1), pp. 61–83.

Douy-Rheims_version, 1609. *The Holy Bible*. s.l.: s.n. http://triggs.djvu.org/djvu-editions.com/BIBLES/DRV/Download.pdf

Dretske, F., 1988. *Explaining Behaviour: Reasons in a World of Causes*. Cambridge, MA: MIT Press.

Edvinsson, R., 2005. *Growth, Accumulation, Crisis: With New Macroeconomic Data for Sweden*. Stockholm: Almqvist & Wiksell.

Edvinsson, R., 2013. New Annual Estimates of Swedish GDP in 1800–2010. *The Economic History Review*, Volume 66, pp. 1101–1126.

Edvinsson, R., 2013. Swedish GDP 1620–1800: Stagnation or Growth?. *Cliometrica*, Volume 7(1), pp. 37–60.

Edvinsson, R., 2015. Recalculating Swedish pre-census demographic data: Was there acceleration in early modern population growth?. *Cliometrica*, Volume 9(2), pp. 167–191.

Edvinsson, R. & Nordlund Edvinsson, T., 2017. New Estimates of Time Use in Sweden 1950–2012. *Journal of European Economic History*, Volume XLVI(2), pp. 77–113.

Eigenraam, M. & Obst, C., 2018. Extending the Production Boundary of the System of National Accounts (SNA) to Classify and Account for Ecosystem Services. *Ecosystem Health and Sustainability*, Volume 4(11), pp. 247–260.

Eisner, M., 2013. What causes large-scale variation in homicide rates?. In: H. Kortüm & J. Heinze, eds. *Aggression in humans and other primates: Biology, Psychology, Sociology*. Berlin; Boston: De Gruyter, pp. 137–161.

Ellerman, D., 2021. *Putting Jurisprudence Back Into Economics: What is Really Wrong With Today's Neoclassical Theory*. Cham, Switzerland: Springer.

Eltis, W., 2000. *The Classical Theory of Economic Growth*. Second Edition. Basingstoke: Palgrave.

Felipe, J., 2006. A Decade of Debate About the Sources of Growth in East Asia. How Much do we Know About Why Some Countries Grow Faster Than Others?. *Estudios de Economía Aplicada*, Volume 24(1), pp. 181–220.

Felipe, J. & Fisher, F., 2003. Aggregation in Production Functions: What Applied Economists Should Know. *Metroeconomica – International Review of Economics*, Volume 54(2&3), pp. 208–262.

Fioramonti, L., 2017. *The World after GDP: Economics, Politics and International Relations in the Post-Growth Era*. Cambridge; Malden: Polity.

Fogel, R., 1964. *American Economic Growth: Essays in Econometric History*. Baltimore: The Johns Hopkins Press.

Folbre, N. & Wagman, B., 1993. Counting Housework: New Estimates of Real Product in the United States, 1800–1860. *The Journal of Economic History*, Volume 53(2), pp. 275–288.

Foray, D., 2004. *The Economics of Knowledge*. Cambridge and London: The MIT Press.

Foray, D., 2004. *The Economics of Knowledge*. Cambridge and London: The MIT Press.

Foucault, M., 1991. *Discipline and Punish: The Birth of a Prison*. London: Penguin.

Fuentes, A., 2018. How Humans and Apes are Different, and Why it Matters. *Journal of Anthropological Research*, Volume 74(2), pp. 151–167.

Galor, O., 2011. *Unified Growth Theory*. Princeton; Oxford: Princeton University Press.

Galor, O. & Weil, D. N., 2000. Population, Technology, and Growth: From Malthusian Stagnation to the Demographic Transition and Beyond. *American Economic Review*, Volume 90(4), pp. 806–828.

Garson, J., 2021. *"Modal Logic", The Stanford Encyclopedia of Philosophy (Summer 2021 Edition)*, E. N. Zalta (ed.). [Online] Available at: https://plato.stanford.edu/archives/sum2021/entries/logic-modal/ [Accessed 2 January 2022].

Georgescu-Roegen, N., 1975. Energy and Economic Myths. *Southern Economic Journal*, Volume 41, pp. 347–381.

George, T., 2021. *"Hermeneutics", The Stanford Encyclopedia of Philosophy (Fall 2021 Edition)*, E. N. Zalta (ed.). [Online] Available at: https://plato.stanford.edu/archives/fall2021/entries/hermeneutics/ [Accessed 25 December 2021].

Gerschenkron, A., 1947. The Soviet Indices of Industrial Production. *The Review of Economic Statistics*, Volume 29(4), pp. 217–226.

Gershuny, J., 2011. *Time-Use Surveys and the Measurement of National Well-Being.* Swansea: Office for National Statistics.

Gittinger, J., 2017. The Rhetoric of Violence, Religion and Purity in India's Cow Protection Movement. *Journal of Religion and Violence*, Volume 5(2), p. 131–149.

Goldschmidt-Clermont, L., 1993. Monetary Valuation of Non-Market Productive Time – Methodological Considerations. *Review of Income and Wealth*, Volume 39(4), pp. 419–433.

Goldstone, J., 1996. Gender, work and culture: Why the Industrial Revolution Came Early to England But Late to China. *Sociological Perspectives*, Volume 39(1), pp. 1–21.

Graeber, D., 2011. *Debt: The First 5,000 Years.* Brooklyn, N.Y.: Melville House.

Gray, R., 2020. The Extended Kardashev Scale. *The Astronomical Journal*, Volume 159(228), pp. 1–5.

Greenstone, G., 2010. The History of Bloodletting. *BC Medical Journal*, Volume 52(1), pp. 12–14.

Grether, D. & Plott, C., 1979. Economic Theory of Choice and the Preference Reversal Phenomenon. *American Economic Review*, Volume 69, pp. 623–638.

Grytten, O., 2021. Revising Growth History: New Estimates of GDP for Norway, 1816–2019. *The Economic History Review*, Volume 75, pp. 181–202.

Habib, I., 2017. Colonialism, Towards a Political Economy of Colonialism. *Social Scientist*, Volume 45(3/4), pp. 9–15.

Haldon, J., 1993. *The State & the Tributary Mode of Production.* London; New York: Verso.

Hamilton, W. D., 1964. The Genetical Evolution of Social Behavior. *Journal of Theoretical Biology*, Volume 7(1), pp. 1–16.

Hanly, P. & Sheerin, C., 2017. Valuing Informal Care in Ireland: Beyond the Traditional Production Boundary. *The Economic and Social Review, Economic and Social Studies*, Volume 48(3), pp. 337–364.

Harris, S., 2011. Does Anātman Rationally Entail Altruism? On Bodhicaryāvatāra 8:101–103. *Journal of Buddhist Ethics*, Volume 18, pp. 93–123.

Harrod, R., 1939. An Essay in Dynamic Theory. *The Economic Journal*, Volume XLIX, pp. 14–33.

Harrod, R., 1939. An Essay in Dynamic Theory. *The Economic Journal*, Volume XLIX (March), pp. 14–33.

Hayek, F., 2008. *The Pure Theory of Capital.* New York and London: Routledge.

Hegel, G. W. F., 1875. *Logic: Being Part of the Encyclopaedia of the Philosophical Sciences.* London: Oxford University Press.

Heinze, J., 2004. Reproductive Conflict in Insect Societies. *Advances in the Study of Behavior*, Volume 34(1), pp. 1–57.

Himmelweit, S., 1995. The Discovery of "Unpaid Work": The Social Consequences of the Expansion of "Work". *Feminist Economics*, Volume 1(2), pp. 1–19.

Ho, D., 1995. Selfhood and Identity in Confucianism, Taoism, Buddhism, and Hinduism: Contrasts With the West. *Journal for the Theory of Social Behaviour*, Volume 25(2), pp. 115–139.

Hoefman, K., Bramson, A., Schoors, K. & Ryckebusch, J., 2018. The Impact of Functional and Social Value on the Price of Goods. *PLOS ONE*.

Hoekstra, R., 2019. *Replacing GDP by 2030: Towards a Common Language flr the Well-being and Sustainability Community.* Cambridge, UK: Cambridge University Press.

Holmes, G. S., 1977. Gregory King and the Social Structure of Pre-Industrial England. *Transactions of the Royal Historical Society*, Volume 27, pp. 41–68.

Hoover, K., 1990. The Logic of Causal Inference: Econometrics and Conditional Analysis of Causation. *Economics and Philosophy*, Volume 6, pp. 207–234.

Houston, D., 1997. Productive-Unproductive Labor: Rest in Peace. *Review of Radical Political Economic*, Volume 29(1), pp. 131–139.

Humphries, J. & Weisdorf, J., 2015. The Wages of Women in England, 1260–1850. *The Journal of Economic History*, Volume 75(2), pp. 405–447.

Hyde, D. & Raffman, D., 2018. *"Sorites Paradox", The Stanford Encyclopedia of Philosophy (Summer 2018 Edition)*, Edward N. Zalta (ed.). [Online] Available at: https://plato.stanford.edu/archives/sum2018/entries/sorites-paradox/ [Accessed 25 December 2021].

Iamblichus, 1918. *The Life of Pythagoras*. Los Angeles: Theosophical Publishing House.

ILO et al., 2004. *Consumer Price Index Manual: Theory and Practice*. Geneva: ILO.

IMDb, 2020. *IMDb*. [Online] Available at: https://www.imdb.com/title/tt11464826/characters/nm7270893

International Monetary Fund et al., 2004. *Producer Price Index Manual: Theory and Practice*. Washington: s.n.

Inter-Secretariat Working Group on National Accounts, 1993. *System of National Accounts 1993*. Brussels; Luxembourg; New York; Paris; Washington: Inter-Secretariat Working Group on National Accounts.

Ironmonger, D., 1996. Priorities for Research on Nonmarket Work. *Feminist Economics*, Volume 2, pp. 149–152.

Itani, T., 2014. *Quaran: English Translation*. Dallas, Beirut: ClearQuran.

Jesus, F. & McCombie, J., 2020. The Illusions of Calculating Total Factor Productivity and Testing Growth Models: From Cobb-Douglas to Solow to Romer. *Journal of Post-Keynesian Economics*, Volume 43(3), p. 470–513.

Jevons, S., 1871. *The Theory of Political Economy*. London: Macmillan and Co.

Jonas, P. S. H., 1970. The Gerschenkron Effect: A Re-Examination. *The Review of Economics and Statistics*, Volume 52(1), pp. 82–86.

Jones, C. & Klenow, P., 2016. Beyond GDP? Welfare across Countries and Time. *American Economic Review*, Volume 106(9), pp. 2426–2457.

Jonsson, G., 1997. Non-market production: What to count and how?. In: J. Eloranta, ed. *Nordiska historiska nationalräkenskaper – Workshop 2 i Järvenpää 20–22 september 1996*.Jyväskylä: University of Jyväskylä.

Kalenkoski, C. & Foster, G., 2016. *The Economics of Multitasking*. New York: Palgrave Macmillan US.

Kallio, K.-M., Kallio, T. & Grossi, G., 2017. Performance Measurement in Universities: Ambiguities in the Use of Quality Versus Quantity in Performance Indicators. *Public Money & Management*, Volume 37(4), pp. 293–300.

Kardashev, N., 1964. Transmission of Information by Extraterrestial Civilizations. *Soviet Astronomy*, Volume 8(2), pp. 217–221.

Kautilya, 1915. *Kautilya's Arthasastra*. Bangalore: Government Press.

Kautilya, V., 2000. *The Kautilya Arthasastra, Part II, An English Translation with Critical and Explanatory Notes*. Delhi: Motilal Banarsidass.

Kelly, K., 1994. *Out of Control: The New Biology of Machines, Social Systems and the Economic World*. Boston: Addison-Wesley.

Keynes, 2010. How to pay for the war. In: D. Moggridge, ed. *Essays in persuasions*. London: Palgrave Macmillan.

Keynes, J. M., 1973. *The General Theory of Empoyment, Interest and Money.* London; Basinstoke: MacMillan; Cambridge University Press.

Khaldun, I., 1967. *Abd Ar Rahman bin Muhammed.* s.l.: s.n. http://www.muslimphilosophy. com/ik/Muqaddimah/

Kim, J., 1973. Causation, Nomic Subsumption, and the Concept of Event. *Journal of Philosophy*, Volume 70, pp. 217–236.

Kitcher, P., 1994. Four ways of "Biologizing" ethics. In: E. Sober, ed. *Conceptual issues in evolutionary Biology.* Cambridge, Massachusetts: The MIT Press, pp. 439–451.

Ko, K. H., 2016. Origins of Human Intelligence: The Chain of Tool-Making and Brain Evolution. *Anthropological Notebooks*, Volume 22(1), pp. 5–22.

Kramer, P. & Bressan, P., 2015. Humans as Superorganisms: How Microbes, Viruses, Imprinted Genes, and Other Selfish Entities Shape Our Behavior. *Perspectives on Psychological Science*, Volume 10(4), pp. 464–481.

Krantz, O., 1987. *Husligt arbete 1800–1980 (Historiska Nationalräkenskaper för Sverige. 6).* Lund: Ekonomisk-historiska föreningen.

Kropotkin, P., 1919. *Mutual Aid: A Factor of Evolution.* New York: Alfred A. Knopf.

Kropotkin, P., 1924. *Ethics: Origin and Development.* London; Calcutta; Sydney: George G. Harrap and Co.

Krugman, P., 2017. *Leprechaun Economics, With Numbers.* [Online] Available at: https:// krugman.blogs.nytimes.com/2017/11/09/leprechaun-economics-with-numbers/

Kudrov, V., 1995. National Accounts and International Comparisons for the Former Soviet Union. *Scandinavian Economic History Review*, Volume 43(1), pp. 147–166.

Kuznets, S., 1934. National Income, 1929–1932. *National Bureau of Economic Research Bulletins*, 49, pp. 1–12. https://www.nber.org/system/files/chapters/c2258/c2258.pdf

Laibman, D., 1992. *Value, Technical Change and Crisis: Explorations in Marxist Economic Theory.* Armonk, New York: ME Sharpe.

Laibman, D., 1999. Productive and Unproductive Labor. A Comment. *Review of Radical Political Economy*, Volume 31(2), pp. 61–73.

Lambert, T. & Kwon, E., 2015. Monopoly Capital and Capitalist Inefficiency. *International Review of Applied Economics*, Volume 29, pp. 533–552.

Lewina, P. & Cachanosky, N., 2018. Substance and Semantics: The Question of Capital. *Journal of Economic Behavior & Organization*, Volume 218, pp. 423–431.

Lewis, D., 1973. Causation. *Journal of Philosophy*, Volume 70, pp. 556–567.

Lindahl, E., Dahlgren, E. & Kock, K., 1937. *National Income of Sweden 1861–1930, part one.* London and Stockholm: s.n.

Lindmark, M., 2019. Greening the national accounts: Basic concepts and a case study of historical environmental accounts for Sweden. In: S. Acar & E. Yeldan, eds. *Handbook of Green Economic.* s.l.: Academic Press, pp. 1–18.

Lipietz, A., 1986. Behind the Crisis: The Exhaustion of a Regime of Accumulation. A 'regulation school' Perspective on some French Empirical Work. *Review of Radical Political Economics*, Volume 18(1–2), pp. 13–32.

Lucas, R., 1988. On the Mechanics of Economic Development. *Journal of Monetary Economics*, Volume 22(1), pp. 3–42.

Lucassen, J., 2021. *The Story of Work: A New History of Humankind.* New Haven: Yale University Press.

Maddison, A., 1991. *Dynamic Forces in Capitalist Development: A Long-Run Comparative View.* New York: Oxford University Press.

Mair, S., 2020. Neoliberal Economics, Planetary Health, and the COVID-19 Pandemic: A Marxist Ecofeminist Analysis. *Lancet Planet Healt*, Volume e588–e596, p. 4.

Malthus, T., 1989. *An Essay on the Principle of Population, volume I and II*. Cambridge: Cambridge University Press.

Mankiw, G., Romer, D. & Weil, D., 1992. A Contribution to the Empirics of Economic Growth. *The Quarterly Journal of Economics*, Volume 107(2), pp. 407–436.

Marginson, S., 1998. Value Creation in the Production of Services: A Note on Marx. *Cambridge Journal of Economics*, Volume 22(5), pp. 573–585.

Marquetti, A., 2003. Analyzing Historical and Regional Patterns of Technical Change From a Classical-Marxian Perspective. *Journal of Economic Behavior & Organization*, Volume 52, pp. 191–200.

Marshall, A., 1890. *Principles of Economics, Volume 1*. New York: MacMillan and co.

Marshall, A., 1997. *Principles of Economics*. New York: Prometheus books.

Martin, J., 1827. *An Account of the Natives of the Tonga Islands, in the South Pacific Ocean, vol 1*. Third ed. London: Edinburgh, Constable and Co., and Hurst, Chance and Co.

Marx, K., 1956. *The Poverty of Philosophy*. Moscow: Foreign Languages Publishing House.

Marx, K., 1965. *Capital, Volume I*. Moscow: Progress Publishers.

Marx, K., 1966. *Capital, Volume III*. Moscow: Progress Publishers.

Marx, K., 1967. *Capital, Volume II*. Moscow: Progress Publishers.

Marx, K., 1969. *Theories of Surplus Value: Volume IV of Capital, Part I*. Moscow: Progress Publishers.

Marx, K., 1977. *A Contribution to the Critique of Political Economy*. Moscow: Progress Publishers.

Marx, K., 1993. *Grundrisse: Foundations of the Critique of Political Economy (Rough Draft)*. London: Penguin Books.

Maslow, A., 1943. A Theory of Human Motivation. *Psychological Review*, Volume 50(4), p. 396.

May, C., 2002. The Political Economy of Proximity: Intellectual Property and the Global Division of Information Labour. *New Political Economy*, Volume 7(3), pp. 317–342.

Ma, Y. & de Jong, H., 2017. Unfolding the Turbulent Century: A Reconstruction of China's Historical National Accounts, 1840–1912. *Review of Income and Wealth*, Volume 65(1), pp. 75–98.

Meek, R., 1973. *Studies in the Labour Theory of Value*. 2nd ed. London: Lawrence and Wishart.

Menger, C., 2007. *Principle of Economics*. Auburn: Ludwig von Mises Institute.

Menzel, C., 2021. *"Modal Logic", The Stanford Encyclopedia of Philosophy (Summer 2021 Edition)*, E. N. Zalta (ed.). [Online] Available at: https://plato.stanford.edu/archives/sum2021/entries/logic-modal/ [Accessed 30 December 2021].

Milburn, O., 2007. The Book of the Young Master of Accountancy: An Ancient Chinese Economics Text. *Journal of the Economic and Social History of the Orient*, Volume 50(1), pp. 19–40.

Mill, J. S., 1885. *Principles Of Political Economy: Abridged, with Critical, Bibliographical, and Explanatory Notes, and a Sketch of the History of Political Economy*. New York: D. Appleton And Company.

Mohun, S., 1996. Productive and unproductive labor in the labor theory of value. *Review of Radical Political Economics*, Volume 28(4), pp. 30–54.

Moldoveanua, M. & Stevenson, H., 2001. The Self as a Problem: The Intra-Personal Coordination of Conflicting Desires. *Journal of Socio-Economics*, Volume 30, pp. 295–330.

Monsalve, F., 2014. Scholastic Just Price Versus Current Market Price: Is. *The European Journal of the History of Economic Thought*, Volume 21(4), pp. 4–20.

Moraitis, A. & Copley, J., 2017. Productive and Unproductive Labour and Social Form: Putting Class Struggle in its Place. *Capital & Class*, Volume 41, pp. 91–114.

More, T., 1516. *Utopia*. s.l.: Autonomedia.

Morin, A., 2006. Levels of Consciousness and Self-Awareness: A Comparison and Integration of Various Neurocognitive Views. *Consciousness and Cognition*, Volume 15, pp. 358–371.

Nagarajan, K. V., 2011. The Code of Hammurabi: An Economic Interpretation. *International Journal of Business and Social Science*, Volume 2(8), pp. 108–116.

Nathan, O., 1944. *Nazi War Finance and Banking*. s.l.: NBER.

Nelson, J., 1995. Feminism and Economics. *The Journal of Economic Perspectives*, Volume 9(2), pp. 131–148.

Niehans, J., 1994. *A History of Economic Theory: Classic Contributions, 1720–1980*. s.l.: Softshell Books.

Nordhaus, W. & Tobin, J., 1973. Is Growth Obsolete?. In: *The Measurement of Economic and Social Performance*. s.l.: NBER, pp. 509–564.

North, D., 1991. Institutions. *Journal of Economic Perspectives*, Volume 5(1), pp. 97–112.

Nyberg, A., 1995. *Hemarbetets volym och värde*. Linköping: s.n.

Nyberg, A., 1997. Makt, kön och BNP. In: G. Ahrne & I. Persson, eds. *Familj, makt och jämställdhet: rapport till utredningen om fördelningen av ekonomisk makt och ekonomiska resurser mellan kvinnor och män, SOU 1997:138*. Stockholm: s.n.

O'Connor, J., 1975. Productive and Unproductive Labor. *Politics & Society*, Volume 5(3), pp. 297–336.

Okasha, S., 2006. *Evolution and Levels of Selection*. Oxford: Clarendon Press.

Olsen, E., 2017. Productive and unproductive labor. In: D. Brennan, D. Kristjanson-Gural, C. Mulder & E. Olsen, eds. *Routledge handbook of marxian economics*. New York: Routledge, pp. 122–134.

Perrotta, C., 2003. The Legacy of the Past: Ancient Economic Thought on Wealth and Development. *The European Journal of the History of Economic Thought*, Volume 10(2), pp. 177–229.

Perrotta, C., 2018. *Unproductive Labour in Political Economy: The History of an Idea*. London: Routledge.

Persky, J., 2000. The Neoclassical Advent: American Economics at the Turn of the 20th Century. *Journal of Economic Perspectives*, Volume 14(1), pp. 95–108.

Petty, W., 1662. *A Treatise of Taxes & Contributions*. [Online] Available at: http://www.hargaden.com/enda/wp-content/petty_taxescontributions.pdf

Petty, W., 1662. *A Treatise of Taxes and Contributions*. London: N. Brooke.

Phelps, E., 1961. The Golden Rule of Accumulation: A Fable for Growthmen. *The American Economic Review*, Volume 51(4), pp. 638–643.

Pigou, A., 1920. *The Economics of Welfare*. London: MacMillan and Co.

Pigou, A. C., 1920. *The Economics of Welfare*. London: Macmillan.

Piketty, T., 2014. *Capital in the Twenty-First Century. A. Goldhammer, Trans.* Cambridge, Mass. Cambridge, Mass: Belknap Press.

Plato, n.d. *Euthydemus*. [Online] Available at: http://perseus.uchicago.edu/perseus-cgi/citequery3.pl?dbname=GreekTexts&query=Pl.%20Euthd.&getid=1

Plekhanov, G., 1947. *The Development of the Monist View of History*. London: Lawrence & Wishart.

Quick, P., 2004. Subsistence Wages and Household Production: Clearing the Way for an Analysis of Class and Gender. *Review of Radical Political Economy*, Volume 36(1), pp. 20–36.

Rawls, J., 1972. *A Theory of Justice*. Cambridge, MA: Harvard University Press.

Reid, M., 1934. *Economics of Household Production*. New York: John Wiley and Sons.

Ricardo, D., 1969. *The Principles of Political Economy and Taxations*. London: Dent.

Riccardini, F., 2015. Towards Satellite Accounts on Education and Human Capital in OECD Countries. In: F. Maggino, ed. *A New Research Agenda for Improvements of Quality of Life*. Cham: Springer, pp. 205–230.

Roberts, K., 1999. *Leisure in Contemporary Society*. Wallingford, UK: CAB International.

Robinson, J., 1938. The Classification of Inventions. *Review of Economic Studies*, Volume V, pp. 334–361.

Robinson, J., 1960. *Exercises in Economic Analysis*. s.l.: Macmillan.

Robinson, J., 1962. *Economic Philosophy*. London: Routledge.

Robinson, J., 1962. *Essays in the Theory of Economic Growth*. New York: St Martin's Press.

Robinson, J., 1966. *An Essay on Marxian Economics*. 2nd ed. London: MacMillan; St Martin's Press.

Romer, D., 1996. *Advanced Macroeconomics*. New York: McGraw-Hill, New York.

Romer, P., 1990. Endogenous Technological Change. *Journal of Political Economy 90 (October, Part 2), pp. S71-S102*, Volume 90, pp. S71–S102.

Rothbard, M., 1976. New Light on the Prehistory of the Austrian School. In: E. Dolan, ed. *The Foundations of Modern Austrian Economics*. Kansas City: Sheed and Ward, pp. 52–74.

Roxburgh, S. H., Berry, S. L., Buckley, T. N., Barnes, B. & Roderick, M. L., 2005. What is NPP? Inconsistent accounting of respiratory fluxes in the definition of net primary production. *Functional Ecology*, Volume 19, p. 378–382.

Roy, T., 2002. Economic History and Modern India: Redefining the Link. *Journal of Economic Perspectives*, Volume 16(3), pp. 109–130.

Ryder, A., 1955. *Panchatantra of Vishnu Sharma*. Chicago: University of Chicago Press.

Rymes, T., 1971. *On Concepts of Capital and Technical Change*. London: Cambridge University Press.

Said, E., 2003. Blind Imperial Arrogance. *Los Angeles Times*, 20 July.

Samuelson, P., 1938. A note on the pure theory of consumers' behaviour. *Economica. New Series*, Volume 17, pp. 61–71.

Santana, C., 2021. We Come in Peace? A Rational Approach to METI. *Space Policy*, Volume 57.

Savran, S. & Tonak, A., 1999. Productive and Unproductive Labour: An Attempt at Clarification and Classification. *Capital & Class*, Volume 23(2), pp. 113–152.

Schepelmann, P., Goossens, Y. & Makipaa, A., 2010. *Towards Sustainable Development: Alternatives to GDP to measure progress*. [Online] Available at: https://epub.wupperinst.org/files/3486/WS42.pdf [Accessed 10 8 2021].

Schroeder, M., 2021. *"Value Theory", The Stanford Encyclopedia of Philosophy (Fall 2021 Edition)*, Edward N. Zalta (ed.). [Online] Available at: https://plato.stanford.edu/archives/fall2021/entries/value-theory/ [Accessed 2 January 2022].

Schrödinger, E., 1967. *What is Life? The Physical Aspect of the Living Cell with Mind and Matter*. Cambridge: Cambridge University Press.

Schumpeter, J., 1954. *History of Economic Analysis*. New York: Oxford University Press.

Schumpeter, J., 1975. *Capitalism, Socialism and Democracy*. New York: HarperPerennial.

Schumpeter, J., 1982. *Business Cycles*. Philadelphia: Porcupine Press.

Schumpeter, J., 1994. *History of Economic Analysis*. London: Routledge.

Screpanti, E., 2019. *Labour and Value: Rethinking Marx's Theory of Exploitation*. Cambridge, UK: Open Book Publishers.

Searle, J., 1983. *Intentionality*. Cambridge: Cambridge University Press.

Sedlcek, T. & Havel, V., 2011. *Economics of Good and Evil: The Quest for Economic Meaning from Gilgamesh to Wall Street*. Oxford: Oxford University Press.

Selase, A. E., Xing, C., Agbadze, O. K. & Thompson, B. E., 2015. The General Overview of the Phrase 'Fuzzy Logic'. *International Journal of Engineering, Management & Sciences*, Volume 2(5), pp. 68–73.

Selgin, G., 1988. Praxeology and Understanding: An Analysis of the Controversy in Austrian Economics. *The Review of Austrian Economics*, Volume 2, pp. 19–58.

Sen, A., 1989. Development as Capability Expansion. *Journal of Development Planning*, Volume 19, pp. 41–58.

Sen, A., 1999. *Commodities and Capabilities*. Dehli; New York: Oxford University Press.

Senior, N., 1850. *Political Economy*. London: John Joseph Griffin & Co.

Shaikh, A. & Tonak, A., 1994. *Measuring the Wealth of Nations: The Political Economy of National Accounts*. New York: Cambridge University Press.

Shankaracharya, A., 1909. *The Sarva-Siddhanta-Sangraha*. Madras: The Superindendent, Government Press.

Shapiro, M. & Wilco, D., 1996. Mismeasurement in the Consumer Price Index: An Evaluation. *NBER Macroeconomics Annual*, Volume 11, pp. 93–142.

Sherwin, R., 1974. Hedonic Prices and Implicit Markets: Product Differentiation in Pure Competition. *Journal of Political Economy*, Volume 82(1), pp. 34–55.

Simpson, D., 1983. Joseph Schumpeter and the Austrian Shool of Economics. *Journal of Economic Studies,* Volume 10, pp. 18–28.

Sîn-lēqi-unninni, 1998. *Epic of Gilgamesh*. s.l.: s.n. http://www.ancienttexts.org/library/mesopotamian/gilgamesh/

Smith, A., 1976. *The Theory of Moral Sentiments*. Oxford: Oxford University Press.

Smith, A., 1979. *The Wealth of Nations*. London: Penguin books.

Smith, A., 1999. *The Wealth of Nations Books IV-V*. London: Routledge.

Smith, V., 1985. John Stuart Mill's Famous Distinction Between Production and Distribution. *Economics and Philosophy*, Volume 1(2), pp. 267–284.

Solow, R., 1956. A Contribution to the Theory of Economic Growth. *The Quarterly Journal of Economics*, Volume LXX, pp. 65–94.

Solow, R., 1994. Perspectives on Growth Theory. *Journal of Economic Perspectives*, 8(1), pp. 45–54.

Soter, S., 2006. What is a Planet?. *The Astronomical Journal*, Volume 132, pp. 2513–2519.

Stiglitz, J., Sen, A. & Fitoussi, J.-P., 2009. *Report by the Commission on the Measurement of Economic Performance and Social Progress*. [Online] Available at: https://web.archive.org/web/20150721025729/ http://www.stiglitz-sen-fitoussi.fr/documents/rapport_angla [Accessed 2019].

Stiglitz, J. & Uzawa, H., 1969. *Readings in the Modern Theory of Growth*. Cambridge: The MIT Press.

Studenski, P., 1958. *The Income of Nations. Theory, Measurement, and Analysis: Past and Present. A Study in Applies Economics and Statistics*. New York: New York University Press, Washington Square.

Sweezy, P., 1942. *Theory of Capitalist Development*. London: Dobson Books Ltd.

Söderberg, J., 2010. Long-term trends in real wages of labourers. In: R. Edvinsson, T. Jacobson & D. Waldenström, eds. *Historical Monetary and Financial Statistics for Sweden: Exchange rates, Prices and Wages 1277-2008*. Stockholm: Ekerlids Förlag; Sveriges Riksbank, pp. 453–478.

Taylor, D. & Strutton, D., 2016. Taylor, D.G. and Strutton, D. (2016), "Does Facebook usage lead to conspicuous consumption? The role of envy, narcissism and self-promotion. *Journal of Research in Interactive Marketing*, Volume 10(3), pp. 231–248.

Tedeschi, R., 2018. The Irish GDP in 2016. After the disaster comes a dilemma. *Questioni di Economia e Finanza, Banca d'Italia*, Issue 471.

Tennie, C., Bandini, E., van Schaik, C. & Hopper, L., 2020. The zone of latent solutions and its relevance to understanding ape cultures. *Biology & Philosophy*, Volume 35(55).

Tilly, C., 1985. War making and state making as organized crime. In: P. Evans, D. Rueschemeyer & T. Skocpol, eds. *Bringing the state back*. Cambridge: Cambridge University Press, pp. 169–187.

Tily, G., 2009. John Maynard Keynes and the Development of National Accounts in Britain, 1895–1941. *The Review of Income and Wealth*, Volume 55(2), pp. 331–359.

Tomer, C. & Jürgen, H., 2015. Ants Adjust their Pheromone Deposition to a Changing Environment and their Probability of Making Errors. *Proceedings of the Royal Society B*, Volume 20150679, p. 282.

Tzu, L., 1988. *Tao Te Ching*. New York: HarperPerennial.

United Nations et al. 2003. *Integrated Environment and Economic Accounting 2003*. s.l.: United Nations.

United Nations et al. 2009. *System of National Accounts 2008*. New York.: United Nations.

United Nations et al. 2014. *System of Environmental-Economic Accounting 2012*. New York: United Nations.

United Nations, 1953. *A System of National Accounts and Supporting Tables*. New York: United Nations.

United Nations, 1968. *A System of National Accounts*. New York: United Nations.

United Nations, 1971. Basic Principles of the System of Balances of the National Economy, 1971. United Nations; New York. New York: United Nations.

United Nations, 2020. *Human Development Report 2020. The next frontier. Human development and the Anthropocene*. New York: United Nations.

Uzawa, H., 1961. On a Two-Sector Model of Economic Growth. *The Review of Economic Studies*, Volume 29(1), pp. 40–47.

van den Bergh, J., 2001. Ecological economics: Themes, Approaches, and Differences with Environmental Economics. *Regional Environmental Change*, Volume 2(1), pp. 13–23.

van der Linden, M. & García, M. R., 2016. *On Coerced Labor: Work and Compulsion after Chattel Slavery*. Leiden; Boston: Brill.

Vaz-Curado, S. & Mueller, A., 2019. The Concept of Entrepreneur of Schumpeter in Comparison to Kirzner. *MISES: Interdisciplinary Journal of Philosophy Law and Economics*, Volume 7(3), pp. 613–642.

Veblen, T., 1899. *The Theory of the Leisure Class*. s.l.: https://www.gutenberg.org/files/833/833-h/833-h.htm.

Veblen, T., 1904. *The Theory of Business Enterprise*. New York: Scribner's sons.

Veblen, T., 1908. Professor Clark's Economics. *Quarterly Journal of Economics*, Volume 22(1), pp. 147–195.

Visser, W. & McIntosh, A., 1998. History of Usury Prohibition: A Short Review of the Historical Critique of Usury. *Accounting History Review*, Volume 8(2), pp. 175–189.

Vogel, V. et al., 2010. The Worldwide Expansion of the Argentine Ant. *Diversity and Distributions*, Volume 16, pp. 170–186.

von Böhm-Bawerek, E., 1907. Capital and Interest Once More: II. A Relapse to the Productivity Theory. *The Quarterly Journal of Economics*, Volume 21(2), pp. 247–282.

von Böhm-Bawerk, E., 1890. *Capital and Interest, a Critical History of Economical Theory.* London: Macmillan and Co.

von Böhm-Bawerk, E., 1898. *Karl Marx and the Close of His System: A Criticism.* London: T. Fisher Unwin.

von Hayek, F., 1942. Scientism and the Study of Society. Part I. *Economica*, Volume 9, pp. 267–291.

von Hayek, F., 2001. *The Road to Serfdom.* London: Routledge.

von Mises, L., 1949. *Human Action.* New York: Yale University Press.

Vorzimmer, P., 1969. Darwin, Malthus, and the Theory of Natural Selection. *Journal of the History of Ideas*, Volume 30(4), pp. 527–542.

Wade, M., 1977. An experimental study of group selection. *Evolution*, Volume 34, pp. 134–153.

Waerness, K., 1987. On the rationality of caring. In: A. S. Sassoon, ed. *Women and the state.* London: Hutchinson, pp. 207–234.

Wallis, J. & North, D., 1986. Measuring the transaction sector in the American economy, 1870-1970. In: S. Engerman & R. Gallman, eds. *Long-term factors in American economic growth.* s.l.: University of Chicago Press.

Walsh, T., 2017. The Singularity May Never Be Near. *AI Magazine*, Volume 38(3), pp. 58–62.

Weber, M., 1949. Objectivity in social science and social policy. In: E. A. a. F. H. A. Shils, ed. *The methodology of the social sciences.* New York: Free Press.

Weber, M., 1978. *Economy and Society.* Berkeley, Los Angeles, London: University of California Press.

Whittle, J., 2019. A Critique of Approaches to 'Domestic Work': Women, Work and the Pre-Industrial Economy. *Past & Present*, Volume 243(1), pp. 35–70.

Wilson, D. & Wilson, E., 2008. Evolution for the good of the group. *American Scientist*, Volume 96(5), pp. 380–389.

Wilson, E., 1971. *The Insect Societies.* Cambridge. Massachusetts: Belknap Press of Harvard University Press.

Wilson, E., 1975. *Sociobiology: The New Synthesis.* Cambridge Massachusetts: Belknap.

Wilson, E., 2005. Kin Selection as the Key to Altruism: its Rise and Fall. *Social Research*, Volume 72(1), pp. 1–8.

Winiecki, J., 2011. *The Distorted World of Soviet Type Economics.* New York: Routledge.

Wood, C., 1997. The First World/Third Party Criterion: A Feminist Critique of Production Boundaries in Economics. *Feminist Economics*, Volume 3(3), pp. 47–68.

World Bank Group, 2018. *The Changing Wealth: Building a Sustainable Future.* Washington: World Bank Group.

World Bank, 1993. *Planned economies. A guide to the data. 1993 edition featuring economies of the former Soviet Union.* Washington D.C.: s.n.

Zhuangzi, 2013. *The Complete Works of Zhuangzi.* New York: Colombia University Press.

Zinner, D. & Wheeler, B., 2013. Aggression in Humans and Other Primates: Biology, Psychology, Sociology. In: H. Kortüm & J. Heinze, eds. *Aggression in Humans and Other Primates: Biology, Psychology, Sociology.* Berlin; Boston: De Gruyter, pp. 41–85.

Index

Printed in the United States
by Baker & Taylor Publisher Services